The New Local Government Series

No. 23

LOCAL GOVERNMENT IN BRITAIN SINCE REORGANISATION

The New Local Government Series
Series Editor: Professor Peter G. Richards

LOCAL GOVERNMENT IN BRITAIN SINCE REORGANISATION

ALAN ALEXANDER

Lecturer in Politics, University of Reading

London
GEORGE ALLEN & UNWIN
Boston   ·   Sydney

George Allen & Unwin (Publishers) Ltd,
40 Museum Street, London WC1A 1LU, UK

George Allen & Unwin (Publishers) Ltd,
Park Lane, Hemel Hempstead, Herts HP2 4TE, UK

Allen & Unwin, Inc.,
9 Winchester Terrace, Winchester, Mass. 01890, USA

George Allen & Unwin Australia Pty Ltd,
8 Napier Street, North Sydney, NSW 2060, Australia

First published in 1982

British Library Cataloguing in Publication Data

Alexander, Alan
    Local government in Britain sinc reorganisation.
    —(The New local government ies; no. 23)
    1. Local government—Er nd
    I. Title   II. Series
    352.042   JS30
    ISBN 0-0 52100-2
    ISB. -04-352101-0 Pbk

Library of Congress Cataloging in Publication Data

Alexander, Alan, 1943–
    Local government in Britain since reorganization.
    (The New local government series; no. 23)
    Includes index.
    1 Local government—Great Britain.   I. Title.
    JS3095 1982.A39   352.041   82-1793
    ISBN 0-04-352100-2   AACR2
    ISBN 0-04-352101-0 (pbk.)

Set in 10 on 11 point Times by Preface Ltd, Salisbury, Wilts.
and printed in Great Britain
by Billing and Sons Ltd, Guildford, London and Worcester

CONTENTS

PREFACE

The idea for this book began to germinate during the time when I changed from being a member of the council of the old County Borough of Reading to being a member of the new Berkshire County Council. The fieldwork upon which it is largely based did not begin until after the county council elections of 1977 when the electors of Abbey Ward, Reading, dispensed with my services as a councillor. I suppose I should thank them for providing me with the time to write the book.

During such a long period of gestation and production an author collects many debts. Any attempt to thank individually all of those officers and members who gave time to be interviewed, to reply to subsequent queries, and to complete questionnaires would run the risk of offending both those who were omitted and those who preferred to do good by stealth. I hope they will accept my thanks anonymously.

There are, however, some people whose contribution is such that it must be identified. First of all, my thanks are due to Professor Peter Campbell, whose wisdom and insights inform much of the book. The work of transcribing most of the more than eighty interviews indicated in the appendix was undertaken with unfailing cheerfulness and accuracy by Mrs Catherine Davies who, but for her tragic and untimely death, would also have typed the book itself. My thanks here are a poor substitute for the impossibility of thanking her personally. Mrs Sue Papandreou, who stepped into the breach at a fairly late stage, produced drafts and final copy with a speed and efficiency that my uneven pattern of work hardly deserved.

Two institutions contributed greatly. The library of the Local Government Operational Research Unit, Reading, allowed me to borrow material and to keep it longer than most librarians would tolerate. The fieldwork was made possible by a grant from the Nuffield Foundation without which the book could never have been written.

Finally, I owe the greatest debt to my wife Morag whose encouragement ensured the book's completion and whose editorial pencil got rid of more infelicities and obfuscations than I can count. For those that remain, for all errors, omissions and solecisms, I take full responsibility.

ALAN ALEXANDER
Wokingham, Berkshire
March 1981

To my parents

Chapter 1

THE RATIONALE OF REFORM

The local government systems of England and Wales and Scotland have undergone, since their piecemeal growth between medieval and Victorian times, only two major structural reorganisations. Neither can be regarded as an outstandingly successful exercise in institutional reform. Both were the results of a general consensus that change, consolidation and rationalisation were necessary and both bore the marks of the inevitable compromises reached in Parliament when it is considering the reform of political institutions.

There can be no doubt that it was the flaws in the first reorganisation together with population changes and the expansion of the scope of government that led to the slow growth in the twentieth century of a conviction that a further major change was necessary. It is, on the face of it, surprising that it took so long for that conviction to issue in legislative form.

The passage of the County Councils Act 1888 (and of the County Councils (Scotland) Act 1889) arose from two complementary pressures. First, it was highly anomalous for county government to remain undemocratic and unrepresentative. Municipal government and the provision of poor relief had been placed on an elective footing by the Municipal Corporations Act 1835 and the Poor Law Amendment Act 1834, and both of these Acts had been the work of the first reformed Parliament. Thus, from 1835, with boroughs, poor law unions and the House of Commons democratised, the continued government of the counties by appointed justices of the peace, who sat at quarter sessions and levied rates for county purposes, became progressively more difficult to defend. Secondly, there was a utilitarian appreciation of the need to rationalise and standardise the structure of local institutions. The 1888 legislation, supplemented by the provisions of the District Councils Act 1894, achieved the objectives implied by the pressures for reform: it established a democratic system of local government throughout the country and, in formal institutional terms, it created a uniform structure.

But it did so only at the cost of a major parliamentary concession which not only ensured the immediate obsolescence of the new structure but also created classes of local authorities whose deep mutual antagonism would be an obstacle to reform even when disinterested observers were unanimous that change was essential. Before the

1

1888 legislation was introduced, there was general agreement that if county government were democratised, the enabling legislation would need to preserve the independence and local autonomy of England's major industrial cities. The Royal Sanitary Commission of 1869, whose report was the original catalyst to the rationalisation of subnational government in England and Wales, had referred to the impossibility of ignoring existing representative institutions when change was under consideration. The government accepted this view and introduced the 1888 legislation with the intention of creating, for the ten most populous cities, a new local government unit. This was to be a single-tier, all-purpose authority – the county borough. During the passage of the Bill through Parliament, however, the qualifying population for county borough status was reduced from 150,000 to 50,000. This concession, together with the extension of the right to county borough status to ancient cathedral cities, led to the establishment not of ten but of sixty-one county boroughs. The exclusion of about a quarter of the population (and therefore the tax base) from the jurisdiction of the new counties and the drawing of county borough boundaries on the basis of existing parochial areas ensured that the new system would be unable easily to adapt to major social, economic and demographic change.

For the new system was set up on the eve of the explosion of suburbanisation that followed the long period of urbanisation to which the reforms of the late nineteenth century had been an institutional response. From early in the twentieth century until it was demonstrated by the reform of London's local government in the 1960s that major structural change in local government institutions was possible, there was widespread dissatisfaction with the system. This dissatisfaction expressed itself in official inquiries, minor amending legislation and, most significantly, in what Richard Crossman, the minister on whose initiative the Redcliffe-Maud Commission was appointed, called 'the war between the county councils and the county borough authorities' (Crossman, 1975, p. 65). This 'war' was fought over three central concerns of local institutions – territory, tax base and status. It arose, quite simply, from the inherent conflicts in a structure that implied a belief in the autonomy of urban centres but that did not provide an effective mechanism whereby that structure could respond to demographic change.

The local government system, before the end of the first two decades of the new century, was showing the strains of the conflict between the opposing classes of authority created in 1888: county boroughs wanted to expand; major urban districts which passed the 50,000 population threshold wanted county borough status; counties opposed any further loss of territory and tax base. As Redcliffe-Maud was to say in 1969, 'local government areas no longer correspond[ed] to the pattern of life and work' (Redcliffe-Maud, Cmnd 4040, 1969,

Vol. 1, para. 85), but from the 1920s onwards there was a widely held conviction among politicians and officials at both national and local level that this misfit between society and its governing institutions could be remedied by tinkering rather than by major reorganisation.

The process by which central government and local authorities reached a consensus in the 1960s that something comprehensive must be done about subnational government in Britain can be viewed in two ways. On one view, it is an example, albeit an exaggerated one, of the normal method of policy-making in Britain. As Bruce Wood says in the first sentence of his book on the process of local government reform, 'Policy-making is a lengthy and complex process in Britain' (Wood, 1976, p. 17). Wood's book deals with the period between 1966 and 1974, but it is possible to see the many inquiries, commissions, legislative changes, negotiations, and discussions with interested parties as part of a bargaining process extended over almost fifty years by a perceived need to proceed by consent and to avoid major upheavals.

Evidence to support this view is not hard to find. In the terms of reference of the Ullswater Commission which investigated London's government in 1922–3 and of the Onslow Commission which, between 1925 and 1930, published three reports on the working of the local government system in the rest of England and Wales, there are clear indications of the determination of successive governments to defend the status quo in structure and to preserve the increasingly obsolescent and inefficient division between town and country. The pace of demographic change in the interwar period was made clear in 1940 with the publication of the Barlow Commission's report on the distribution of the industrial population (Cmnd 6153, 1940) but even after the war, in a period of major social, economic and industrial change, the Labour government appointed a Local Government Boundary Commission whose remit excluded it from considering functions. It was thus restricted to recommending changes of area and status within the existing structure and with the existing distribution of functions. The government's response to the commission's complaint that its job was thus rendered all but impossible (House of Commons Papers, 1948) was its summary abolition. Even when ministers concluded, in 1957, that the problems of local government in the metropolis were urgent enough to be referred to a Royal Commission, they were persuaded to proceed in the rest of England and Wales by the appointment of new Local Government Commissions to consider piecemeal the problems of particular areas. Although the Special Review Area procedure enabled the commissions to make recommendations on area, status and functions, the decision-making process associated with the reviews militated strongly in favour of maintaining the status quo (Jones, G. W., 1963, pp. 175–6).

On this view, then, the achievement of a consensus in favour of major reform depended upon the gradual demonstration of the failure of all other methods of change. On the other view, the process is lengthened by the power of vested interests and by the fact that those most opposed to any particular change have the greatest access to decision-makers. There is, of course, a sense in which this mode of explanation is not wholly distinct from the one just considered, but rather a variant of it. For the search for consensus among institutions and individuals who are in direct competition for the same commodities – territory, tax base and status – inevitably gives to each participant in the process a virtual veto on any proposal which is not seen to be to its advantage. Certainly, the representative bodies of local government were encouraged by ministers to believe that central government would not proceed with any change to which they were individually or severally opposed. It is possible, therefore, to see the restricted terms of reference of the Local Government Boundary Commission of 1945 and of the Local Government Commissions of 1958 as the result of a consultative process that pandered to the preservation of the vested interests of the various classes of authority as represented by the local authority associations – the Association of Municipal Corporations (AMC), the County Councils Association (CCA), the Urban District Councils Association (UDCA), and the Rural District Councils Association (RDCA).

But the nature of the relationship between central government and local authorities in Britain is itself an obstacle to major institutional change. Local authorities are subordinate institutions that derive all power and status from legislation passed by Parliament. They are also local centres of political power that have, in the twentieth century, become not only increasingly partisan in their own right, but also indispensable to national politicians in the achievement of their policy goals. Whether the concern of national politicians is with the general needs of economic management or with particular plans for personal services such as housing, education and social services, their life will be easier if they have to deal with sympathetic rather than hostile local authorities.

In policy-making, this concern manifests itself in ways that are sometimes mutually contradictory. First, in determining the structure of local government, national politicians will seek to maximise their party's advantage under any new arrangements. Secondly, in drawing new local government areas, ministers will be aware that the parliamentary Boundary Commissions try to follow local government boundaries when they redistribute parliamentary constituencies. It was a major disadvantage of the Local Government Commissions of 1958 that their recommendations depended for implementation on ministerial orders. For, as both Sir Keith Joseph (Brand, 1974, p. 141) and Richard Crossman (Crossman, 1975, p. 64) found as the responsible minister, this procedure ensured that parliamentary pressure would be most intense where it mattered most – at the point of political decision.

Thirdly, a concern with the relationships between central and local government can affect the process of institutional change because ministers want to avoid the strained relations that may result from any proposal for change that affects classes of authority in different ways. These concerns, taken together with the close integration of the representative bodies of local government into the process of policy-making, amounted to a huge log-jam of vested interest standing in the way of major change.

Although this institutional resistance to change continued to dominate the local government worlds of England outside London, Wales and Scotland through the 1950s and into the 1960s, it had begun to be broken down in the metropolis by the appointment, in 1957, of the Herbert Commission (Herbert, Cmnd 1164, 1960) to investigate the local government of Greater London. The path to reform in the capital was a long and tortuous one, culminating in a bitterly contested legislative process in the course of which a number of concessions were made which ensured that the final shape of the institutions was considerably different from that envisaged by the Royal Commission. The significance of the process to the reform of local government elsewhere in Britain, however, was twofold. First, despite the length and difficulty of the progress from the appointment of the Royal Commission in 1957 to legislation in 1963 to implementation in 1964–5, it demonstrated that it was feasible to redesign completely a local government system without causing the provision of services to grind to a halt. Secondly, it showed the usefulness of the Royal Commission procedure as a catalyst to change that was proof against the dead hand of the vested interests of existing power centres, in this case the London County Council (LCC) and the existing metropolitan boroughs, none of which survived the changes. And thirdly, the process of change in London was completed just at the time when the inadequacies of the Local Government Commissions as agents of reform in the rest of England and Wales were becoming clear.

The new system of local government in London came into operation a few months after the 1964 general election which brought Labour to power and Richard Crossman to the Ministry of Housing and Local Government. As his diaries clearly show, Crossman inherited, and at first publicly accepted, the settled departmental view that 'the only practical reforms [were] likely to come . . . from the Local Government Commission' but parliamentary pressures of the kind mentioned earlier caused him privately to doubt whether the local government system could be made either rational or efficient so long as the existing classes of authority were preserved (Crossman, 1975,

p. 65). The eventual outcome of his conversion was an announcement to the AMC conference in September 1965 that he proposed to appoint an authoritative committee of inquiry to conduct a thorough and unfettered review of the entire local government system. The appointment of the Royal Commission on Local Government in England and its counterpart in Scotland were formally announced in February 1966.

It is important to note here that resistance to major reorganisation was greater in England than in Wales or Scotland. Before Crossman's 'conversion' in 1965, the newly established Welsh Office had begun a series of consultations on the reform of local government in Wales. It was a matter of some discontent in the principality that the concrete proposals for change which resulted from the initiatives of the Welsh Office were continually shelved while the reports of the English and Scottish commissions were awaited. And despite the fact that the process of investigation and consultation had been wholly distinct from that in England, reform was eventually achieved through a single Act of Parliament for both countries.

Although the Labour government decided to proceed in Scotland by a Royal Commission, under the chairmanship of Lord Wheatley, a senior Court of Session judge who was also a former Labour MP, whose remit was identical to that for England, there was evidence that departmental thinking about the local government structure was further advanced and more radical in the Scottish Office than it was in either the Ministry of Housing and Local Government or the Welsh Office. In 1963 the government had published a White Paper (Cmnd 2067) that proposed changes that were more far-reaching than any that might have been expected to emerge from the investigations and recommendations of the Local Government Commissions in England and Wales. Although its contents were to be of historical interest only, as an input to the Royal Commission's inquiries, the white paper was indicative of a growing belief that local institutions throughout Britain had outlived their usefulness and that major reorganisation, rather than mere tinkering, was the only way forward.

The investigations and reports of the two Royal Commissions were an irresistible stimulus to some kind of nationwide reorganisation of the local government system. In retrospect, however, it is possible to argue that the compromises that so flawed the final legislation as to make the system in England and Wales very difficult to operate, and with which most of this book is concerned, were facilitated by the failure of the Redcliffe-Maud Commission to be either unanimous or, in the case of the majority report, internally consistent. It would be inappropriate here to analyse in detail the conclusions and recommendations of the commissions. But there are certain aspects of the pre-legislative stage of reform that have an important bearing on the process of political bargaining that led to the introduction by the

Conservative government of two-tier local government throughout England and Wales.

The diagnosis in the majority report of the Redcliffe-Maud Commission (Cmnd 4040, 1969, Vol. I), and one that was shared by Mr Derek Senior in his *Memorandum of Dissent* (Cmnd 4040–I, 1969, Vol. II), was that 'the most fatal flaw' (Cmnd 4040, para. 85) in the existing structure was the rigid separation of town and country. The prescription of the majority – and it was the majority report that determined the direction of public debate (Wood, 1976, p. 84) – was a move to a system of unitary local authorities, except in the three major conurbations of Birmingham, Manchester and Liverpool, where a two-tier system, not unlike that introduced in London in 1964, was proposed. These general conclusions were radical enough to commend themselves to the Labour government that received the report: as the Herbert Commission had done in London, Redcliffe-Maud proposed to abolish all existing authorities and classes of authority. But by being conservative on boundaries – the majority report said that 'the new . . . pattern should . . . stem from the existing one' and that new boundaries would differ from old ones 'only where the advantage seemed unquestionable' (Redcliffe-Maud, Cmnd 4040, 1969, Vol. I, paras 9(X) and 280) – and by being less than convincing in its defence of the unitary authority as the appropriate unit throughout non-metropolitan England, the commission provided ammunition for those who found its structural radicalism unacceptable.

Comparison with the Herbert Commission report is instructive in two further ways. First, one of the major research studies commissioned by Redcliffe-Maud (Redcliffe-Maud, *Research Study 2*, 1968) was of the process and performance of reform in London, so, as was argued above, there was a clear continuity between the process of change in London and that elsewhere. Secondly, in party political terms, the path to reorganisation in London had been very smooth: a Conservative government appointed the Royal Commission, received the report just after an election in which it had greatly increased its parliamentary majority, and was therefore in a position to ensure the passage of legislation that it considered to be both defensible in the light of the Commission's report and advantageous politically. Governments, of course, are not bound to accept the conclusions of Royal Commissions they appoint. But the power to choose the chairman and members and to define terms of reference makes it more likely that a commission will come up with conclusions that the appointing government will accept. And where the legislation is carried through by that government the line between investigation and legislation is likely to be more direct than is the case when a change of government intervenes.

In the cases of Redcliffe-Maud and Wheatley, however, the reports were delivered in mid-1969 to an unpopular government nearing the end of its parliamentary term. Given the need to consult widely, to publish a considered government response and subsequently to push a controversial measure through Parliament, the time-scale would have been extended enough even without the intervention of a general election, which was due to take place by the spring of 1971. The integration into the policy process of interested parties, in particular the local authority associations, presupposes a degree of negotiability and readiness to compromise. When an election is imminent and the major parties are not agreed on the general principles of institutional change, there is greater scope for those whose position differs from that of the government to delay in the hope of postponing final decisions until after the election. As Wood shows, this was precisely the tactic of the CCA, employed in the knowledge that the Conservative Party had opposed the establishment of the Royal Commissions and was moving towards a modest, county-based reorganisation with a two-tier structure throughout the country. So, despite the Labour government's attempt to accelerate the process by declaring certain points non-negotiable in its White Paper (Cmnd 4276, 1970), the period between the publication of the Royal Commission report and the publication of a Bill was one in which compromise and concession were at a premium. And to this process the commissioners had given a number of hostages to fortune, first by being divided, and second by being less than vigorous in their defence of the preferred solution of the majority. The process of legislative compromise and its effects on the new system are examined in Chapter 2.

By the end of the 1960s, then, there had been created a consensus that a major reorganisation of the local government system was not only inevitable but urgent. The incoming Conservative government in 1970 did not consider the option of doing nothing: in particular, the new minister responsible for local government, Peter Walker, was committed to a major reduction in the number of authorities as an essential precondition of making the entire system more efficient. But, despite the Royal Commission findings – perhaps, in the case of England, because of them – there was still no consensus about the fundamental principles upon which the new system should be based. The major political parties differed radically upon the crucial question of whether a new system should have one tier or two. And this disagreement, which was in some ways a proxy for their contrasting political interests, was of central significance to the achievement, or non-achievement, of successful institutional change.

Major changes to the political institutions of a developed democracy have, in general, two purposes. First, they should improve the workings of institutions and so raise the quality of the services they provide. Secondly, where the issue of reform is controversial – and in a party democracy this means disputed between the major political parties, or by the vested interests, or by both – change should take the matter 'off the agenda' for a very considerable time. These are the general criteria against which the success of change can be measured and, as such, they constitute continuing reference points for the rest of this book.

But there are also particular criteria, derived from the justifications offered for reform and the expectations of its authors as expressed during the long period of discussion, legislation and implementation. These, too, inform the analysis that follows and it is as well to articulate them clearly.

A close textual analysis of ministerial speeches, parliamentary debates, reactions of the local authority associations and the publications and propaganda of the pressure groups concerned with local government would yield a long list of fears, hopes and *ante facto* justifications of the new system. For the purposes of analysis and assessment, however, they can be reduced to four central principles upon which the new system was to be founded: efficiency, comprehensibility, local autonomy and conclusiveness.

The goal of efficiency was generally regarded as the most significant of the four. There was general agreement that the number of authorities existing before reorganisation – in England and Wales outside London there were just under 1,400 local authorities and in Scotland there were 331 – no longer made efficient local government possible and constituted an obstacle to the effective and equitable provision of services. It was also anticipated that an increase in the size and resources of individual authorities would make possible improvements in management structures and decision-making processes which would increase the efficiency of local government and enable it to employ professional staff of a higher quality and to attract a greater number of able councillors from a wider social, educational and professional background.

The second objective was comprehensibility. The intention was to create a system of local government that could be easily understood by the man in the street and in which the distribution of functions, and hence the lines of political responsibility, were clearcut. In the old system, confusion was said to have arisen not only from the obsolescence of county borough and other boundaries, but also from the various schemes of delegation, particularly in education, from county councils to county districts. There were, moreover, many areas in which *ad hoc* institutions and joint bodies of various kinds had been set up to administer and/or co-ordinate services that did not respect outdated local government boundaries. Bodies of this sort, which were typically indirectly elected by local authorities in their area and to which public access was at best indirect, functioned in the provision of police, fire, water and planning services.

The intention to strengthen local autonomy runs as a *leitmotive* through the whole history of central–local relations in Britain, and the creation in 1974 of fewer and larger authorities was expected to be accompanied by a reduction in the amount of central direction and a consequent strengthening of local autonomy. The 1971 White Paper (Cmnd 4584, 1971*b*) said that the government intended 'to allow authorities the maximum discretion to make their decisions' and to reduce to a minimum 'over a thousand statutory controls by central government over local government' that had accumulated since 1888. Later, Peter Walker said that he was 'discussing with each of [his] Cabinet colleagues those thousands of controls' (AMC, 1971, p. 11) that might be removed. Actual performance in this field is examined in detail in Chapter 7.

But it is not only the number and quality of specific statutory controls that determine the nature of the central–local relationship. Political autonomy relies on the possession of a power to tax and to spend; local authorities in a unitary state derive that power from national government. At the time of reorganisation, there was a widely held view that the question of local government finance had been insufficiently examined and that reorganisation offered an opportunity to remedy the deficiency and to modernise the structure of local taxation. A White Paper (Cmnd 4741, 1971*c*) was published in 1971 and a Committee of Inquiry was appointed in 1974, but no major changes resulted until 1980. The implications of the changes in the system of central assistance for the financing of local government are considered in Chapter 7.

Finally, after such a long period of gestation, it was hoped by its authors that the reorganisation they proposed would be conclusive, that it would create a structure that would be responsive to demographic change in a way that had been impossible for the 1888 system and that the question of local government reform would be answered for at least a generation. As Peter Walker put it in his speech introducing the second reading of his Bill, 'When the Bill reaches the statute book we shall have ended the uncertainty that has bedevilled local government since the war' (*Hansard*, 16 November 1971).

The remainder of this book is an attempt to evaluate the success or failure of a major institutional change and to assess how far the new systems have lived up to the expectations that were used to justify their establishment.

Chapter 2

THE NEW STRUCTURE: EXPECTATIONS

Writing in 1964, for a conference on the Anglo-American aspects of urban planning whose deliberations were collected and published as *The Regional City*, Derek Senior said, 'Wherever you draw it, a boundary will cut across problems' (Senior, 1966, p. 20). Few of the protagonists of local government reform, and even fewer of those who practice as officers and members in the systems that emerged from that process, would disagree with Senior's view. After six years of the new systems, however, it is clear that the combination of conservatism on boundaries that began, as was noted in the previous chapter, with the Royal Commission report, and the parliamentary and political compromises that characterised the period between publication of the report and the passage of the Local Government Act 1972, had the effect of maximising rather than minimising the problems that inevitably arise from the redrawing of local authority boundaries.

But in the structure of subnational government, boundaries are not only spatial and geographic. They also delineate the allocation of functions and the distribution of political power. And it is impossible to describe and evaluate the performance of the new institutions of local government without first discussing the practical difficulties that have to be overcome in any system of government in which there are a number of autonomous, or semi-autonomous, levels.

THE PROBLEM OF TWO-TIER LOCAL GOVERNMENT

Clearly any multi-level system will require a structure of communication between levels and, possibly, some mechanism for the resolution of conflict where agreement is unobtainable. Thus, in federal systems, there arises a system of political consultation between the levels of government, together with a process of judicial arbitration, particularly of those issues which political negotiation fails to settle. In Britain the structure of liaison between national government and local government *as a whole* is made relatively simple by the centralised nature of law-making and the subordinate position of local government. Generally speaking, central government has the power to ensure that in any major dispute its view will prevail, either by the application of existing laws or by the passage of new ones. This relationship is considered in Chapter 7.

The relationships between the tiers *within* local government create much more serious problems. Relationships between the tiers in any conceivable pattern of democratic local government are likely to be fraught with difficulties. These difficulties arise from sources that are often outside the control of local government precisely because they are consequences of its subordinate status. First, all local government units derive their legal powers from central legislation and to this extent they are all equal before the law, despite the manifest inequalities of resources, population and functions that exist among them. So here, potentially at least, is a source of conflict: equality of constitutional status and inequality of function and power. Secondly, in any geographical area, all tiers of local government will consider themselves to represent the people of the area, for all are elected and, notwithstanding their limited legal autonomy as subordinate units of government, all will claim the legitimacy that arises from the process of democratic election. Thus, to add to the problem of equality of status, there is the inevitable conflict that proceeds from the existence of more than one directly elected institution serving the same population. In any dispute, each authority may claim, with some force, to speak for the people of the area. Thirdly, the perceptions that local institutions have of their status and authority are affected by factors less concrete than legislation and the processes of democratic election. They reflect also such intangibles as historic development, civic pride, and the identification of people with particular areas and institutions. Thus any multi-level structure of local government will be affected by pre-existing loyalties and if the structure does not treat competing loyalties equitably, its inherent difficulties will be compounded. This source of difficulty is not new, as the creation of county boroughs in the 1888 legislation suggests, but it will be argued here that the absence of equity in dealing with it is an important cause of the apparent impermanence of the new system.

The first and most significant political decision about the shape of the new local government system was that it should everywhere have two tiers. The Royal Commission had argued the case for two-tier local government in the three major conurban areas around Birmingham, Liverpool and Manchester but had proposed a system of unitary authorities elsewhere. In the debate on the Labour government White Paper (Cmnd 4276, 1970) the Conservative opposition had committed itself to the establishment of a two-tier structure, and this commitment was reproduced in the Conservative manifesto for the General Election of 1970. It is not difficult to see why such a structure was attractive to Conservatives. First of all, it accords with a strain of romantic localism which is to be found in Conservative thinking about local government and with the general antagonism of some Conservatives to what is often described as 'big government'.

Conservatives generally regarded the unitary authorities proposed first by Redcliffe-Maud and then by the Labour government as too remote to be democratic. But, as with all attempts to devise local government systems, the objective of local democracy was not always compatible with the goal of efficiency. Despite recent arguments to the contrary (Sharpe, 1978a, 1978b) there was little dispute at the time of reorganisation about the need to create larger local government units, which were universally thought likely to produce a higher standard of service at a lower unit cost. The fact that there was little hard evidence to support this view (Redcliffe-Maud, *Research Studies 2 and 3*, 1968; Stanyer, 1973, p. 122) did not prevent it from having a considerable influence on the course of reform. The new Conservative minister in charge of local government, Peter Walker, was identified with the cause of institutional modernisation and efficiency and he was therefore unwilling to sacrifice the presumed benefits of larger units on the altar of the party's affection for localism. The process of intra-party compromise pointed very directly towards a two tier system. Thus, in introducing his measure at second reading, Walker justified the creation of the lower tier on grounds which demonstrate the effects of history, localism and efficiency on the construction of a compromise solution: 'I considered it important that many of our boroughs and county boroughs, and our rural districts and urban districts, should be able to make decisions on matters that very much affected their local communities' (*Hansard*, 16 November 1971).

The second reason for the Conservatives' attraction to the two-tier solution was more overtly party political. It was no secret that Labour's acceptance of the unitary principle had been informed, as are all decisions about political institutions that have power to affect public policy, by the calculation of partisan advantage. So also was the Conservative decision to have a two-tier system in which the upper tier would be based on the existing counties, the centres of Conservative strength in local government. It is not necessary to agree with the Labour MP who detected in the Bill 'a pervading stench of gerrymander' (*Hansard*, 16 November 1971) to conclude that partisan considerations were influential in this first, major strategic compromise upon which the new system was built. They were also influential, perhaps more blatantly so, in some of the consequential decisions.

The first major implication of the decision to have a two-tier structure was that it immediately became impossible to treat existing local authorities equally. The old system was composed of counties, county districts and county boroughs. In the new system, counties (and, with amalgamations, county districts) would survive; county boroughs would disappear. And no amount of official argument to the contrary would convince the county boroughs that the new structure was based on anything other than the preservation and enhancement of one class of major authority and the degradation of the other. This is the most important single contributory factor to the failure of the new systems on the test of conclusiveness, for the dissatisfaction of the county boroughs, and in particular of those large county boroughs that would not form the basis of metropolitan districts, ensured a legacy of disgruntlement and injured pride. In such circumstances, any claim to have 'ended the uncertainty' (Walker, *Hansard*, 16 November 1971) by taking the question of local government off the agenda would be difficult to maintain.

It is instructive here to compare the reorganisation of 1974 with the reform of local government in London in 1964–5. In London a major premiss of reform was that no existing authority would survive the changes. Thus the London County Council (LCC), all of the existing metropolitan boroughs, the county boroughs of East Ham, West Ham and Croydon, and some county districts all disappeared. (The only concession to the existing institutional structure was the somewhat anomalous decision to create the Inner London Education Authority (ILEA) as a single-purpose body to preserve the integrity of the education service provided by the LCC.) All of these authorities fought, with varying degrees of ferocity, to maintain their existence. But once the legislation was passed none could claim with any conviction to have been treated unfairly when compared with any other.

In 1974 the outcome was very different. Major county boroughs in the non-metropolitan areas were subsumed into counties with which their relationship had hitherto been merely geographic or, in the cases of Bristol and Hull, into counties they felt to have been created for the primary purpose of subsuming them. To take four examples (from different parts of England), the county boroughs of Norwich, Southampton, Plymouth and Nottingham, with populations ranging from 120,000 to 300,000 and all having municipal charters dating from the Middle Ages, ceased to be all-purpose local authorities. They did not even have the compensation of having their boundaries as new districts expanded to bring in the suburbs which for many years had drawn on them, without paying rates, for services not provided by the county district councils that governed the suburbs.

Nor were these cities exceptional. Outside the areas which were to become metropolitan counties there were, in England, forty-two county boroughs. Of these, twenty-seven became district councils without any change to their boundaries. The Royal Commission report had provided some warrant for this conservatism on boundaries when it said, 'The new local government pattern should so far as practicable stem from the existing one' (Redcliffe-Maud, Cmnd 4040, 1969, Vol. I, para. 85) and the Conservative govern-

ment in its White Paper had said that, 'The bigger cities and towns
will retain their identities' (Cmnd 4584, 1971*b*), a view that was
reiterated by Walker in his speech introducing the second reading of
his Bill. But the maintenance of existing boundaries in so many major
urban areas could not but emphasise the reduction in status that the
new system implied. The earliest moves to recover some of the
powers they had 'lost' were made, within months of the new authorities becoming executive, by the nine most populous former county
boroughs in England outside the metropolitan counties. None of
these cities had had its boundaries varied when it became a district
council area. The effects of this kind of continuity on the performance
of the new systems are considerable and will be looked at in some
detail later. It should be noted here, however, that the objective of
retaining the identity of existing cities, while laudable in itself,
ensured that the loss of power and status of many of the county
boroughs would not be disguised by their incorporation of surrounding suburban areas. This conservatism, though clearly intended to
ease acceptance of the new arrangements, was therefore incompatible with the objective of conclusiveness.

In terms of civic pride, and political interest, it would have been
hard for these cities to accept that they were no longer to be independent providers of education and social services, nor to have unfettered control over the physical environment, whatever the changes
imposed by national legislation. Indeed, this difficulty was at the
heart of the failure of the county boroughs' representative body, the
AMC, to produce a coherent response to any of the proposals for
change that emerged between 1969 and 1972. What made the Conservative government's proposals particularly difficult to accept, and
ensured that this lack of acceptability would adversely affect the functioning of the new system, was that the other existing major
authorities – the county councils – not only continued to exist with
only minimal changes to their boundaries but acquired the function of
providing in the cities the services whose removal meant the end of
the county boroughs as all-purpose authorities. Under the proposals
of the Royal Commission and of the Labour government, county
boroughs would have disappeared, but so also would county councils
in favour of unitary authorities. Ancient cities would not have been
happy with such a structure, but it would have been difficult, as it was
in London in 1964, to point to inequity of treatment as a justification
for continuing hostility to the new system.

But it was more than civic pride and *amour propre* that conditioned
the response of the county boroughs. There was also an important
partisan dimension. Many county boroughs, of which those exemplified above are four, were often governed by councils with Labour
majorities. This was true of very few counties and there was little

reason to expect that Labour would control many more counties in the new system. Certainly in the first elections to the new county councils, Labour gained an absolute majority on only six English and four Welsh counties, and this at a time when the Conservatives were at the nadir of their popularity in the country. After the county elections in 1977, Durham was the only county in England to have a Labour-controlled council. Thus, in the major urban areas (outside the six metropolitan counties which will be considered later), the important policy fields of education and social services were seen to be effectively closed to Labour influence. The Labour leader of a major former county borough said, on resigning from the city council after reorganisation, 'The city council is no longer an instrument for bringing socialism to the people of Southampton', expressing graphically a view held in many other towns and cities.

THE METROPOLITAN COUNTIES

In the six metropolitan counties of the West Midlands, Greater Manchester, Merseyside, South Yorkshire, West Yorkshire and Tyne and Wear, the situation created by the demise of the county boroughs was similar in principle to the position in the rest of the country but soon began to show important differences in practice. These differences arose from a distribution of functions that ensured that in these areas the lower-tier district authorities, all but three of which were based upon, or included within their territory, one or more former county boroughs, would be more important in the direct provision of local government services than the metropolitan counties. Nevertheless, the superimposition of a strategic upper tier of local government quickly became a source of resentment and of varying degrees of irritation to officers and members of authorities which for centuries had wielded considerable unfettered power over their localities. As will be illustrated in some detail later, such resentment was particularly keenly felt, with important consequences for the functioning and likely permanence of the new structure, in those metropolitan districts derived from the cities which had considered themselves to be the regional centres of the areas in which the new metropolitan counties were given jurisdiction.

The second major implication of the decision 'that the reorganised system should everywhere be based on two forms of operational authorities' (Cmnd 4584, 1971*b*) was a need to decide upon the allocation of local government functions between the tiers. In the metropolitan counties the allocation was governed by principles that could scarcely be applied to the rest of the country, for it was easier to make the system there fit the twin goals of democracy and efficiency. Both the Royal Commission and the Labour government in its White

Paper had accepted that there was a need in the conurban areas for an authority, not unlike the Greater London Council (GLC) in its structure and functions, that would be able to take on the role of strategic and environmental planning and the provision of emergency services (that is, fire, police) over an area wider than that which might be appropriate for the provision of the more personal services of education, social services and housing. Also the establishment of the metropolitan counties in densely populated urban areas ensured that most of the lower-tier authorities would have populations large enough, by the criteria then prevailing, to enable them to provide these personal services. The Royal Commission had concluded that, for its unitary authorities and for those providing the personal services in the metropolitan areas, a minimum population level of 250,000 would be desirable (Redcliffe-Maud, Cmnd 4040, 1969, Vol. I, para. 289) and the Conservative government's White Paper accepted that, 'With functions such as education and the personal social services . . . the units appropriate to the provision of these services should have populations broadly within the range of 250,000 to 1,000,000' (Cmnd 4584, 1971*b*, para. 12). In the event, the lower-tier metropolitan authorities had populations covering a rather wider range, from South Tyneside (Tyne and Wear) with 172,990 at reorganisation to Birmingham (West Midlands) with almost 1·1 million.

It is worth noting, however, that the smallest metropolitan district was 57 per cent larger in population than the smallest county in England (Isle of Wight) and 74 per cent larger than the smallest county of all (Powys in mid-Wales). Even if one excludes these extremes, on the grounds of the preservation of the Isle of Wight as a separate county at a very late stage in the legislative process and what the chief executive of Powys County Council describes as 'the sparsity factor' in depopulated central Wales, there was a range between the smallest non-metropolitan *county* (Northumberland) and the largest metropolitan *district* (Birmingham) proposed in Walker's Bill of from 283,310 to almost 1·1 million, and only four non-metropolitan counties had populations bigger than that of the new lower-tier authority in Birmingham. Perhaps the only fair conclusion to be drawn from these comparisons is that despite the willingness of ministers and others to accept the recommendations of the Royal Commission as minimum, maximum and optimum population levels for the new authorities, the difficulties which academic researchers (Redcliffe-Maud, *Research Studies 3 and 4*, 1968; Redcliffe-Maud, Cmnd 4040, 1969, Vol. I, paras 217–21; Stanyer, 1973, pp. 138–9) found in demonstrating any link between size and efficiency were mirrored by the difficulties which politicians found in making the local government areas of a complex society conform to preconceived desirable levels of population.

It was possible to argue credibly that the lower-tier authorities in the metropolitan areas were big enough to provide the education, social services and housing functions efficiently, while preserving enough local identification for the objective of maintaining and strengthening local democracy also to be achieved. This division of function was in line with advice given to government not only by Redcliffe-Maud (Cmnd 4040, 1969, Vol. I, para. 248), but by Wheatley in Scotland (Wheatley, Cmnd 4150, 1969,) and in 1968 by the Seebohm Committee report on the personal social services (Seebohm, 1968, Cmnd 3703), that one authority should be responsible for housing, social services and education. Finally, only in the three metropolitan districts that did not contain a county borough (Knowsley in Merseyside; Tameside and Trafford in Greater Manchester) would it be necessary to create service departments from scratch. Even here the basic components of social services and education departments existed in the form of divisions of previous county authorities and, in the case of Knowsley, the status of two of its constituent authorities as excepted districts under the Education Acts.

The pattern of authorities and functions that emerged for the metropolitan counties was, therefore, as shown in Table 2.1. Broadly speaking, the categorical distinction which the Royal Commission had articulated between the 'environmental services' and the 'personal services' is reflected in the allocation of functions. The operation of the new system in the metropolitan counties is analysed in detail in the next chapter, but three points should be noted here: first,

Table 2.1 *Distribution of Major Functions[a] in Metropolitan Counties*.

Metropolitan Counties (6)	Metropolitan Districts (36)
Police[b]	Education
Fire	Social services
Consumer protection	Housing
Major roads	Local roads
Structure planning	Development control
Passenger transport	Amenities
Refuse disposal	Refuse collection

[a]For more detailed allocation of functions including areas of concurrent or overlapping jurisdiction see Department of the Environment, *Local Government in England and Wales: A Guide to the New System* (London: HMSO, 1974).

[b]Tyne and Wear has a joint police authority with Northumberland County Council.

a generally sensible division of function may reduce the potentiality for conflict between the tiers, but it will not remove the need for liaison; secondly, even within this sensible division of function it is immediately clear that the existence of shared responsibility in three fields – roads, planning, and refuse collection and disposal – was a possible source of tension between the tiers; and third, as Leach and Moore have argued (1979*a*, 1979*b*; Leach, 1977) the clearly pre-eminent position of the districts in the provision of services, as opposed to the planning of the environment, was bound to affect the performance of the system.

THE NON-METROPOLITAN COUNTIES

The allocation of functions between the tiers in the non-metropolitan, or shire, counties was more difficult for it was necessary to try to combine objectives that were inherently incompatible. Thus the objective of simplification was difficult to reconcile with the imposi tion in former unitary county borough areas of a two-tier structure with which they were unfamiliar. The goal of increased efficiency, particularly as measured by an increase in the calibre of members and officers in the new authorities, depended for its achievement on ensuring that the lower-tier authorities had a range of functions that would allow them to regard themselves, and be regarded, as more than glorified parish councils grafted on to the system as a localist makeweight for the remote bureaucracy of the upper-tier authorities. This condition clearly implied that district councils in the shires would have to be given responsibility for one major personal service. If this were to be so, and if the objective of achieving reorganisation with as little disruption as possible to existing arrangements were also to be met, then the housing function nominated itself, for it was the only one which was already the responsibility of all the classes of authority which, whether by metamorphosis or amalgamations, would consti- tute the new districts. For under the County Councils Act 1888, supplemented by the District Councils Act 1894, county boroughs, urban districts and rural districts were all housing authorities: there was no other local authority function of any significance for which all had responsibility.

It is being argued here that the decision to divide the personal services – to give education and social services to the county councils and housing to the districts – was an inevitable, even logical, conse- quence of the decision to have a two-tier system; that the allocation of functions in the shire counties was not, in other words, the result of rational, political decision-making. As Wood says (1976, p. 108), 'Without housing, the new districts would have so few important tasks that the new structure would be close to a unitary model', an eventuality that would have been inconsistent with Walker's 'insistence on the importance of districts as service providers'. Walker himself, however, places a different gloss on this decision, and one that illustrates once again the effects of localism and efficiency in Conservative thinking. In 1978 he described the process thus: 'The manner in which the functions were distributed was to list all the functions and . . . if a function could be done efficiently at a lower level, it was put at a lower level' (Interview with the author, 14 September 1978).

Whatever the reasons for the decision, it ensured that for the local authorities serving more than 75 per cent of the population of England and Wales the goal of unifying (or, in the case of the former county boroughs outside the metropolitan areas, keeping unified) the provision of the personal services of education, social services and housing would not be realised. It also ensured that, in addition to the structural need for liaison that would have arisen in any two-tier system, there was added a need for liaison between cognate functions provided by different authorities. As will be analysed in detail in the next chapter, this was a consequence of the allocation of functions in the shire counties that cast serious doubt on the capacity of the new system to pass the tests of efficiency, comprehensibility and conclusiveness. An examination of central–local relations in the years since 1974 (Chapter 7) also calls in question the performance of the reorganised system on the test of preserving and strengthening local autonomy, for the nature of such relations is, of course, conditioned by both the structural shape of, and the distribution of functions within, subnational government.

This brief examination of the statutory allocation of functions in the shire counties is completed by noting two other areas where responsibility was divided between the counties and the districts: planning and (except in Wales) refuse collection and disposal. Of these, the decision on planning was by far the more important. Not only did the distribution of functions contained in the Local Government Act 1972 greatly increase the number of planning authorities, with the consequent risk of tension and need for liaison between statutorily autonomous bodies, it also raised the possibility of throwing into confusion a system of strategic land-use planning and local development control that had scarcely begun, to operate. The first major planning act passed since 1947 had been the Town and Country Planning Act 1968. This Act had laid on county councils and, in the old system, county boroughs, a duty to produce structure plans as strategic indicators of planning policies in the medium to long term. The problem is succinctly stated by Brazier and Harris (1975, p. 255) when they point out that 'The 1972 Local Government Act . . . superimposed a two-tier local government structure on the unitary approach of the 1968 Town and Country Planning Act, and divided the planning process . . .' The procedural and institutional effects of this division are discussed in the next chapter. At this stage it should be noted that before the implementation of the 1972 Act there were 138 planning authorities in England and Wales outside London, although many districts and boroughs had planning powers delegated to them by county councils; the total after implementation was 422. Also the future of the planning function in the new system highlights again the likely differences in performance between the metropolitan and non-metropolitan areas of England. For although the change to a bifurcated planning process applied to both, its effect was likely to be influenced by the history of the planning function in the two parts of the reorganised structure. In particular, it was bound to be important that in the lower-tier authorities of the six metropolitan counties, with the three exceptions of Trafford, Tameside and Knowsley which did not include a former county borough, there already existed one or more planning departments, and even in the three exceptional metropolitan districts one or more of the constituent municipal boroughs or urban districts had had planning powers delegated to them by the county council. Thus it was the six upper-tier authorities, charged with the intellectually more stimulating task of strategic planning (as opposed to local planning and development control), that had to establish planning departments from scratch.

In the shire counties only those districts that were identical to, or were based upon, a county borough approached the reallocation of functions in the planning field with a staff experienced in all matters of planning and development control. In other districts, any professional planning staff who were available for transfer to the new authorities had experience only in the exercise of development control functions delegated to their councils by the county council. Thus, with the exception of those counties – Avon, Humberside and Cleveland – that were not based on an existing county council area, it was the lower-tier authority, responsible for the less professionally attractive, but arguably more publicly sensitive, function of local planning and development control, that had to provide themselves, sometimes absolutely from scratch, with a planning staff. Many commentators (Richards, 1975; Buxton, 1974; Smart, 1972) were apprehensive about the effects on the efficiency of the planning process of a short- to medium-term scarcity of professional planners. And the Department of the Environment, in offering advice on *Co-operation between Authorities* (Circular 74/73, 1973*b*), was clearly aware that there was a potential source of inefficiency and system malfunction in a structural change which, at the time of implementation, demanded that staff who had hitherto discharged either the direct or the delegated

Table 2.2 *Distribution of Major Functions*[a] *in English Shire Counties and Welsh Counties.*

Counties (47)	Districts (333)
Education	Housing
Social services	Development control
Structure planning	Passenger transport undertakings
Passenger transport co-ordination	Local roads
Major roads	Refuse collection[b]
Refuse disposal[b]	
Police[c]	
Fire	

[a]For more detailed allocation of functions, including areas of concurrent or overlapping jurisdiction see Department of the Environment, *Local Government in England and Wales: A Guide to the New System* (London: HMSO, 1974).

[b]In Wales both refuse collection and refuse disposal are district council functions.

[c]There are joint police authorities for the following groups of counties: Avon and Somerset; Devon and Cornwall; Dyfed and Powys; Hampshire and Isle of Wight; Tyne and Wear and Northumberland (Northumbria Police Authority); Clwyd and Gwynedd (North Wales Police Authority); Mid, South and West Glamorgan (South Wales Police Authority); East Sussex and West Sussex (Sussex Police Authority); Berkshire, Buckinghamshire and Oxfordshire (Thames Valley Police Authority); Hereford and Worcester and Shropshire (West Mercia Police Authority).

functions of 138 planning authorities should now discharge the statutory functions of 422.

The pattern of authorities and the distribution of major functions in England and Wales outside London and the metropolitan counties is shown in Table 2.2.

It will be noted from the allocation of functions that there would be a need for liaison on roads, planning, passenger transport and the collection and disposal of refuse, all services in which both levels of authority had statutory responsibilities. Further, the division of the personal services, with housing at one level and social services and education at the other, raised the probability, already noted, of a need for liaison between closely related services not provided by the same authority. The structure of liaison and its effects on the performance of the system are examined in Chapter 3.

BOUNDARY CONSERVATISM AND INSTITUTIONAL UNIFORMITY

The new system that became operational on 1 April 1974 had certain other characteristics which might have been expected to affect its functioning. It is as well to examine them briefly before going on to look at the workings of the new local authorities: they relate to boundaries, to the imposition of a uniform structure in all the non-metropolitan counties of England and Wales, to the agency arrangements that were possible between authorities and classes of authorities, and to statutory provisions relating to civic dignities and the status, style and title of authorities.

On boundaries it is important to note two consequences that have not yet been considered which arise from the conservative nature of the changes. First, it was decided, as was indicated earlier, to disturb as few existing boundaries as possible in order that reorganisation could proceed with a minimum of disruption. This meant that once the county boundaries were set by the legislation the district boundaries at the lower tier would be recommended by the Local Government Boundary Commission and they would be drawn by amalgamating existing districts where that was necessary to achieve an acceptable population level or, as in the case of the former county boroughs noted earlier, by designating the area of an existing authority as the area of a new one.

A measure of the degree of conservatism in the drawing of district boundaries can be derived from the following figures. Of the 296 non-metropolitan districts in England, 187 were created by the amalgamation of two or more former authorities or by the designation of an existing council area as that of a successor authority. This figure included the twenty-seven unchanged county boroughs noted earlier, together with fourteen former municipal boroughs or urban districts that became shire districts with no changes to their areas. Of the thirty-seven Welsh districts, seventeen arose from amalgamation of districts. These figures, however, tend to exaggerate the extent of the changes, for in the 109 English districts in which the boundaries of former authorities were altered, the changes were often very minor or were the consequence of the antecedent changes to county boundaries or of the need to make district boundaries compatible with the designated areas of new towns. The details are given in Table 2.3.

As a result of this conservative approach to existing local government boundaries, combined with the effects of widely varying population densities across England, the range of population levels in the non-metropolitan districts is very wide indeed, thus intensifying the difficulties that would arise, in any case, from the differences of resources among constitutionally equal authorities. At the time of reorganisation, the biggest non-metropolitan district in England (Bristol) had a population of 421,800 (bigger, incidentally, than all but six of the metropolitan districts, than four non-metropolitan English counties, than all but two of the Welsh counties) and the smallest (Teesdale in Co. Durham) had a population of 24,060. In resource terms, the difference can be expressed by comparing the rateable

Table 2.3 *Non-Metropolitan Districts in England and Wales (composition by reference to former administrative areas).*

A. *England*

Former county borough: boundaries unchanged	27
Former municipal borough/urban district: boundaries unchanged	14
Amalgamation of two or more former authorities: boundaries unchanged	146
Amalgamation with boundary changes to follow new county boundaries	35
Amalgamation with boundary changes to follow designated new town areas	20
Amalgamation with boundary changes affecting not more than two parishes	16
Others: i.e. more substantial boundary changes	38
Total	296

B. *Wales*

Former county borough: boundaries unchanged	0
Former municipal borough: boundaries unchanged	1
Amalgamation of two or more former authorities: boundaries unchanged	16
Amalgamation with boundary changes to follow new county boundaries	10
Amalgamation with boundary changes affecting not more than two parishes	5
Others: i.e. more substantial boundary changes	5
Total	37

values of these two extremes: Bristol with £56·6 million and Teesdale with £1·9 million.

The Local Government Act 1972 specified the areas of the new counties and delegated the determination of district council boundaries to the Secretary of State for the Environment who would act on the recommendations of a specially constituted Local Government Boundary Commission. These recommendations developed from the commission's investigations, its consideration of local wishes and its visits to the localities that were to be affected. But the determining criteria were those laid down by the Conservative government, first in their 1971 White Paper (Cmnd 4584, 1971b) and then in the guidelines for the commission published by the Department of the Environment (Circular 58/71, 1971) inviting proposals on district boundaries from local authorities and others. The clearest indication of the combination of localism and exaggerated respect for existing boundaries that continued, even after the major decision on a two-tier structure had been taken, to inform Conservative thinking on the shape of the new system at the district council level is found in guideline no. 5, quoted by the Local Government Boundary Commission in its *First Report* (Cmnd 5148, 1972):

> Wherever reasonably practicable a new district should comprise the whole of one or more existing county boroughs and county districts . . . Because of the need to concentrate on the main pattern of the new districts, new boundaries which do not follow the boundary of an existing local government unit or electoral area should be proposed only in special circumstances.

It should be noted that not all of the guidelines were mutually compatible: maintaining the identity of large towns was not compatible with a population range of 75,000 to 100,000; the injunction that 'only very exceptionally should a district be proposed with a population under 40,000' was not always compatible with the need to have regard to 'the wishes of local inhabitants' and 'the pattern of community life', and the commission had to ignore the minimum population level guideline in fourteen cases. Finally, as Richards points out (1975, p. 16), the maintenance of the identity of large towns not only cut across the 'dominant theme' of merging town and country but produced potentially unstable configurations. The towns of Bath, Cambridge, Hereford and Scunthorpe were each completely surrounded by one other district council area. All of these consequences of the conservative (and Conservative) approach to boundaries would affect the performance of the new system, at least on the tests of efficiency and conclusiveness and perhaps also on that of comprehensibility.

The second consequence of the conservative approach to the redrawing of local government boundaries affected the metropolitan areas. In particular, the durability of the new system was likely to be affected by the decision of the Conservative government, first indicated in its White Paper (Cmnd 4584, 1971*b*) to draw the county boundaries more tightly around the existing built-up area than had been the intention of the Labour government (Cmnd 4276, 1970) in a recommendation that followed closely the principles of the majority report of the Royal Commission. The Conservative government White Paper said that 'where it is impossible to meet all housing and redevelopment needs within the county boundaries, the answer will lie in development well outside the metropolitan area', a clear departure from Labour's view that 'the Commission were right to draw wide boundaries for these areas, taking in parts of the surrounding country'. On the face of it, it is difficult to resist the conclusion that there was a party political division lurking behind this difference of view. Certainly, as the secretary of state acknowledged in the second reading debate (*Hansard*, 16 November 1971), there was 'a straight difference of view in planning terms' about whether local authority boundaries around developed areas should be used as a means to contain urban sprawl or whether these areas should be given extended boundaries to enable them to meet their own further development needs. But the possibility of inter-authority disputes, given the likelihood that, as in London, a metropolitan authority that was often Labour-controlled would be surrounded by shire counties that were invariably Conservative-controlled, was very real indeed. With tightly drawn boundaries, as the Labour spokesman in the Commons John Silkin pointed out, development would 'rely on the co-operation of the planning authorities of the metropolitan counties and their neighbours coming to our rescue' (*Hansard*, 16 November 1971). He went on, in a sentence that is worth bearing in mind when considering the performance of the new system in the metropolitan areas: 'I wish that I could say that this sort of co-operation always works, but it does not. It creates considerable conflict, confusion, altercation and, above all, delay.'

The imposition throughout non-metropolitan England and Wales of a uniform structure of counties and districts created a number of apparently anomalous arrangements. These anomalies arose from the need to reconcile the original strategic compromise on structure with the results of parliamentary bargaining, the search for partisan advantage, and the effects of earlier, localised, attempts at local government reform.

At a very late stage in the legislative process, an amendment in the House of Lords succeeded in detaching the Isle of Wight from the proposed new county of Hampshire and 'reconstituting' it as a separate county. With a population of just under 110,000, the island would otherwise have been an ideally sized district in the new Hampshire, conforming to the optimum size requirements of the government guidelines to the Local Government Boundary Commission and, as an offshore island, satisfying better than most the criteria of community of interest and the wishes of local inhabitants, at least in so far as their first choice, continued existence as a separate county, was not on offer. With the success of the local campaign to avoid amalgamation with Hampshire, there was much to be said for recognising the exceptional nature of the island, as the government did in the case of the western and northern isles when local government in Scotland was reorganised the following year, and constituting it as a unitary authority. But the government had set its face against the unitary principle and so two district councils were created for the Isle of Wight when the criteria of efficiency and comprehensibility pointed very clearly to the creation of a single authority. In practice, by the use of shared facilities and agency arrangements of a sort to be described and evaluated in the next chapter, about 80 per cent of local government services on the island are provided by the county council. Thus it can be argued that uniformity of structure, in this case, has led to over-government, with three councils and ninety-nine elected members for a population of not much more than 100,000.

For the county of Cleveland the establishment of two-tier local government was particularly traumatic, for the Bill was passed only four years after the creation, by the amalgamation of Middlesbrough, Stockton-on-Tees, Thornaby-on-Tees, Redcar and their surrounding areas, of the unitary County Borough of Teesside. Now with the incorporation of the County Borough of Hartlepool as the basis of a new district and the division of Teesside county borough into three new districts, the new County of Cleveland became the only local government area in Britain in which the number of local authorities, and therefore the number of elected members, increased as a result of reorganisation. Again the need for uniformity ensured this result, but it could hardly be seen as an improvement either in the efficiency of local government in Teesside or in its comprehensibility to local people.

As a final example of the impact of the need for uniformity in structure the County of South Glamorgan should be considered. For here it is impossible to exclude from consideration of the decisions consequent on the commitment to a two-tier structure the importance of the search for partisan advantage in the form of the boundary gerrymander. As Wood says 'Cardiff was just about the only pocket of Conservative Party strength in south Wales' (1976, p. 127), and it is generally agreed in Wales and elsewhere that the creation of the county of South Glamorgan was prompted by the need to ensure some Conservative voice in the provision of county council services in south Wales. The new county looked when it was proposed in 1971 'very like the City of Cardiff with large boundary extensions' (Wood, 1976, p. 127). The creation within it of a second district, the Vale of Glamorgan based on the old Barry municipal borough, may have satisfied the need for uniformity in structure but it did not remove the taint of gerrymander and has left a legacy of bitterness in the new county of Mid Glamorgan, which was relatively impoverished by the loss of Cardiff's rateable value. Also, as in the Isle of Wight, agency arrangements and shared staff have ensured that South Glamorgan does not function in the way that a two-tier system is intended to do. Dissatisfaction with the dismemberment of Glamorgan continues in south Wales and has the same effect on the performance of the new system there as has the disgruntlement of the former county boroughs in England. Again it is difficult to see how a structure based on a widely recognised, and almost as widely resented, gerrymander can be expected to pass the test of conclusiveness. Indeed in local government circles in south Wales the one regret at the Labour government's failure in 1979 to secure the establishment of a Welsh Assembly was that it removed the immediate prospect of further reforms of the structure of local government.

THE INTRODUCTION OF AGENCY ARRANGEMENTS

The 'agency clause' of the Local Government Act 1972 has had a very significant effect on the performance of the new system, as will become clear in the next chapter. Its elevation from a relatively uncontentious clause designed to increase the flexibility with which individual authorities might approach their statutory duties into an alteration to the statutory distribution of functions that amounted to a major derogation from the principles underlying the establishment of a two-tier system is an important example of the effects of parliamentary compromise on the credibility and likely durability of the reformed structure.

During the debates on the Bill members representing the now-obsolescent county boroughs complained about the proposed allocation of functions. The 'standard defence' (Wood, 1976, p. 150) resorted to by ministers against these complaints was that the agency clause would provide the necessary flexibility in the performance of local government responsibilities. The clause (Clause 101, Local Government Act 1972) allows one authority to act as the agent of another in the performance of its duties. Precisely, the Act says that 'a local authority may arrange for the discharge of any of their functions . . . by any other local authority in England and Wales' although by subsequent clauses the emergency services, education and the social services are excluded from the scope of agency arrangements. These exclusions ensured that by far the most significant area in which agency agreements would be negotiated would be highways construction and maintenance, a field in which the obsolescent county boroughs and the major urban districts already had responsibilities and fully staffed departments to discharge them. The circular (Department of the Environment, Circular 131/72, 1972) which the government issued to give guidance on the practical implications of agency also nominated planning, consumer protection, libraries and refuse disposal as suitable services for the negotiation of agreements, and it is not without interest that in two of these, planning and refuse removal (as well as highways), statutory responsibility was shared between two levels of local government.

Four points about the immediate effects of agency on the new system should be noted and should be borne in mind when the operation of the system is examined in the next chapter. First, there is little doubt that the provision for the negotiation of agency agreements eased the process of implementation, for in many authorities it allowed the preservation of an existing department despite the fact that the statutory responsibility for the service provided by the department had passed to another authority. Ministers had used this prospective benefit as an answer to parliamentary critics of the abolition of the county boroughs and there is little doubt that it was regarded politically, if not legally, as a means of enhancing the proposed role of non-metropolitan districts, especially those former county boroughs that regarded responsibility for housing as insufficient to maintain their status as major authorities.

Secondly, and this follows very directly from the point about preserving the integrity of departments, the use of the agency clause was likely to exacerbate the 'former county borough' problem referred to earlier. Circular 131/72 had said, more in hope than expectation it might be thought, that 'where the previous distribution of responsibilities has been modified by the Act, agency agreements should not be regarded simply as a means of one authority to "claw back" from another the services which were provided by its predecessor'. Not only were they likely to be so regarded, ministers had positively encouraged borough Members of Parliament so to regard them. The agency system thus added to the perceptions of the likely impermanence of the new arrangements which had arisen from the inequitable treatment of the county boroughs as compared with the counties. It also helped to increase the credibility of the case made for adjustments to the statutory distribution of functions, first by the 'big nine' former county boroughs and later by many others, which eventually issued in the Labour government's proposals in 1979 for 'organic change' (Cmnd 7457, 1979*a*). These proposals are considered later (Chapter 8) but it should be noted here that this effect of agency can scarcely be seen as contributing to the stability or permanence of the new structure of local government.

Thirdly, the employment of the agency clause was certain to increase and complicate the need for liaison arrangements between authorities. Agency agreements were likely to be complex enough for purely administrative and legal reasons, and paragraph 20 of Circular 131/72 listed four matters that might have to be spelt out in some detail – functions delegated and discretion allowed to the agent, staff and property arrangements, duration of agreement and provision for variations, and budgetary and financial control arrangements between the authorities involved. These imply a lot of liaison, both at member level on policy and at officer level on implementation. If it was likely, or even possible, that the agreement would be regarded, despite the pious hopes of the authors of the circular, as a means of clawing-back powers 'lost' in the Act, then the process of liaison might be embittered, extended and made more expensive.

Finally, the whole notion of agency had major implications for the comprehensibility and simplicity of the new local government system. What had been promised was a clear and unambiguous allocation of functions; not even the statutory distribution of responsibility had achieved that. But the superimposition of agency on an already complicated allocation ensured that, in much of the country, any claim to have simplified local government and to have made it easier for the ordinary person to understand would be so weak as to be laughable. It also ensured that the processes of public accountability and democratic control would be so convoluted as to raise serious doubts about their effectiveness.

STATUS, STYLES AND TITLES

The provisions about the preservation of ancient civic dignities and the status, style and title of local authorities were also likely to affect the performance of the new system. While it is not suggested that these provisions (contained in sections 245 to 249 of the Local Government Act 1972) are in any sense as important as the matters of boundaries, uniformity and agency just considered, the point remains that the preservation, particularly in the cases of large former county boroughs, of the ancient titles of borough and city added a further reason to conclude that the settlement of the local government structure contained in the Act might not be considered to be absolutely final. There is some evidence in official sources that the government may have been aware of the possibility that these matters of style, title and dignity might not be wholly divorced from the more highly charged matters of the allocation of functions and the comparison of the powers and duties of the new authorities with those of the old. As with agency, the practicalities of the arrangements regarding *Status of Authorities*, *Civic Dignities, Etc*. were dealt with in a circular (Department of the Environment, Circular 51/73, 1973a) in which the government found it necessary to tell those new councils that might wish to exercise their right to petition the Crown for a borough charter that such charters 'will be confined to matters of status, dignities and ceremonial'. In short, the maintenance of styles and titles – borough, city, mayor – associated with the old system might be a minor additional encouragement to those new authorities which might wish to seek the early recovery of some of the powers lost in the reorganisation. Finally the provision that, in the areas of the smaller boroughs of the old system, parishes might retain their councils as 'successor parishes' and opt for the title of 'town council' with their chairman styled 'town mayor' raised complicated questions of precedence within districts which might be a minor complication in the functioning of the new structure. This possibility also arose in the case of old boroughs within the area of new councils that did not apply for borough status for the whole of the new district. In these cases, the district councillors for the area of the old borough were designated 'charter trustees' and enabled to elect one of their number as 'town mayor'. As with the decision to preserve the identity of major towns and cities, these concessions may have eased acceptance of the new system but they also created some minor continuing stresses within it.

Chapter 3

THE NEW STRUCTURE: PERFORMANCE

As soon as it was clear that the new system of local government in England and Wales would be a two-tier one in which new counties, except in the metropolitan areas, would be the dominant authorities, the existing authorities began to establish steering committees to organise the transition. It is not the purpose of this book to duplicate the study by Richards (1975) of the process of implementation, but it should be noted that these committees, set up under section 264 of the Local Government Act 1972, received a large amount of advice on liaison arrangements offered in advance of the new councils becoming executive on 1 April 1974. The conclusions arrived at by such committees more often than not formed the basis for the liaison arrangements introduced in 1974 and it is with these arrangements and their practical workings that this chapter is principally concerned. It is intended that a picture of the operation of the new structure will emerge from this examination and that this picture will provide a basis upon which to evaluate the performance of the new institutions.

Clearly, the Department of the Environment as the ministry responsible both for the implementation of the Act and the operation of the new system realised that both the shape of the system and the allocation of functions within it necessitated the issue to new authorities of detailed and specific advice on inter-authority relations. On 21 February 1974 the Department of the Environment issued, as a Circular, a consolidated 'list of all orders and regulations made, and most of the circulars and consultation papers issued between 26 October 1972 and 8 February 1974'. The total number of documents listed was 195 and although only a few had a general bearing on the operation of the new structure, the amount of advice does indicate the complexity of this sort of major institutional change.

In addition to this direct advice from the department, the steering committees (and later the new authorities) had before them the recommendations of a study group set up in 1971 by the Secretary of State for the Environment and the local authority associations 'to examine management principles and structures'. The report of this study group, under the chairmanship of M. A. Bains, then clerk of Kent County Council became known universally in local government as the 'Bains Report', and while the majority of its recommendations related to the internal management of local authorities and will therefore be considered in the next chapter, it also contained a chapter on 'Working arrangements between the new authorities' and, as such, it had a pervasive effect on the nature of the liaison machinery adopted in the individual counties.

The major recommendation of the Bains Report was that any joint bodies established for the purpose of liaison between the tiers in the new counties should be designed 'to co-ordinate the interaction between all county and district functions' (Bains, 1972, para. 8.6). It explicitly advised against the alternative of having 'joint committees in respect of each major function or service' (Bains, 1972, para. 8.7) on the grounds that such committees would not be conducive to the adoption of what it calls the 'community approach to the problems and needs of areas'. It is difficult not to conclude, on the basis of the research for this book, that the so-called 'community approach' draws its superficial attractiveness as a guiding principle of liaison from a view of the local government world that discounts the importance of statutory autonomy, independence, *amour propre* and local politics, partisan and otherwise. The reasons for such a conclusion will emerge in the course of the analysis of the machinery of liaison that follows.

It should be noted, first of all, that the initial designs for liaison were produced, as it were, *in abstracto* by the joint committees set up under the Local Government Act to organise the transition from one system of local government to another. These committees had a wide range of matters to decide, most of which would be once-for-all issues of a purely mechanical and practical kind and which would not continue to affect the new system once it became operational. It was, of course, essential to settle such matters as the transfer and ownership of assets, the movement of staff from one authority or class of authority to another and the continuity of services during the changeover period. But matters of that kind, if they involved political interest at all, involved that of a dying system. Members and officers of the old authorities might wish to extract a maximum of advantage from the process of change, especially if they saw clearly where their own interests would lie after it. But in these areas of discussion they would be dealing with matters of fact which, where they raised matters not amenable to agreement locally, could be settled by the direction of ministers called in to break a deadlock. On staffing matters these committees operated under advice and guidance from the Local Government Staff Commission, a body specially created by the Act and appointed by the Secretary of State for the Environment to ensure that the position of existing local government staff was adequately protected. This left little room for discretion or manœuvre on the part of the joint committee.

In the case of recommending arrangements for organising contacts and liaison between the tiers, the members of joint committees found themselves faced with the need to consider a continuing political and administrative process in which they would not jointly have any interest. The members of these committees were drawn from among the councillors and officers of obsolescent authorities, many of whom were either opposed to the whole idea of change in so far as it meant the demise of authorities to which they had owed loyalty for a very long time or were opposed to the particular kind of change which the 1972 Act imposed. It was much simpler to concentrate on the concrete matters of transfer referred to above, and on the internal arrangements necessary for the individual new councils than to consider the much more conjectural question of how to organise relations among these new authorities. Perhaps, also, there was some reluctance to enter this political thicket before the partisan composition and policy objectives of the new authorities were known. Whatever the reasons for it, the outcome across the country was a very general implementation of the major liaison recommendations of the Bains Report.

These arrangements arose, then, from a fairly uncritical acceptance of the Bains recommendations, supported by direct advice from the Department of the Environment, particularly in Circular 131/72 (1972) on agency arrangements and Circular 74/73 (1973*b*) on co-operation between authorities on planning matters. These documents had in common an assumption that the relationship between the tiers in the new system would be a co-operative one. Bains, for example, uses the term 'community approach' in a way which assumes that the will to co-operate in determining the shape and content of public services in particular localities would overcome the structural difficulties created by a reorganisation that not only ensured a need for liaison everywhere, but also maximised rather than minimised the number of policy fields in which there would arise occasions for liaison. Bains was clear that its terms of reference did not permit it to make specific recommendations concerning 'provisions relating to the discharge of functions' (Bains, 1972, para. 8.2) and it is probable that its exclusion from this sort of consideration caused it to make recommendations that were both unspecific and optimistic. It is possible also that the preparation of the report by a group of senior local government officers, working under only the 'general direction' (Bains, 1972, p. v.) of a steering group of members drawn from obsolescent local authority associations, contributed to a downplaying of the more politically sensitive problems of liaison. More generally, also, there was an understandable reluctance to say anything that might be interpreted as an attempt to abridge the freedom of new authorities to make their own arrangements.

Nor were the Department of the Environment circulars any more ready to be specific in their recognition of the problems that might surround the process of inter-authority liaison. Circular 131/72 (1972) repeated the words which Walker had used in the House of Commons and which might be read as a guarded admission of the difficulties inherent in his new system: ' . . . if one is to have two levels in local government, then from the time this commences they should work together in a spirit of co-operation not of hostility and rivalry'. Looked at in the light of the fieldwork on which this book is based, that statement seems optimistic to a fault for there is much evidence that many authorities have regarded the county–district relationship as an adversary one rather than as a co-operative one.

But the circular was optimistic in another way, and one that is of particular relevance to the argument introduced in Chapter 2 that the inequity of treatment between classes of authority amounted to a serious structural flaw which would have an effect on the functioning of the new system. In this context it is worth quoting in full the relevant passage from paragraph 11 of Circular 131/72 (1972):

> Suggestions that agency arrangements might be made in particular cases should not be regarded as a reallocation of statutory responsibilities contrary to the way in which these are defined in the Local Government Act; nor, where the previous distribution of responsibilities has been modified by the Act, should they be regarded simply as a means for one authority to 'claw back' from another the services which were provided by its predecessor.

The evidence is that in many counties agency agreements were regarded by district councils in exactly the way that the circular discouraged. Such an approach to agency has an important continuing effect on the system in that it encourages large districts, especially the more important former county boroughs in the shire counties, to believe, first, that they have 'lost' less than they actually have and, secondly, that the loss may, in any case, be temporary. These factors will be considered in more detail in the discussions of the operation of agency arrangements and of the formal proposals for 'organic change' published in 1979.

The advice offered in the circular (Department of the Environment, Circular 74/73, 1973*b*) on the operation of the divided planning function was, if anything, even less specific than that of either Bains or Circular 131/72. The circular said that 'though concerned with a particular function, [it] does not attempt to prescribe what arrangements for co-operation should be set up in particular areas' and expressed the somewhat pious view that 'the test of the effectiveness of the arrangements will be the extent to which the public will receive the planning service it is entitled to expect'. There were references to the need for 'flexible local arrangements and understandings' (here echoing almost exactly similar exhortations in both Bains and Circular 131/72), to the need to avoid laying down 'rigid rules and procedures' and to the desirability of creating 'some form of machinery . . . at member level to give direction and impetus to the partnership'. On this last point, once again, the government referred to the Bains advice against committees dealing with individual services and, once again, it makes an assumption that an attitude of co-operation and constructiveness would be automatically available everywhere. Finally, the circular announced that 'the Secretaries of State are confident that authorities have available a sound basis for partnership'. The soundness of that basis now has to be evaluated in the light of the evidence that members and officers have found the division of the planning function more troublesome than any other specific decision on the allocation of functions, and that the next Conservative government to come to office after reorganisation has found it necessary to legislate, in the Local Government, Planning and Land Act 1980, to simplify the distribution of planning powers. More generally, the optimism which pervades all of the official advice is much at variance with the experience of members and officers in all services and in most counties in operating the complex processes of liaison made inevitable by the two-tier system set up by the Act. The remainder of this chapter will deal in some detail with the practical processes of liaison between authorites and with the specific problems encountered in certain functional areas.

COUNTY-WIDE LIAISON

The most common form of county-wide liaison, both in the metropolitan and non-metropolitan areas, was organised through the kind of county joint committee envisaged by Bains. In only nine of the forty-five English metropolitan and non-metropolitan counties did the process of liaison involve joint committees dealing with particular services and some of these, such as the joint highways committees between Cambridgeshire and the district councils serving Cambridge and Peterborough, should be viewed as *ad hoc* institutions to deal with exceptional problems arising from the presence of a minority of urban areas in a predominantly rural county. Conversely, only thirteen of the new counties in England and Wales began to operate the system in 1974 without a county liaison committee, representing the county council and all of the district councils within it. These bodies typically have a membership composed of the chairman of the county council, the leader of the county council and the chairman of the policy committee of the county council, together with their opposite numbers from each of the district councils within the county. These members are usually supported by their chief executives and, when necessary, by other chief officers and other chairmen. Clearly, such committees can become very large indeed, especially in those counties, such as Essex, Hampshire and Kent, that have a large number of districts, and there is little doubt that their generally poor performance and their tendency, throughout the country, to fall into disuse are partly because of their size. Bodies of this size and composition lend themselves more to position-taking than to the process of constructive compromise envisaged by ministers, Bains and the pre-reorganisation circulars. As one chief executive put it: 'Many of the districts feel that this is a very formal way of somebody standing up in alphabetical order of districts and giving a comment and no real discussion across the table.'

These county-wide joint committees were very important in the transitional phase between the old system and the new, but the general pattern has been for them to decline very substantially in significance and effectiveness thereafter. Two comments from chief executives will illustrate the point; both are officers of major districts in shire counties, the first in a former county borough:

I think that it was important that the counties demonstrated that they were interested enough in liaison to set them up. I think . . . they are not very effective.

There is sometimes a little difficulty in finding enough items for an agenda but it is necessary as a public relations exercise.

The difficulty in finding enough for the county joint liaison committees to discuss is very widespread and, in the shire counties in particular, a major reason is that, in the words of one chief executive, 'there are very few across-the-board problems: most problems are district to county'. The result of this has been a general decline in the frequency of meetings and, in some counties, a decision to drop them altogether in favour of *ad hoc* meetings when necessary. It is clear, also, that abandonment in some counties owed much to the opportunity that these committees gave for the public expression of the hostilities inherent in the two-tier structure. In particular, the problems of lost status deeply conditioned the approach which many former county boroughs brought to this form of inter-authority liaison. Indeed, Leach and Moore (1979*a*, p. 169) say that 'the attitude of the county and districts . . . to the 1974 reorganisation' is 'crucial to an understanding of the pattern of county/district relations' and they comment also on the remarkable 'resilience of attitudes formed at reorganisation'.

The effects of this 'former county borough (FCB)' problem are most intense in the metropolitan counties although they are also felt elsewhere, a point to which attention will be directed in another context later. In the metropolitan counties, however, the problems of status and former status have been so acute that they have, in several cases, led to the complete or partial collapse of formal liaison mechanisms between the tiers of local government. In both West Yorkshire and South Yorkshire all liaison quickly became the subject of informal officer-to-officer contact, occasionally complemented by discussions between leading political figures. In West Yorkshire the process by which the formal liaison arrangements between the county council and the five metropolitan district councils were abandoned is exemplified by the following comment from a former chief executive of the city of Leeds: 'It got so bad . . . that . . . I've seen an occasion when we've spent three hours arguing about the minutes of the previous meeting . . .' In the case of South Yorkshire, the formal processes of liaison between the county and the four metropolitan districts failed, in the words of one participant, when the leader of the county council 'took his bat home', a remark which, whether accurate or not, is typical of an inter-authority relationship described by yet another metropolitan county chief executive as 'years of open warfare'.

In the metropolitan counties the effects on the operation of the two-tier local government system of matters of status derive from three distinct sources. First, as was indicated in the previous chapter, only three of the thirty-six lower-tier authorities in these counties are neither based upon, nor contain within them, one or more former county boroughs. Only Tameside and Trafford in Greater Manchester and Knowsley in Merseyside were formed entirely from authorities that had any experience of two-tier local government. As one of these chief executives put it, 'We think that we understand two-tier government in a way that no one else does', but for the other thirty-three metropolitan districts, based as they were on former county boroughs and with their boundaries drawn tightly around urban areas, the superimposition of an upper tier of local government was considered to be unnecessary as well as both intrusive and duplicative.

Secondly, as Leach and Moore (1979*a*, p. 174) point out, the distribution of functions in the metropolitan areas is such as to make the so-called lower-tier authorities the predominant providers of local government services. Comparing the two kinds of two-tier system now in operation in England and Wales, Leach and Moore say: 'In the shire counties, the balance of power is tilted very much towards the county; whilst in the metropolitan counties it is tilted very much towards the district' and it is clear that this imbalance in the metropolitan areas increases the feelings of the districts that the county council is a redundant institution that creates over-government, duplication and tension in the provision of services. Leach and Moore

(1979*a*, p. 175) also note that several metropolitan counties are engaged in 'a painful search for a distinctive indentity', a conclusion supported by the investigations conducted for this book in all six of the metropolitan counties. The effect on the operation of the system of the distribution of functions is significant enough to merit extended treatment here before going on to look at the third source of status-related strain, the position of former regional centres.

The allocation of functions in the metropolitan areas leaves the county council without any personal service to administer and with only the emergency services and consumer protection as areas of exclusive jurisdiction. In the case of the police service, moreover, the amount of discretion left to the council, working through its police committee, is very strictly limited by the twin influences of Home Office regulations and the independence of chief constables in operational matters. Where there is a joint police authority, the amount of power left to the individual local authority is reduced still further. In other major areas of provision, responsibility was either shared with the districts, as in the cases of planning and refuse collection and disposal, or likely to be the subject, at least initially, of agency arrangements with the districts, as in the case of major roads. The final responsibility, passenger transport, involved making the county council the passenger transport authority, but detached the administration of the service by making it the business of a passenger transport executive. Both in the statutory allocation of functions and in the operational arrangements necessary for their discharge, the metropolitan counties were disadvantaged. They had to establish themselves from scratch and it was inevitable, therefore, that they would rely heavily in their early years on the political experience and professional expertise available within their areas. Both of these commodities were, more often than not, in the control not of the counties themselves but of the district councils as successor authorities to the county boroughs on which most of them were based.

In the early years after reorganisation, however, the metropolitan counties began to become more self-assertive in an attempt to give a semblance of reality to their notional statutory position as strategic, even subregional, planning authorities. The effect of this search for an operational role which they could regard as commensurate with their statutory position is graphically described in this comment from the chief executive of a metropolitan borough: 'The breakdown of relations with the county council stemmed from a structure that gave the metropolitan counties too little to do and therefore their members and officers were determined to make the most of the highways and planning functions.' Similarly, another city chief executive referred to the fact that his council, formerly 'an all-purpose authority, accustomed to doing things' did not take kindly to 'anybody that got in their way'. And with a distribution of functions which left this former county borough with statutory responsibility for education, social services and housing, and agency agreements with the county council covering highways and traffic management, it found itself after reorganisation doing most of the things it had done before. Its statutory change in status was not reflected in practice and both officers and members, here as in other metropolitan districts, were resentful of the very presence of the county council and bound to resist any attempt by the county council to enhance its role and increase its influence in the area administered by the district. In short, the relationship between the tiers in all the metropolitan areas is an adversary one rather than a co-operative one. The effectiveness of the new system and its ability to pass the tests of efficiency and permanence cannot be judged other than unfavourably, especially when the chief executives of two metropolitan districts in the same county can say, in one case, 'We treat the county very much at arm's length' and, in the other, 'We've basically written [the county council] off'.

Thus the prospects of a co-operative relationship or, in the Bains phrase, 'a community approach' in the metropolitan counties were reduced by the effect of status on the new system in two significant ways. First, there was the effect on the new system of the status carried forward from the old, especially by the former county boroughs whose powers and, through the extensive use of agency, functions were scarcely reduced. And secondly, there was the attempt by the new counties, after the initial problems of establishing themselves had been solved, to provide themselves with a range of powers and an amount of influence that was consistent with their notional status as subregional, strategic authorities.

The third and final way in which questions of status have affected the performance of the system in the metropolitan counties is, in some ways, an extension and intensification of the 'former county borough' problem referred to earlier. In all six of the metropolitan counties, the county–district relationship is worst, and mutual distrust and antagonism deepest, between the county council and the district based upon that former city that considered itself to be the historic regional centre. Thus Birmingham, Liverpool, Manchester, Sheffield, Leeds and Newcastle resent even more than the other metropolitan districts the loss of their all-purpose status and local government independence and autonomy. The reason for this is simply enough described but has a complex and pervasive effect on the new system. To take Birmingham as an example, it is clear that before reorganisation the city had an influence and standing in the West Midlands that extended further than the local government area over which the all-purpose county borough authority had jurisdiction. That influence, that capacity to affect the development of the entire area, whether apparent or real in the old system, is now seen to have found an institutional home in the West Midlands County Council. And the same applies, *mutatis mutandis*, to the other cities mentioned above and their surrounding counties. Dixon (1978, p. 65) makes the following observation about the relationship between Leeds and West Yorkshire:

> The county argued that it alone should carry out this function [foreign borrowing] for the county as a whole which brought the counter arguments by Leeds that its name was best known in Europe, the name of West Yorkshire being hardly known at all . . . and should therefore be designated the 'lead' authority for this purpose.

Additionally, these historic regional centres now have to accept an equality of status with other metropolitan districts that they did not have to accept with other county boroughs before reorganisation. As the chief executive of one county said:

> I think the local authority which formerly regarded itself as having some semi-regional standing . . . has lost out . . . and when it occasionally tries to reassert it, the other districts on the whole prefer the county to the old city. It's not an easy relationship.

The structure and process of liaison in the non-metropolitan counties are also affected by the questions of status and former status raised by the inequity of treatment of former authorities in the 1972 Act. As a general statement, it can be said that just as the transition to the new authorities was easiest in those counties whose boundaries changed little and which did not absorb a former county borough, so also has the process of liaison been happier there. Given the variety of the changes made in the 1972 Act, it is not surprising that there are exceptions to this overall picture. It is, however, an indicator of the fact that uncomplicated and harmonious relations across the tiers of local government are the exception rather than the rule that the same examples are quoted regularly by both members and officers. The relationship, for example, between Essex County Council and the district council which took over the unchanged area of the former County Borough of Southend is generally regarded as excellent. The whole process of liaison in East Sussex, a county that was formed by the amalgamation of a former county area with three former county boroughs (Brighton, Eastbourne and Hastings), all of which became district council areas with unchanged boundaries, is so harmonious that it is one of the few counties in which the district councils do not find it useful to meet separately from the county council. There is no county branch of the Association of District Councils (ADC), nor is there any other forum in which the districts attempt, as is commonly done in other parts of the country, to formulate a common view on matters of discussion, liaison and dispute between the tiers of local government. Despite this picture of harmony and co-operation, however, the decision not to establish a county branch of the ADC was not unanimous. But according to one chief executive, who thought that there was a need for such inter-district liaison, 'the view prevailed . . . [that] it would be a source of division between county and districts'.

But these are the exceptional cases. Reorganisation involved the incorporation of one or more former county boroughs in twenty-seven of the thirty-nine English non-metropolitan counties and in four of the eight Welsh counties. In almost all of them the quality of liaison, and therefore the effectiveness of the new system of local government, has been adversely affected by the continuing disgruntlement of the officers and members of former county boroughs now serving district councils whose only significant area of exclusive jurisdiction is housing. And there is an awareness in those counties that do not contain a former county borough and where the process of liaison is effective and harmonious that this may be the result, at least in part, of the fact that none of the districts is a former all-purpose authority. This view is exemplified in the comment of the chief executive of one such county that 'had there been one big county borough it might have upset the apple cart'.

This last comment may also have a more general significance in its reference to the possible effect on the system of liaison of a big county borough, for it is impossible not to consider the likelihood that the effect of the 'former county borough' problem on the workings of the new system varied with the size of the borough concerned. Certainly, it has been, and continues to be, most acute in those counties that contain the so-called 'big nine' – those former county boroughs outside the metropolitan counties that have populations of more than 200,000. As was mentioned in the previous chapter, these nine – Bristol, Nottingham, Leicester, Hull, Stoke-on-Trent, Plymouth, Derby, Southampton, Portsmouth – launched a campaign in June 1974 to regain the powers they had lost in a reorganisation that had become effective only two months before and that sort of stance was not conducive to good relations in their own counties. Even here, however, the picture has been variable. County–district relations are worst between Bristol and Avon and between Hull and Humberside for in these two cases a number of strains are present, all of which militate against the smooth functioning of the system. First, each city formed the basis for the new county into which it was incorporated and to which it 'lost' its powers in education, social services and strategic planning. The classification given by Richards (1975, p. 14) to these two new counties (and to Cleveland), 'Amalgamation of former county boroughs with surrounding hinterland', is not only accurately descriptive; it is also suggestive of one of the structural reasons for bad relations between city and county in the new system. For, in addition to their own loss of authority, Bristol and Hull have the constant comparison of their own long history of independent local government with the passage of that authority to new councils with no history at all. Secondly, the proportion of the county's population and resources (as measured by rateable value) contained within the boundaries of these cities is high (as it is with seven of the 'big nine'): Bristol has 46 per cent of the population and 54 per cent of the rateable value of the county of Avon; Hull has 33 per cent of the population and 30 per cent of the rateable value of Humberside. In both cases, it is difficult for the cities to accept equality of status with other districts in their county, none of which comes anywhere near them in population or resources and only two of which (Bath in Avon, Grimsby in Humberside) have ever been all-purpose authorities. Thirdly, in terms of party politics, the dominant political party in both these cities feels itself to be permanently disadvantaged by the creation of the county council. Hull is almost permanently controlled by the Labour Party, while the political control of Humberside will probably alternate between Labour and Conservative, with the latter likely to win more often than the former; Bristol is more often Labour than Conservative, while the Labour victory in Avon in 1981 is likely to prove to be exceptional. Fourthly, their position comparatively with the English metropolitan districts, with their much wider range of powers, is a constant reminder of the extent of their loss of authority: only six metropolitan districts have bigger populations than Bristol, and Hull has a bigger population than eighteen metropolitan districts.

Some of these characteristics also apply to others of the 'big nine' – Leicester, for example, provides 35 per cent of the population and 37 per cent of the rateable value of Leicestershire – but it is the combination of factors that compounds and deepens the problem of county–district relations in Humberside and Avon. Also, the combination of sources of disharmony makes it very difficult to envisage the relationship being improved, as it has been in the cases of others of the 'big nine' by liaison at the party political level. In Devon, for example, the situation has been improved by the fact that the positions of Leader of the County Council and Leader of Plymouth City Council were held by the same individual, an example of the usefulness of having 'dual' members that is not replicated throughout the country. And in Hampshire some of the heat has been taken out of the relationship between the county council and Southampton because at the time of the publication of the Labour government's 'organic change' proposals in 1979 (Cmnd 7457, 1979*a*) the Leader of the City Council was personally opposed to the proposals, as well as being a leading member of the controlling group on the county council. Despite these exceptions, however, there is no evidence to suggest that the 'big nine', as a group, are any more resigned to a long-term acceptance of their position than they were in 1974. For party political reasons, to which attention will be directed later, the chances of securing change in the short to medium term were greatly reduced when the Labour government lost office in 1979. But the fact that they have not abandoned all hope of change, together with the adjustments to the distribution of planning functions by legislation passed in the Local Government, Planning and Land Act 1980, ensures that county–district relations in the eight counties concerned will not be entirely harmonious.

Further evidence of the possible link between status, size and the performance of the new system is found in the campaign, mounted between 1977 and 1978, by a group of non-metropolitan districts who described themselves, somewhat cumbersomely, as 'The Cities and Boroughs of medium size'.|This group – comprising thirteen districts based on thirteen former county boroughs and four based on five former municipal boroughs, three of which (Poole, Swindon and Slough) had entertained hope of county borough status in the old system – pressed for a more limited adjustment in the distribution of functions than that sought by the 'big nine', but they added a further twelve counties in which there were major lower-tier authorities that had expressed public dissatisfaction with the status quo. The relevance of size of authority is suggested first by the title chosen by the group and, more specifically, by the fact that in each of the statements it published – on planning, social services, and highways and traffic management – the districts concerned were described as 'authorities all of whom [sic] have an urban nucleus of between 100,000 and 200,000 people, i.e. the substantial urban authorities in the non-/metropolitan areas'. Nor is it surprising that the criterion of size of authority should be applied by those seeking to change a system they considered to be unsound for, as was discussed in the previous chapter, the chimera of optimum size had dominated the process by which reorganisation had been achieved.

A further cuase of strain in the non-metropolitan counties, and therefore a further indicator of why there has been a general tendency towards the atrophy of the county liaison committee as an institution of liaison, is the difference in outlook and needs between the counties and the urban centres which are former county boroughs or former major urban districts. To an extent the conflict here is, of course, bound to be party political, arising from the resentment of Labour (or sometimes Labour) cities at their absorption into counties dominated by the Conservatives. But the failure of party political liaison between the tiers suggests that, even where there is no partisan divide to be crossed, the interests of cohesive urban centres are perceived to be quite separate from those of the rural-dominated counties. They may, also, be quite separate from the interests of other district councils, especially where the former county borough is the only urbanised area in the county. This point is vividly made in the following comment from the chief executive of Ipswich, a medium-sized former county borough in a very rural county:

> I find myself quite often sitting at meetings with my fellow chief executives and they are all avidly interested in one subject which has absolutely no relevance to me and I am trying to raise other subjects that they just don't want to hear about. The members find it as well.

Nor is this conflict restricted to liaison at the local level. The very wide range of sizes of population and rateable values among the non-metropolitan districts, together with their socio-economic variety from agricultural communities to suburbia to major industrial and commercial cities, also has an effect on the functioning of the ADC at national level, as the view expressed by a former chief executive of Cardiff suggests: 'I attend their [the ADC's] meetings . . . and I find they want to spend all their time talking about cesspool emptying and so on. When you talk about the problems of big cities most of them are lost' (the late H. V. Mansfield).

Thus far, the consideration of county-wide liaison in the metropolitan and non-metropolitan counties has been concerned with the processes and institutions of inter-authority contact at member or political level. As with all other aspects of local government, however, members' functions in the field of liaison are always supported, and sometimes dominated, by the work of officers. The key institution of this officer-, or administrative-level liaison is the meeting of chief executives of the county and of the county districts. There are very few counties in which the chief executives' meeting is not the linchpin of the whole machinery of inter-authority liaison and the resilience of this institution contrasts sharply with the decline in the significance of county liaison committees.

To understand how liaison now works in English and Welsh local government it is essential to recognise the disjunction between the theory and the practice of the officer's role. This disjunction affects all facets of the work of local authorities and it has been further complicated by the introduction, to be considered in Chapter 4, of processes of corporate management and of the post of chief executive. The problem of the relationship between officers and members, and the source of the failure of the theory and practice of the officer's role to coincide, is a variant of the ancient difficulty of separating policy and administration. In theory, officers advise members who take decisions. Specifically, the chief executive, in spite of his misleading title, is the chief policy adviser to his members generally, and to the controlling political group in particular. In the field of liaison, chief executives are increasingly cast in the role of decision-makers because of the action of many members in removing themselves from the field altogether in response to the difficulties already described.

But even before the atrophy of formal liaison committees enhanced their significance, chief executives were already in a strong position to influence the process of liaison. This strength arose from four sources related to the introduction, structure and administration of the new local government system.

First, in the process of transition from one local government system to another, the position of the chief executive of each authority was often crucial. The Local Government Act had required the designation of some officer as the 'proper officer' of the authority for the receipt of all communications concerning implementation (and indeed to be responsible for the discharge of certain statutory functions) and this designation normally fell to the chief executive, thus ensuring that in the earliest stages of the new system the processes of liaison and co-ordination would centre on the chief executives. Such a concentration was facilitated, also, by the preoccupation of members of the new authorities with the creation of their internal management structures and the questions of selection, patronage and politics which that raised. At a very early stage, then, chief executives, through their involvement in negotiating transitional arrangements, agency agreements and schemes of co-operation in shared functions, were enabled to establish close personal relationships that eventually became essential to the continued operation of the two-tier system. The personal networks of contacts among local government chief executives and other chief officers have become an important part of the process by which the structure copes with political and administrative strain.

The second source of strength arises from the rules that governed the recruitment of staff for the new authorities and it relates very closely to the point just made about the importance of personal contacts. The Local Government Staff Commission (which was appointd by the secretary of state, under the terms of the Local Government Act, to consider the staffing problems of reorganisation) insisted that in the non-metropolitan districts the 'pool' from which chief executives could be recruited should, in the first instance, be restricted to the local government service within the area of the new county in which a district was situated. Among the advantages of this restriction, to quote Richards (1975, p. 133), was that 'it ensured that a high proportion of new appointees would have local knowledge'. In the context of the continuing process of liaison, it also ensured that many chief executives in the districts were drawn from middle-rank positions in county councils and former county boroughs and so they brought with them personal knowledge of the prejudices, working practices and preoccupations of departments and of chief officers with whom they would have to consult in the new system. In their analyses of county–district relations Leach and Moore (1979*a*, 1979*b*) attach considerable importance to 'the extent to which key officers have knowledge and experience of the other authority' (1979*a*, p. 171) and they say that 'informal personal relationships . . . were found to be especially important where officers of different authorities had previously worked together for the same authority' (1979*b*, p. 283). The good relations between authorities in East Sussex, noted earlier, is generally thought to have been the result, in part, of a system of officer-to-officer contact and discussion dating back to the period immediately after the publication of the Royal Commission report and to the fact that restricted recruitment ensured that chief executive positions were filled by individuals who had been interacting for a long time. These factors apply, in varying degrees, to the chief executive groups of all the English and Welsh non-metropolitan counties. The chief executives of the new counties and of the metropolitan districts could be recruited from anywhere in England and Wales, except London, but in practice most appointments were made from among local applicants. Thus, to the advantages drawn from being present at the creation, many chief executives' groups could add the strengths of personal acquaintanceship and historical cohesiveness.

The third source of strength for the chief executives is the allocation of functions prescribed by the Local Government Act and described in Chapter 2. This allocation creates a large number of occasions for liaison between authorities. The co-ordination, and increasingly the presentation, of the authority's case during the liaison process falls to the chief executive, often working through a specially designated member of his staff. In the adversary relationship which exists between local authorities, it is essential that an authority's case be coherent and free from internal contradictions. It is desirable, also, that agreement among authorities be reached before public hostilities break out. The tasks of achieving coherence and agreement are typically those of the chief executive, subject only to the general direction of members or, after agreement is reached at officer level, to the endorsement of councils acting individually or jointly through the medium of a county liaison committee.

In the early years of the new system, it was common for the chief executives' meeting to precede by a few weeks the meeting of the county liaison committee and to give preliminary consideration to items that the committee would consider. In some counties, meetings of the local ADC were also phased into the process in an attempt to see, first, if there existed a common district view and, secondly, if agreement between the districts and the county could be achieved. Recommendations would then be made to the liaison committee much in the way that, within a local authority, recommendations progress up the decision ladder from service committee to policy committee and then, if necessary, to full council. Just as the balance between the real contribution of officers and members to policy-making (see Chapters 4 and 5) will depend on the level of political direction coming from members within a particular council, so the relative inputs of chief executives and leading members to the process of liaison will depend on the amount of time, resources and effort members are prepared to expend on inter-authority bargaining. Where members abandon the process, as has widely happened, the allocation of functions demands that liaison continues and so the position of officers, and particularly chief executives, is strengthened. When formal, political or member-level liaison ceases, the meetings of chief executives become a substitute for, rather than a support to, the work of councillors. The implications for democracy and local accountability of this change are profound and obvious, and although it might be argued that closed meetings of chief executives are more 'efficient' than open sessions of liaison committees with their characteristic position-taking, it is less clear that this mode of operation is conducive either to the comprehensibility of the new system or to strengthening its political autonomy.

The allocation of functions in the 1972 Act makes inevitable a continuous need for liaison in planning, in housing and social services, in refuse collection and disposal, in road construction and maintenance and in a wide range of individual functions that have become the subject of agency agreements between authorities. Some consideration will be given later to the nature of the process of interaction in particular service areas. At this stage it is sufficient to note that even where the day-to-day contacts are the responsibility of other officers – chief planning officer, director of social services, surveyor or treasurer – the shape of the system and the adversary relations that characterise it in so many places combine to strengthen the position of the chief executive within an authority and of the chief executives when they act in concert. The complexity of the relationships which chief executives have to oversee, and which arise from the combined effects of having a two-tier system of any kind and of having a distribution of functions between the tiers of a particularly complicating kind, are indicated in the following comments:

> There are constant and daily relationships at officer level because the Local Government Act of 1972 . . . is the biggest dog's breakfast that was ever invented – it is a diabolical thing to operate . . . I am not anti-county. I am just anti the structure. (Metropolitan district chief executive)

> One of the biggest strains of the job of a chief executive is this liaison role because it takes so much time. (Non-metropolitan district/former county borough (FCB) chief executive)

> Before reorganisation one chief officer would have talked to another chief officer and they would have settled it . . . But this [minor interdepartmental problem] meant a full scale formal meeting between the city, the county, the Land Authority for Wales, and the Welsh National Water Authority, and it took the whole of the morning: it came to no firm decision because they all had to go back and consult their chiefs. (The late H. V. Mansfield, Chief Executive, Cardiff City Council)

This last comment introduces yet another complication of the institutional reforms of subnational government and administration which took place in 1974, for not only was local government reformed but certain services, notably water supply and distribution and certain health services, were removed from the control of local government and made the responsibility of appointed statutory authorities. Additionally, in Wales the duties imposed on English and Scottish local authorities under the Community Land Act 1975 were placed on a separate statutory authority, the Land Authority for Wales. All of these bodies deal with matters that directly affect the work of local authorities, thus creating yet further need for liaison. The duty of liaison with these bodies further complicates the work of chief executives and other chief officers. As one chief executive put it, succinctly expressing a view commonly held, 'I think we almost exhaust ourselves at times liaising rather than doing'.

The fourth source of strength for chief executives in the liaison process is the complexity of the administrative arrangements that arise from the existence of a two-tier structure of local government in a state where all local powers are drawn from national legislation and where a high proportion of local services are paid for out of general taxation rather than out of revenue raised locally. The reference in the previous paragraph to the duties laid upon English local authorities by the Community Land Act 1975 introduces an example of how the policy objectives of central government may depend for their realisation on the capacity of local authorities to make the necessary administrative arrangements. The Act laid upon county councils the duty to establish Land Acquisition and Management Schemes (LAMS) in co-operation with the district councils in their areas.

Amongst the particular matters requiring inter-authority negotiation identified in the Act were the following: consideration of the financial and technical resources and experience of authorities and their officers; the division of planning and other functions between the tiers of local government; arrangements for deploying staff and apportioning costs; provisions for settling disputes and for periodic reviews of the scheme. The circular offering advice on the production and administration of LAMS (Department of Environment Circular 121/75, 1975*a*) said that the scheme would form 'the basis for the efficient working' of the Act and would settle 'who does what' in each county, and it considered the desirability of having a joint committee to supervise it. As with other circulars already discussed, the expectations of smooth co-operative working arrangements between authorities were not fulfilled in practice and, indeed, the existence of a two-tier local government system not only complicated the administrative arrangements but also made the implementation of government policy, as expressed in the Act, very problematical.

In many counties the process of producing LAMS was an acrimonious one because the Act was regarded by Conservatives as both doctrinaire and unnecessary. Much bitterness arose where Labour districts believed that Conservative counties were dragging their feet and the composition of committees of members set up to supervise the preparation of LAMS often raised difficult questions of political and institutional representation. Once again, the chief executives' groups became involved and, despite the fact that restrictions on public expenditure all but nullified the intentions of the Act, much time and effort were expended in an attempt to administer it. A particular problem here was that the requirements of the Act threw into sharp relief the already difficult relationships created by the bifurcation, in the 1972 Act, of the planning process. As one authority on the Community Land Act comments:

> There can be little doubt that had the concept of the Community Land Scheme been in the minds of the framers of the Local Government Act, 1972 there would have been a considerable advantage in retaining the county councils as overall local planning authorities and confining 'authorities' under the [Community

Land] Act to district councils . . . thereby wholly separating the planning and land acquisition functions. (Corfield, 1976, p. 135n.)

A further need for administrative liaison arises from the procedures introduced by central government to govern the allocation of borrowing powers to local government. Up until the introduction, in 1980, of controls on capital expenditure, capital projects in local government fell into two major groups: first, there was the 'key sector' in respect of which specific approval had to be sought before the money could be borrowed; secondly, there was the 'locally determined sector' in respect of which control of government borrowing was achieved not by scheme approval, as in the key sector, but by means of block allocations of loan sanctions to county *areas*. The emphasis indicates how this method of control, described in Department of the Environment Circular 66/76, further complicated the relations between the tiers in the new local government system. A quotation from the circular will show how the achievement of the objective of central government to control the quantum of local expenditure, while leaving councils a degree of discretion, was made difficult and potentially convoluted by the need for liaison: 'County areas are the county council and the district councils within a nonmetropolitan county. The county area block allocation is usually administered through a County Allocation Committee and an allocations officer . . .' (Circular 66/76, 1976, para. 19). Once again, there was a need for liaison in a field which combined the politically charged issue of competition for scarce resources with the technical questions of controlling, distributing and accounting for public finance. This was an area where much of the bargaining was done on an officer-to-officer basis, with only the most difficult, and often fundamentally unresolvable, problems being raised at member level.

A similar liaison process arises, with similar implications both for the nature of relationships between authorities and for the position of chief executives, from the arrangements introduced by central government in respect of Transport Supplementary Grant (TSG) submissions. These submissions are made by county councils in the form of a Transport Policy and Programme (TPP) which functions as a bid for grant support for the discharge of the county's functions in the transport and transport co-ordination fields. In describing the arrangements to be made in the counties, Department of the Environment Circular 125/75 (1975*b*) said:

Counties should consult their Districts . . . It is obviously desirable that . . . Counties should involve district authorities as early as possible in the preparation of their TPPs, so that agreed policies may eventually be brought forward for consultation and discussion.

And, as if to imply that this process is likely to involve conflict, it goes on to say that while 'district opinions can be accommodated' by this procedure, 'it is the County's duty to draw up' the policy 'for which they have the necessary powers' (para. 35).

In addition to the administrative causes for liaison already discussed, three others should be noted. First, the Local Government Act made the district councils the rating authorities, and obliged the county councils to precept upon their districts to raise the revenue necessary for county purposes. Although this has little effect upon the decision-making processes and rate-fixing mechanisms of individual authorities, it does cause a further need for inter-authority liaison both as to the timing of rate-fixing meetings and the dates for the collection and inter-authority payment of the monies collected. Although there is some merit in the simplicity inherent in each ratepayer receiving only one demand, such a procedure may blur the lines of responsibility between the decision-makers and those who foot the bill. Also, there has been some evidence that the obligation on districts to collect rates for county purposes has led to friction, especially when the district council does not approve of the policy decisions of the county council. In such circumstances, districts have sometimes included with their rate demands their own explanation of the costs of services amounting to a dissociation from the policies for which the county is raising revenue.

Secondly, it is common for all the superannuation funds for local government employees in a county to be administered by the county council, and clearly this creates a further need for liaison at the administrative level and, where decisions on the investment of funds may be controversial, at the political level also.

Thirdly, the organisation of elections, both parliamentary and local, demands a degree of co-operation among authorites on such matters as the preparation and publication of electors' lists, the use of premises for electoral purposes and the review and redrawing of electoral boundaries. This last process, once again, may raise issues of considerable controversy, as well as cause a need for much administrative liaison.

This analysis of the processes of liaison at the county-wide level is completed by a brief examination of performance in two functional areas: the relationship between housing and social services authorities and the operation of the divided planning functions.

It was noted in Chapter 2 that one objective of reform canvassed by several of the committees and commissions that investigated the subject in the 1960s; that of ensuring that in any new system the personal services of housing, social services and education should be provided by the same authority, could not be achieved in the two-tier system chosen by the Conservative government in 1972. In the early years of the new system, the relationship between counties and districts was affected adversely by the need to agree a means of dealing with a particular problem, homelessness, which in the shire counties was a concern of both social services departments at county level and of housing departments at district level.

Here again, the government tried to induce co-operation by the publication of optimistic advice, this time in Department of the Environment Circular 18/74 *Homelessness* (1974) published less than two months before the new local authorities assumed their responsibilities. According to this circular, it was essential to have 'a corporate and collaborative approach with appropriate machinery to ensure it works' and to this end it exhorted local authorities in the new system to create 'appropriate machinery . . . to provide links between them both at policy and . . . at working level'. Specifically, the circular said that 'In non-metropolitan counties there will need to be regular contact and joint action between county and district councils: new county councils are asked to co-operate with the new district councils in their area'.

The problem of liaison in this field is simple: homelessness is the condition of being without a home and it can only be dealt with by the provision of a dwelling; as a social condition, homelessness is the responsibility of social services departments but dwellings and their allocation are the responsibility of housing departments. When these departments exist in separate authorities, as they do in the non-metropolitan counties, then the process of liaison becomes suffused with such issues as autonomy, independence and *amour propre*, factors that the circular could not consider without tacitly conceding that the distribution of functions, and perhaps the whole new structure that was not yet operational, were seriously flawed.

The difficulties became so great, and the provision of any kind of coherent service to the homeless so problematical, that within a very short time all of the local authority associations were pressing the government to legislate to clarify the position by laying upon housing authorities a statutory duty to house the homeless. This was achieved, in 1977, in the Housing (Homeless Persons) Act, a Private Member's measure passed with government support. But the experience, in the meantime, of local authorities in trying to reach the kind of co-operative arrangements recommended in Circular 18/74 is a classic example of the difficulties inherent in the two-tier system set up in 1974. A view of this process can be gained from a brief examination of the attempt, ultimately unsuccessful, to create in Berkshire, where the author served as a member of the county council from 1973 to 1977, an agreed method of operating the spirit of Circular 18/74.

In Berkshire, the department of social services, with the support of the appropriate committees, sought to establish with the six districts in the county an agreed scheme whereby emergency shelter, if necessary in bed and breakfast accommodation, would be provided for twenty-eight days by the social services department. Thereafter, the responsibility for the provision of shelter, usually by meeting the cost of bed and breakfast accommodation, would pass to the housing authority unless that authority provided permanent accommodation. There can be no doubt that such a scheme would have been fully in accord with the spirit of the circular, but in order to achieve county-wide agreement on it the amount of inter-authority liaison, backed up by the internal decision-making processes of individual councils required to give it effect, was quite staggering. It was necessary to involve the following formal bodies: six county–district liaison committees; seven policy committees; six housing committees; one social services committee; the county–district conference (Berkshire's county liaison committee); and the full councils of the seven authorities. To the time and effort consumed in these meetings must be added the unrecorded, but very numerous, contacts at officer level that were necessary before members could be involved. After all this, moreover, the scheme foundered when one district, Windsor and Maidenhead, failed to endorse it because it decided that its interpretation of the law as it then stood did not give it the power to pay for bed and breakfast accommodation. It argued, quite tenably, that it was empowered to provide shelter but not sustenance, the latter being a social services responsibility. This experience was not unique; its occurrence in other counties was largely responsible for the growth of a consensus for new legislation; but the problem arose directly from the combination, noted in other contexts earlier, of having a two-tier system and a particularly troublesome distribution of functions.

Certain other aspects of the procedural consequences of this separation of closely cognate services should be mentioned. There is some evidence of a decline in the amount of social work support available to the housing departments of districts that were formerly county boroughs and responsible for providing their own social services. To an extent this is attributable to the economic stringency that surrounded the introduction of the new system and the pressure that was thereby put on new counties to 'level down' rather than 'level up' their provision, but it adds to the feelings of the former county boroughs that they have been ill-served by reorganisation. It is worth noting, also, that the political divide between Labour towns and Conservative counties often exacerbates relations at this particular interface and that this was often a contributory factor to the inter-authority wrangles over care of the homeless. In some areas, also, there has been a tendency, as one district chief executive in a former county borough put it, 'to build up within the housing department our own social services department', a process not unrelated to the hope of 'organic change'.

Some of the fatuousness of the inter-authority disputes encouraged by the separation of housing and social services is revealed when the situation regarding homelessness is compared as between the metropolitan and the non-metropolitan counties. In both areas the problems are the same: dealing with homelessness involves expenditure by housing departments and by social services departments. But in the metropolitan counties, because both are departments of the district council, neither members nor officers perceive any financial or political advantage in attempting to off-load responsibility from one department to another. In the shire counties, although the total expenditure will be unchanged, there is seen to be some advantage in passing some of the responsibility to the other authority. It goes without saying, of course, that where there is a partisan divide between the councils, the pressure to act in this way is increased.

Finally, even with the statutory responsibilities of authorities clarified by legislation, the need for continuous, and expensive, liaison between these two closely related services remains. In many counties the social services department is organised on an area basis whereby a social services division is coterminous with the boundaries of one or more district councils. Such an organisational arrangement facilitates the creation of a close working relationship between social workers and housing officers. But, as is the case at many points in the two-tier structure, efficient delivery of the services relies as much, if not more, on good personal relationships and *ad hoc* administrative mechanisms as on the performance of the system created by legislation. As many members and officers put it: 'Any system can be made to work' but, in the case of the housing–social services split, making it work has demanded the commitment of an incalculable amount of scarce resources of time, manpower and money.

The other major area that demands separate consideration under the general heading of county-wide liaison is that of town and country planning. The imposition of a two-tier structure with the planning function divided between the tiers was, as discussed in Chapter 2, potentially incompatible with the unitary approach of the Town and Country Planning Act 1968 as amended in 1971. Despite this, however, the division of responsibility for planning matters in the Local Government Act is superficially sensible and logical: the upper-tier authorities – the counties – have responsibility for the wider, strategic aspects of planning and so retain the structure planning function laid on the old counties and county boroughs in the earlier legislation; the lower-tier authorities – the districts – are given the development control function, the right to receive almost all planning applications and the responsibility, subject to the structure plan and any other county requirements, to prepare local plans.

But as with other 'sensible' distributions of functions in the new system, the need for liaison is inherent and, even in those counties where the relationship is a generally co-operative one, the fact that the distinction between the local and the strategic in planning is often subjective rather than objective demands the creation of effective means of discussion, negotiation and compromise. The need for these mechanisms of liaison, and the consequences for the operation of the entire local government system when they are not effective, is most marked in the metropolitan counties. There, the constant acrimonious disputes on planning matters between districts which, in the majority of cases, are former all-purpose, structure planning authorities and the new county councils, which are in search of an identity and purpose, have been a major contributory factor to the general pattern of inter-authority disharmony. It has also influenced the decision of the government, in the Local Government, Planning and Land Act 1980, to alter the distribution of planning functions in a way designed to reduce the incidence of disputes. It is significant, also, that the field of planning is that in which opinion among members and officers throughout the country came closest to unanimity on the need to amend the 1972 Act.

In Schedule 16, the Local Government Act 1972 defined what was meant by a 'county matter' in planning terms. With the exception of a few specific subjects, principally concerned with mineral extraction, the definition was vague and depended on the opinion of either the district council or the county council, or both. Thus, in many cases, the decision on whether a matter was 'local', and therefore open to determination by a district council, or a 'county matter', and therefore subject either to being referred by the district to the county or to being called in for determination by the county itself, was essentially a subjective one. Because of this, it may raise in very sharp relief issues which are very salient indeed to councillors and their authorities. Many commentators (Leach and Moore, 1979a, 1979b; Friend, 1976; Brazier and Harris, 1975; Buxton, 1974) have pointed to the links connecting planning, politics, autonomy, independence, status and former status and to the need to make the planning process work despite the attitudinising that the structure encourages. This need is served by the creation of complex informal networks of information, negotiation, compromise and decision-making, very few of which are subject to the public scrutiny upon which the credibility, and therefore the comprehensibility, of a democratic system depends.

Although it is difficult to judge whether, to quote again from Circular 74/73 (Department of the Environment, 1973b), 'the public . . . receive[s] the planning service it is entitled to expect', there is some evidence to suggest that the prevention of a serious decline in the quality of the service has owed much to the informal networks among planners and planning authorities, rather than to the formal structure created by the 1972 Act. Turton (1975), in a localised study of planning in Cheshire in the first year of the new system, concluded that the quality and cost of the planning service had not been markedly affected by the structural charges, that the district councils had been more successful as planning authorities than many observers had expected, and that the vast majority of planning applications were determined by the districts without county involvement. It is, perhaps, instructive to examine these conclusions in the light of experience over a longer period and of evidence drawn from a wider area.

First, on costs, Turton's figures appear to relate only to the salary costs of processing planning applications within a single authority. They do not take account of the costs of the liaison arrangements – for example, the preparation and acceptance of a development control agreement with the county council, or the resources claimed by informal networks – which are essential to the performance by a district of its local planning function. He does, however, concede that a satisfactory agreement in Cheshire was reached 'but not without some effort' (Turton, 1975, p. 18). Secondly, on the success of district councils as planning authorities, the facts that applications are being processed, that planning permissions are being granted and that delays do not appear to be much greater in the new system than in the old, surely constitute minimal criteria for success. The intention of reorganisation was to make the system better, not simply to do the same job as well but differently. Also, there is some evidence, particularly in respect of those shire districts based upon former rural districts that had no delegated powers in planning before reorganisation, that the service has actually declined in quality. Thirdly, Turton makes the point that in Cheshire only about 10 per cent of planning applications involve the county council, as against a pre-reorganisation estimate that about 20 per cent of planning applications would be 'county matters' under the Act. In judging the performance of the bifurcated planning system, however, it is not the number of 'county matters' that is important. Rather it is numbers that are disputed between the tiers, the costs of settling disputes, the inter-authority arrangements necessitated by disputes, and the effect of such disputes on the nature of the county–district relationship. The particular nature of the distribution of planning functions has caused a great deal of expenditure on liaison. It has also contributed to the building of the consensus, noted above, that the allocation of planning powers ought to be simplified by amending the 1972 legislation.

DISTRICT-LEVEL LIAISON

As well as creating a need for liaison at the county-wide level, the Local Government Act 1972 created a need for inter-authority contact between counties and individual districts. The most formal type of liaison at this level has been the district joint committee or district liaison committee; institutions of this sort were set up in twenty counties. The composition of such committees varied quite widely across the country, but a common form was a membership comprising nominees from the district council (usually the chairman, the leader of the council, and one or more committee chairmen) and a delegation from the county council made up mainly, but not exclusively, of councillors representing county council electoral areas within the boundaries of the relevant district. As with the county liaison committees, the members are accompanied by their chief executive or his representative and by other officers as required by the agenda. Committee chairmen from the county council are sometimes invited to attend when matters coming within their committees' terms of reference are to be discussed.

Committees of this kind have been subject to the same process of atrophy as has affected the county liaison committees. For despite the widely held view, quoted earlier from one chief executive, that most liaison issues are 'district to county', in the sense that they require consultation between one district and the county rather than across the board, it has generally been found that most issues can be dealt with at officer level – between planners, between the chief housing officer and the director of social services, and so on – and then referred to committees of the individual authorities. Those issues that do necessitate inter-authority meetings of members were found to be best dealt with by *ad hoc* meetings rather than by regularly scheduled ones for which issues were too urgent to wait or for which agenda items had to be invented in the few weeks before the date. As one chief executive put it, expressing a view shared by officers and members in many counties: 'The district liaison committees never really worked and they have fallen into desuetude because we were finding . . . we were either scratching around looking for items or else the meeting was too far ahead.'

It is significant, also, that fewer than half of the new counties established any formal liaison mechanisms at all at the district level. The decline of this form of liaison, then, brings those counties into line with those which realised, for various reasons, that it would not work. First, the occasions for liaison between the county and individual district do not occur on a regular timetable. Secondly, bilateral discussions as a matter of routine would, where relations between the tiers were already fragile because of dissatisfaction with the outcome of reorganisation, offer an opportunity for positions to harden. Thirdly, some districts feel that bilateral liaison provides the county council with an opportunity 'to pick the districts off one by one'. There is much evidence that district councils, aware of the adversary nature of the relationship between the tiers, have realised that there is safety in numbers and strength in a common front. This point will be examined in more detail under the heading of 'inter-district liaison'.

But perhaps the most important reason for the decline in this form of liaison, and to an extent of the county-wide form also, is the fact that committees of this sort can be representative and consultative but they cannot be executive. They cannot take decisions. Even when agreement is reached on how to proceed on a matter involving both sides, implementation will involve action by both councils, and the composition of the liaison committee may not be weighty enough to convince either side that such implementation will follow as a matter of course. If this is so, councils will quickly come to prefer *ad hoc* liaison with the influential and the powerful to regular liaison with the representative and consultative. Quite simply, a deal between the leaders of two councils, supported by appropriate officers, may present a clearer prospect of quick resolution than a public discussion of differences followed by a reference back to two authorities. This cause of the decline in the performance of district liaison committees may be especially important where political leadership in local government is particularly strong and where that strength is allied with continuing disgruntlement at the outcome of reorganisation. Consider, for example, these comments:

Gradually these meetings of district joint committees fell into disuse. Some were formally wrapped up, some died away. The districts said, 'Look, when we want to talk to the county, in view of the power of chairmen of committees, we want to talk to chairmen . . . not to backbench members'. (Non-metropolitan county chief executive)

We have particular problems with two of the cities; first of all . . . they're Labour and everywhere else is Tory. The other factor is they're rather isolationist in their outlook. (Metropolitan county chief executive)

We do tend to accuse the county council of interfering in our job and of tending to be looking for something to do. (Non-metropolitan district/FCB chief executive)

[Some] districts have been determined to make a success of it. Others didn't want to know. For example, [in one district] we're still getting a lot of county-bashing going on. The piece of machinery was there, but you've got to have goodwill on both sides and the determination to make it work. (Non-metropolitan county chief executive)

Perhaps the position is best summed up in the words of the chief executive of a non-metropolitan district who said, 'We have our business and the county council has its business and I don't think you should mess with other people's private business'. It would be difficult to conceive of a clearer or more succinct description of a relationship that is adversarial rather than co-operative.

AGENCY

If the new local government system of England and Wales makes inter-authority liaison inevitable, that inevitability is most marked in those counties where extensive use has been made of clause 101 of the Local Government Act 1972 which allows one authority to act as the agent of another in the discharge of statutory functions. In strictly legal terms the agent occupies, to quote Richards (1975, p. 78), 'a humble position' in that the responsibility for the nature, extent and quality of the service provided remains with the principal. There is much evidence, however, that many district councils differentiate between the legal and the political implications of agency. Since agency agreements, sometimes albeit of a strictly limited kind, are, or have been, in operation in every English and Welsh county, the workings of the agency process have an important effect on the workings of the system in general. The most important service in which agency arrangements have been employed is highways construction and maintenance, but they have also been used in the following services: libraries, consumer protection, architecture, food and drugs inspection, traffic management, and building repair and maintenance. But it is in highways that they have been most significant and much of the analysis that follows relates to that field.

Agency is a bilateral business and it is important to examine, first of all, the motives that led the various classes of authority to enter into agency agreements. In the case of the metropolitan counties, the negotiation of agency agreements, as was implied in another context earlier, was motivated by the intensely practical consideration that they were entirely new authorities without any existing departmental structure or professional expertise. It was, therefore, vital to ensure the continuation of services through the transitional period. All of the metropolitan districts had been formed, in whole or in substantial part, from former authorities which had extensive highway powers. If the counties had not appointed their district councils as their agents, it would not have been possible to maintain the continuity of the service. But even at this early stage the beginnings of the conflicts that surround agency in many counties were apparent, as is clear from this comment from a metropolitan county chief executive: 'We had no resources. They [the new districts] said that we had no depots, we had nothing. We had to get the thing moving . . . we had to give them an agency: it was the most give-away agency you could possibly have . . .'

For the non-metropolitan counties, all of which, except for Avon, Humberside and Cleveland, were based upon old counties which had responsibility for highways in all but the area of former county boroughs and major urban districts, the problem of administering services for which they had no departments did not arise. Here, the motivations for entering into agency arrangements were often closely linked to a desire to ease the transition to the new system and to induce a co-operative relationship between counties and their district councils. And, as Richards points out (1975, p 83), the degree to which counties were likely to deal generously with their districts' claims for agency was influenced by the temporary power given to ministers to arbitrate and direct in disputed cases. The agency clause was also employed to give a statutory foundation for particular local county–district relations: in Surrey 'partnership agreements' were negotiated between the county and some of its districts; in Devon decentralisation of county functions and sharing of officers became an important part of the inter-authority working relationships; and in South Glamorgan the county and the city of Cardiff concluded what was called 'a non-duplication agreement' which prevented the county from establishing a department in a field where the city already had one, and vice versa.

For the district councils the motives for seeking to become agents were both more complex and potentially more disruptive than those of the counties. For these reasons any analysis of the effect of agency on the local government system must concentrate heavily on the experience and attitudes of the district councils and, in particular, those of the former county boroughs. First of all, it is worth repeating that many district councils viewed the use of the agency clause in exactly the way warned against by Circular 131/72 (Department of the Environment, 1972): they saw it as an opportunity to 'claw back' powers that had passed to the counties under the 1972 Act. Especially where it was possible for the agent to acquire a degree of autonomy, usually expressed by granting decision-making powers for capital expenditure up to a certain level, district councillors and their officers could regard agency as providing a significant accretion to their statutory powers. Secondly, there is no doubt that by enabling existing departments to be preserved, particularly in the former county boroughs, agency agreements helped to minimise the disruption of the changeover from one local government system to another. Also, for those districts created by amalgamation of former rural districts, urban districts and municipal boroughs, the negotiation and retention of a highways agency was viewed as a means of enhancing the technical functions given to them as statutory duties and so enabling them to attract a higher calibre of professional officer. This is probably the one way in which agency operates to achieve the objectives of those who introduced the 1972 Act. Thirdly, if there was, as has consistently been argued here, a disposition at district level (particularly in the former county boroughs) not to regard the allocation of powers in the act as final or permanent, it was imperative that major district councils should claim, or negotiate, agency agreements that were as generous as possible. As one former county borough chief executive put it, 'My job is to get as much as I can for the borough council'. This motivation towards agency implies a clear derogation from the statutory allocation of powers and it was, of course, most marked among the 'big nine', as this comment from the chief executive of one of them indicates:

We are a great city and we will always be so and, whatever the local government institutions, it is imperative that we should be able to talk to the county on equal terms . . . If you can't do that, you might as well have parish council status.

Just as the motivations leading authorities to enter agency arrangements differed according to the class of authority, so experience of their practical operation varies. But the general conclusion must be that the operation of the agency clause has made the new local government system in England and Wales more confusing, more inefficient, more expensive and more impermanent than was anticipated by those who conceived, introduced and ensured the passage of the 1972 Act.

In the metropolitan counties, as might be inferred from the earlier discussion of county-wide liaison, it soon became clear that there was a fundamental conflict of interest between the need to get things going at the outset of the new system and the desire of the county councils to establish their position as major institutions of subnational government. The need to terminate, or fundamentally to renegotiate, agency agreements has been raised, either formally or informally, in all but one of the metropolitan counties. The exception is West Yorkshire where there is a two-way agency with the engineering function performed by the county and architecture by the districts. This has prevented a major confrontation on the specific question of agency. Even there, however, the relationship on agency is characterised by 'constant bellyaching' between the authorities, though this may be part of the generally bad relations in West Yorkshire that were noted earlier. In the other five metropolitan counties, by 1978–9, when agency agreements made for five years were coming up for renewal, termination or renegotiation, most leading officers and members would have shared the view of one chief executive in a Greater Manchester district when he said, 'We are into a brawl about agency'. Thus the existence of agency exacerbated the bad relations caused by the allocation of functions and by the difficulties faced by the metropolitan counties in establishing their identities.

The attitudes of many non-metropolitan counties to the operation of agency have been affected more by considerations of budgetary and technical control than by considerations of power, influence and status. Within a fairly short time after the new system came into operation many shire county councils began to express to those of their districts that had extensive agency powers, especially in the highways field, concern about wasteful expenditure. But it was not until after the 1977 county council elections that the change of attitude began to harden into attempts to terminate, or at least to renegotiate, existing agreements. In these elections the Conservatives made extensive gains, taking control from Labour in some counties and greatly consolidating their strength in others. It is not suggested that attitudes to agency are determined party politically: rather the consolidation of the position of the dominant party in the shire counties allowed the county councils to be more assertive towards the districts than before.

The position of the counties, and the response of the districts, reveal once again how the two-tier system militates against the co-operative and constructive approach its progenitors claimed to anticipate. And, as Leach and Moore (1979*b*, p. 284) point out, agency agreements, by virtue of their status as the documentary expression of inter-authority liaison, provided a specific battleground upon which tension could find an outlet. But it was hardly surprising that the counties should seek to economise where they could: not only were they feeling the effects of inflation and, after 1976, of the increasingly severe restraints on public expenditure; they were also affected adversely by the alterations in the distribution formula for the rate support grant paid by central government in aid of local services. In addition, many county engineers, surveyors and treasurers, who had been unenthusiastic about agency from the start, genuinely believed that it was leading to a decline in both financial control and technical standards. As the chief executive of a large shire county put it: 'A number of districts have not been as careful as they might have been in exercising control over levels of expenditure . . . County surveyor will still say that it would have been cheaper, more effective and easier if he'd taken it all right from the start.'

Many district councils, even when they were controlled by the same politcal party as the county to which they were agents, were disposed to dispute the county case on all particulars. It is difficult to decide the rights and wrongs of specific disputes in specific counties, but it is clear that the positions taken by district councils were influenced by considerations of status and the effect on their range of functions that agency was perceived to have. Few members, and fewer chief officers, however, will argue that agency is not wasteful. But it is striking that many districts, mainly former county boroughs, argue that though it costs them money, with a consequent effect on their rates, their contribution to the administrative costs (and their contribution can only be administrative, for the primary costs are met by the principal) of agency is money well spent. This was especially true, as the following remark from the chief executive of a medium-sized former county borough reveals, in the period between 1976 and 1979 when many districts entertained hopes of organic change: 'We have been losing money regularly on it. We don't mind that . . . because we have an involvement . . . in preparing and influencing schemes.' Perhaps the impossibility of separating the question of agency from other matters of status and liaison is indicated, however, by the view expressed by several county chief executives that their councils were prepared to spend money on agency because it helped to lubricate their interaction with the districts.

If attitudes to agency are, in practice, directly affected by questions of status and the allocation of powers in the 1972 Act, there is much greater degree of consensus throughout local government that, in principle, agency is undesirable. Only a minority of members and officers believe that agency arrangements contribute to the efficiency and comprehensibility of the local government system. The following comments from officers serving authorities of various classes, histories and sizes are representative of a general current of opinion:

Agency is ridiculous – you either do the job or you don't . . . For one authority to provide the money and the other authority to spend it is bound to cause difficulties. (Non-metropolitan district/FCB chief executive)

I think it is much easier if you have got the entire responsibility than when it is divided, with somebody providing all the cash and you getting all the kicks. (Welsh district chief executive)

You invest power in one place or another. On agencies, these beastly concurrent powers are causing all sorts of trouble. (Large metropolitan district chief executive)

A relationship which is rewarding neither to politicians nor to officers. (Metropolitan district chief executive)

In conclusion, the tension between principle and practice on the question of agency is perhaps encapsulated in this remark from the chief executive of a non-metropolitan county:

There has been duplication of work ... Is cost the only criterion? ... It is important to have the local community involved ... Somebody, and not me as an officer, has got to make a judgement weighing something called democracy and involvement against financial benefit.

INTER-DISTRICT LIAISON

This extended analysis of the liaison arrangements necessitated by the new local government structure is completed by examining briefly the process of inter-district liaison. That district councils in almost all counties have found it necessary and useful to have a forum for discussion that does not involve the county council is further *prima facie* evidence that they have come to view the relationship between the tiers as an adversary one. The most common institution for this purpose is the county branch of the ADC and such a branch was established in at least twenty-six of the thirty-nine non-metropolitan counties and in six of the eight Welsh counties. In the metropolitan counties, because both county and districts are eligible for membership in the Association of Metropolitan Authorities (AMA), a local branch of that organisation could not serve as a forum for inter-district liaison. Thus the arrangements in the metropolitan counties have been rather more *ad hoc*, a good example being the South Yorkshire Joint Consultative Committee which, according to one of the chief executives, 'arose from feelings that the South Yorkshire County Council was picking the boroughs off one by one on agency'. What is significant, however, is not the institutional form, but the fact that lower-tier authorities have come to see a need for concerted action against the county council. Indeed, in the metropolitan counties, the deeply adversarial nature of the relationship between the tiers is emphasised by the fact that inter-district liaison machinery has been developed and strengthened, just as county-wide liaison institutions have declined or been abandoned.

In many non-metropolitan counties, also, district members and officers attach more importance to their relations with other district councils than to their relationship with the county council. On matters where disagreement between counties and districts has been deepest – agency, planning, organic change – district councils have striven, with remarkable success, to co-ordinate their views and to present a common front to the county councils. It is significant that, in many counties, district councils with no direct interest in the subject in dispute between one or more of their number and the county council have given public support to the district view, a clear indication that they consider that, in general, district interests ought to be defended. It may also be that districts, having experienced the new system in operation, see a common front as a way of redressing the imbalance of local government power that arises from the distribution of functions in the 1972 Act. In Humberside, for example, districts that have little or no agency powers have supported the efforts of the City of Hull to maintain and extend the agencies it has from the county council. Even more significant, perhaps, is the fact that county branches of the ADC, and indeeed the ADC nationally, maintained a united view on the question of 'organic change' and were persuaded not to oppose the 'big nine' and 'the cities and boroughs of medium size' in their campaigns for a reallocation of local government powers. The changes sought by these campaigns would, on the most liberal interpretation, have affected only about one-third of district councils, although only four of the thirty-nine shire counties would have been completely untouched (Stewart *et al.*, 1978, p. 12). Despite this, however, inter-district liaison produced a remarkably united response.

It is clear that district councils, as a class, are perceived as having interests that conflict with those of the counties. This is a damning indictment of a major institutional reform that was intended to end uncertainty and to bring to a conclusion the wrangles – on autonomy, tax base and status – that had characterised the old system.

Chapter 4

RECEIVED WISDOM OF CORPORATE
MANAGEMENT

The title of this chapter deliberately implies a value judgement, but one that can be supported by evidence gathered throughout the country. It is that the widespread, almost uniform, introduction in the new local authorities of England and Wales of the trappings, if not always the reality, of corporate management was often the result of an uncritical acceptance of the prescriptions of the Bains Report (Bains, 1972). This acceptance, moreover, was frequently unaccompanied, especially in the shire counties and districts, by either a real understanding of the techniques, or an accurate perception of the political consequences, implied by the new approach.

The search for a more efficient method of organising the internal management and decision-making processes of local authorities occurred at the same time as the process of investigation and report to which so many of Britain's public authorities were subject in the 1960s and early 1970s. In 1967 the Maud Committee on the Management of Local Government (Maud, 1967) had given official recognition to the concerns of many local government officers that the iterative, incremental approach to policy-making characteristic of local authorities was inefficient, wasteful and inimical to an economic and cost-effective delivery of public services. The committee's report led most major local authorities, that is to say counties and county boroughs as well as authorities in Greater London, to review their internal organisation (Greenwood *et al*., 1971, p. 1). In this period also, a number of major authorities, led by the GLC, began to introduce rational/comprehensive policy-making systems, imported from the USA or from private business, or from both, chief among which was PPBS – Planning, Programming and Budgeting Systems – the brainchild of the US Department of Defense under the direction of Secretary Robert McNamara in the early 1960s. In some authorities, notably Leeds, Hull, Sheffield and Liverpool, changes in management systems and committee structures were introduced as a result of studies commissioned from outside management consultancies. Even before the report of the Royal Commission added its weight to a growing consensus in favour of internal reorganisation, therefore, there was considerable evidence of a reformist trend among local government managers and professionals.

But it was the appointment of the Study Group on Local Authority Management Structures, and the publication of its report as an integral part of the movement towards major structural change in the local government system between 1970 and 1972, that provided the vital push towards uniformity. The report was advisory only, having neither the coercive authority of legislation nor, on the face of it, the quasi-legislative influence of a departmental circular. The Bains Study Group was set up in 1971 jointly by the Secretary of State for the Environment and the local authority associations. The report was published the following year, just before the Local Government Act 1972 completed its passage through Parliament. There were four important reasons why the Bains Report affected the process of change in English and Welsh local government so decisively. (A parallel process in Scotland, influenced by the Paterson Report [Paterson, 1973] is considered in Chapter 6.)

First, there is no doubt that those to whom the report was initially directed, principally the officers and members serving on the joint committees set up to organise the transition to the new system, were very receptive to advice emanating from a source they regarded as authoritative. As the discussion on the introduction of liaison arrangements (Chapter 3) showed, there was little disposition, especially on the part of those whose work in the new system would be in authorities created by amalgamations and major boundary changes, to reject advice which would ease the immediate problems of change. Also, there is some evidence that where reorganisation involved the shotgun marriage of two or more previously powerful authorities, the Bains recommendations operated as an independent arbiter between them. One chief executive described the process thus: 'Most authorities took Bains when things were very difficult: there was nobody really in post; everybody was saying, "How the hell do we get out of this?" And we got out of it by using Bains.'

Secondly, the evangelical flavour of the Bains Report, together with its inclusion of model management and committee structures for all the new classes of authorities, draft terms of reference for policy committees, and a job specification for a chief executive, chimed with the objective of efficiency that was noted in Chapter 1 as an important justification for the whole process of reform. It was also in the mainstream of the process whereby there had grown up an orthodoxy about the need for rational/comprehensive policy planning in local government. Dearlove (1979, chs 5 and 6) provides a stimulating account of the growth of this orthodoxy which involved such bodies as the Maud Committee, the Institute of Municipal Treasurers and Accountants (IMTA), the Local Authority Management Services and Computer Advisory Committee (LAMSAC) and the Institute of Local Government Studies (INLOGOV) of the University of Birmingham, as well as many independent academic commentators. It is not necessary to accept the wider political inferences drawn by Dearlove from his examination of this process to conclude that very few of the officers involved in the transition to a new local government system could have escaped its influence.

Thirdly, the influence of the report, or at the very least a knowledge of its existence, at member level was ensured by the request of the secretary of state that all newly elected councillors in the new authorities be provided with a copy. Not all new councils acceded to this request, but it is likely that all leading members were apprised of the report's contents by their officers and that it was available on request to others. There is no evidence that the report was as widely read by members as by officers. In this, as in many other matters of high technical complexity, most members were content to accept the advice of officers who, on questions of internal organisation, accepted the advice of Bains. Nevertheless, the fact that the secretary of state thought it important enough to request a wide circulation contributed to the widespread implementation of the report's major recommendations.

Fourthly, the attitude of the secretary of state to the quality of the recommendations was designed to impute to Bains an importance equal to that of the structural changes necessitated by the legislation. In his foreword to the report, Walker wrote:

> If every newly elected member and every newly appointed officer . . . studies this report carefully and *sees that those suggestions appropriate are applied to the work of his new authority* then local government in the future is going to be far more efficient and effective than ever before. (Bains, 1972, p. vii, emphasis added)

Thus management change was seen as inseparable from, and indeed as an important constituent of, the process of reform and reorganisation.

The recommendations of the Bains Report covered almost the whole field of decision-making and management in the new local authorities. (The exception was that the consideration given to the role of members was perfunctory to the point of unhelpfulness.) But the major innovations it envisaged were threefold: the appointment of a chief executive 'as leader of the officers of the authority and principal adviser to the Council on matters of general policy' (Bains, 1972, p. 125); the creation of a policy and resources committee 'to provide co-ordinated advice to the Council in the setting of its plans, objectives and priorities' (p. 124); and the establishment of a management team of principal chief officers 'responsible, under the chief executive's leadership, for the general co-ordination of the implementation of those plans' (pp. 125–6). The incidence of the adoption of each of these innovations gives a preliminary impression of the effect of Bains on the early development of the new local authorities.

Hinings *et al.* (1975a) surveyed the new authorities and among replies received from all the new shire counties in England, all but one of the metropolitan counties, 91 per cent of metropolitan districts and 64 per cent of shire districts, they found only one respondent – a shire district – that did not have a chief executive officer as envisaged by Bains. Even more revealing, because it deals with the qualitative as well as the quantitative influence of Bains, is a survey conducted in 1976 by the Society of Local Authority Chief Executives (SOLACE, 1977, p. 22) which investigated the extent to which the Bains job description for a chief executive (Bains, 1972, app. J, p. 165) had been adopted in the new authorities. The results, based on a response rate of 70 per cent to a questionnaire sent to all local authorities, are given in Table 4.1.

It will be noted that of the authorities that replied to the SOLACE survey, 85 per cent had chief executives whose job descriptions had been directly influenced by the recommendations of the Bains Report. Further evidence of the specific influence of Bains is found in Hinings *et al.* (1975a, p. 18). The report had argued very strongly (Bains, 1972, para. 5.27, p. 45) that the chief executive should have no departmental responsibilities. Only 31 per cent of the authorities surveyed by Greenwood *et al.* did not have such a 'free-standing' chief executive. However, there is some evidence, to be presented later, that this was a recommendation that many councils found more

Table 4.1 *Job Descriptions of Chief Executives in England and Wales.*

	Counties		Districts		All Authorities	
	n	*%*	*n*	*%*	*n*	*%*
Pure Bains[a]	10	24	104	42·5	114	40
Bains rephrased[b]	18	43	60	24·5	78	27
Bains + clerk[c]	7	17	44	18	51	18
Other	1	2	7	3	8	3
None/No response	6	14	30	12	36	12
Totals	42	100	245	100	287	100

Source: SOLACE (1977), p. 22.
[a]Indicates adoption of the Bains description unamended.
[b]Indicates a rewording of the Bains description with no change of substance.
[c]Indicates adoption of the Bains description with traditional clerk's duties added.
Note: SOLACE found that 11 per cent of chief executives had no job description.

Table 4.2 *Adoption of Policy Committees and Management Teams in England and Wales.*

Class of Authority	Percentage with Policy Committee	Percentage with Management Team
Counties	100	100
Metropolitan districts	100	100
Shire districts	94	99

Source: Hinings *et al.* (1975*a*), p. 17.

acceptable when setting up their management structures than in operating them.

On the establishment of a policy and resources committee (or a locally named equivalent) and a management team, the performance of the new authorities was just as uniform as in the case of the creation of the post of chief executive and even more uniform than in the designation of the duties of that post. Hinings *et al.* (1975*a*, p. 17), basing their figures on responses from all the counties in England, from all the metropolitan districts and from 64 per cent of the shire districts, show once again the pervasive influence of the corporate ideas espoused and proselytised by Bains. Their findings are shown in Table 4.2.

It is possible, however, that these figures exaggerate the adoption rate for policy committees among the shire districts. A significant number (seven), of the randomly selected districts investigated for this book had not, in 1974, set up a policy committee, although some of them had done so at a later stage.

In the interviews with chief executives through which much of the evidence for the present analysis was gathered there was expressed a general conviction that the effect of Bains on the decisions about management and committee structures taken by the new authorities had been very great indeed. Significantly, no respondent suggested that he or his authority had ignored the report, although a small number of councils had decided quite deliberately either to reject most of the recommendations or to set up institutions that differed considerably from those it recommended. The flavour of responses of both kinds is indicated in the following comments:

I think Bains said 'turn over in bed' and we all turned over. (Non-metropolitan district chief executive)

Bains clearly indicated that it was more or less wrong not to have a chief executive. (Non-metropolitan district chief executive)

I think, if anything, there was a sort of anti-Bains feeling, although we did adopt some of the Bains proposals. (Non-metropolitan county chief executive)

They [the members] approached Bains . . . rather warily and said, 'We are not having any of this chief executive stuff'. (Welsh district clerk and chief executive [sic])

I have never been a Bains man, so we rejected entirely the Bains concept. (Metropolitan county chief executive)

The argument that the recommendations of Bains were received generally (though not invariably) uncritically and implemented almost universally is, apparently, sustained by the facts. However, given the upheaval involved in such a major structural change as local government reorganisation, and the experience of officers in being appointed and members in being elected to new authorities which, especially in the shire districts, were often very much larger than those to which they were accustomed, such initial homogeneity was perhaps not surprising. In assessing the new management systems and their effects on local government and decision-making it is important to go deeper than the structures and processes arising from the local application of national recommendations. It is essential to examine how the major innovations – the office of chief executive, the officers' management team and the policy committee – work in practice and are viewed by those involved in the day-to-day management of local government. The remainder of this chapter is devoted to such an examination, and the question of the relationship between these management and decision-making institutions and the increased partisanship which characterises the new councils is considered in Chapter 5.

THE OFFICE OF CHIEF EXECUTIVE

When the new pattern of local authorities was finalised in the Local Government Act 1972, there were established 422 new councils all of which, potentially, would be in search of a paid staff to be led by a chief executive. Richards (1975, pp. 58–9) has considered the practical difficulties involved in this process and it would be redundant to cover that ground again. However, for the purpose of assessing the contribution to the workings of local government of the office of chief executive it is useful to look at the background and qualifications of those who were appointed to these posts. SOLACE (1977, pp. 9–10) provides figures (Table 4.3) for the professional qualifications of the 340 chief executives who responded to the 1975 survey and, although

Table 4.3 *Professional Qualifications of Chief Executives (in percentages)*.

Profession	%
Lawyers	69
Accountants	14
Administrators[a]	12
Chartered secretaries	9
Valuers	3
Planners	3
Engineers/Surveyors	2
Architects	1
Others	1

Source: SOLACE (1977), pp. 9–10.
[a]Denotes holders of Diploma in Public Administration, Diploma in Municipal Administration or Diploma in Management Studies.

they refer to Scotland and London as well as to England and Wales, the percentages would not differ significantly if the figures referred only to England and Wales. It should be noted that because some chief executives have more than one qualification and some have none, the percentages do not sum to one hundred.

There is clearly a preponderance of lawyers, but the figures mask some variations among classes of authorities with 'the legal tradition ... strongest in the counties and weakest in the non-metropolitan districts' (SOLACE, 1977, p. 19). Both the preponderance of lawyers and the distinction between classes of authority are supported by the fact that of the randomly selected districts whose chief executives were interviewed for this book 74 per cent had chief executives who were lawyers, while among the counties, some of which were deliberately chosen and some randomly selected (see Appendix), 90 per cent of chief executives were lawyers. In the appointments made since reorganisation there is some evidence that the domination of the lawyers is being reduced (SOLACE, 1977, p. 10) and there is no reason why a chief executive should come to the post better equipped from one professional discipline than another. This is especially, but not exclusively, so where the chief executive has no department.

SOLACE is clearly concerned about the need to train chief executives in management (1977, pp. 12–16) and it is clear that the preponderance of lawyers in the first round of appointments reflects the fact that 'the Clerk of an old authority was an obvious choice for the chief executive of a successor authority' (SOLACE, 1977, p. 10) for, in the old system, clerks (most of whom were lawyers), and to a lesser extent treasurers, were the only chief officers who had a 'central' advisory role at all comparable to that envisaged by Bains for chief executives. The frequency with which these 'continuation' appointments were made raises important questions about the extent to which an officer who was designated 'clerk' on 31 March 1974 and 'chief executive' on 1 April 1974 acted differently in the latter post from the way he had acted in the former. Clearly, many appointments of this sort were received with a mixture of cynicism and scepticism by people both outside and inside local government, and sometimes by the appointees themselves, as is evident from the following comments:

A lot of people were just appointed, who are incompetent, because they were there. (Non-metropolitan district chief executive)

I suffered translation to chief executive in 1974. (Non-metropolitan county chief exective)

We wanted to preserve the basic elements, perhaps dressed up in a different form, of the clerk to the County Council and the deputy . . . The clerk had always acted as the Council's principal policy advisor. (Non-metropolitan county chief executive)

Bains spelled out in intelligible words what we would have been doing anyway. (Non-metropolitan district/FCB chief executive)

But a clearer and more comprehensive picture will emerge from an examination of the performance of chief executives, particularly as it relates to the other major innovation on the officer side – the officers' management team.

Given the widespread adoption of the Bains job description for a chief executive (Bains, 1972, app. J, p. 165), or of variants of it, it is useful to examine the performance of chief executives, and to assess the significance for local government of the institution of chief executive, in the light of the specific roles identified by Bains. The important substantive functions of a chief executive are, first, to be 'leader of the officers' management team', secondly, to be 'the Council's principal adviser on matters of general policy' and, thirdly, to maintain 'good internal and external relations'.

THE CHIEF EXECUTIVE AND THE MANAGEMENT TEAM

On the matter of leadership of the management team the Bains model required that the chief executive be given 'authority over all other officers', an innovation which many chief executives, especially those who had served as town clerks in the county boroughs, consider to be simply the formalisation of a relationship to which they were already accustomed. In practice, however, the degree to which a chief executive provides leadership depends on two aspects of his performance: the organisation of management team agendas and the form of decision-making within the management team. There is a certain circularity in the relationship between chief executive and management team: to an extent the chief executive's position relies on the cohesiveness, corporateness and effectiveness of the management team; and the management team depends for these qualities on the position of the chief executive. This is a consequence of the vagueness of Bains on the functions of the management team. In paragraph 5.47 Bains admitted that the study group had found it 'difficult to lay down any specific terms of reference' (Bains, 1972). Such difficulty clearly arose from the realisation that the notion of having a chief executive as a *leader* of a team of any kind implied that chief officers – as members of that team, who had, in many cases, been used to running departments as quasi-independent fiefdoms – should, 'on occasion . . . subordinate their own particular interest to that of the authority as a whole' (Bains, 1972, p. 49). It is obviously impossible to define in advance the sort of issue upon which such self-abnegation will be expected. Thus agenda management may be a crucially important process for a chief executive.

Bains was more definite on the desirable outcome of the interaction between the chief executive and the management team. In general, reports and recommendations from the management team were expected to be unanimous, but it was anticipated that provision would be made for the expression of a strongly held minority view (Bains, 1972, p. 50). This form of decision-making, placing as it does a premium on unanimity, has significant implications for the position and performance of the chief executive.

On agenda management, the material procedural point that will help to determine the nature of the chief executive's performance in relation to the management team is whether or not he 'filters' the items that emerge for consideration. Some items, of course, have to be referred: questions raised by the decisions of central government, for example on the implications of the rate support grant settlement; or, in those authorities which have a strongly initiative political leadership, matters specifically sent to the management team by the controlling group. Items that emerge from individual departments, however, offer a chief executive a continuous opportunity to assert his leadership. A 'strong' chief executive will scrutinise all such items and will see it as his responsibility, on occasion, to tell a chief officer either that an item is not a suitable matter for management team consideration at all, or that the time is not opportune for its discussion. A 'weak' chief executive will allow chief officers to place items on the management team agenda on demand. Despite its vagueness about the management team and the chief executive's relationship with it, the clear implication of the Bains Report both in its argument and in its recommended job description, is in favour of the strong rather than the weak model.

Of the sixty-one English and Welsh chief executives interviewed for this study, only twenty-seven could be described as strong chief executives on this criterion. The others divide almost equally between those who, as a matter of deliberate practice, do not perform this filtering role and those for whom the issue did not arise, often because their management team equated to the Bains concept in name only, if at all. These figures suggest that the influence of Bains, as expressed in the figures in Tables 4.1 and 4.2, may be more apparent than real, more form than substance. There is evidence that the reasons for this relate to the position of the management team in the decision-making and political structure of the council. This is a point to which further attention will be given when the form of management teams and their relationship to policy formation is considered later in this chapter and in Chapter 5.

Among those chief executives who did operate a filter on management team agenda items, there was a general perception that this function was of considerable importance to their position as chief executive. It is seen, also, as having significance in demonstrating the chief executive's leadership position and in showing that the distinction between the chief executive and the chief officers is both substantial and hierarchical: the strong chief executive is rather more than *primus inter pares*. The following quotations are illustrative of the views of this group.

I chair the meeting and I tell them what they're going to discuss on the agenda. (Non-metropolitan district chief executive)

It is left to me to pick those items that the team should talk about. (Non-metropolitan district chief executive)

Some of my chief officers tended to use management team as a decision-making process to relieve themselves of that burden. (Non-metropolitan district chief executive)

I settle the agenda . . . I don't use it to be obstructive in any way. There have been the odd occasions when I have said that others' reports . . . are premature and that's where I exercise a sort of sifting role. (Non-metropolitan county chief executive)

There is a basic instruction to every chief officer that if they are wanting to propose a change of policy or a new policy, it must be routed through the management group. (Non-metropolitan district/FCB chief executive)

Both the office of chief executive and the institution of the management team are designed to be aids to, rather than substitutes for, political decision-making and the democratic determination of priorities. For this reason the criterion of the form of decision-taking employed in the management team is more important than that of agenda management in assessing the performance of the new institutions. In the great majority of local authorities, elected members are reactive rather than initiative in relation to the policy process and because of this the recommendations that emerge from management team and the process by which these recommendations are produced are of central significance to the workings of authorities. The choice before a chief executive is whether he will seek consensus or majority decisions or whether he will 'lead from the front' and seek to direct his management team towards a preferred conclusion. It is not suggested that these alternatives are completely mutually exclusive: only that, in the context of a decision-making process aiming towards unanimity, they are helpful in classifying and evaluating chief executives' performance.

Using this criterion a chief executive would be classified as 'strong' if he assumed in management team a leadership role, ready to steer the discussion and, as a matter of course rather than as a last resort, to impose a conclusion on a divided team. In so acting, he would reflect Bains's view of him as the council's principal policy adviser and the hierarchical relationship implied in Bains's view that 'the corporate management concept suggests that each of the chief officers acts as the chief executive's deputy' (Bains, 1972, para. 5.31, p. 46). If his approach were to seek consensus as a matter of course and to impose a conclusion only exceptionally then a chief executive would be classified as 'weak'.

The findings here differ considerably from those on the criterion of agenda management: only sixteen of the sixty-one chief executives interviewed could be classified without qualification as 'leaders' or 'strong', while twenty-seven were classified as 'consensus seekers' or 'weak'. In eighteen cases the interviews did not yield enough information to reach a clear view, though in four of these cases there must be some doubt as to whether the meetings of officers amount in any meaningful way to a management team.

Once again, the evidence seems to undermine the preliminary conclusions on the influence of Bains. It suggests that in many authorities that influence was, at worst, superficial in that it led to a widespread adoption of corporate management forms. At best, it was catalytic in that it stimulated the new authorities (as were the old authorities by the Maud Committee in 1967) to examine their procedures and to create management structures and processes best suited to local circumstances.

THE CHIEF EXECUTIVE AS 'PRINCIPAL POLICY ADVISER'

The second important role of the chief executive, as specified in the Bains job description, was to act as 'the Council's principal adviser on matters of general policy'. Any evaluation of chief executives in this role inevitably impinges upon the analysis of the effects on the local government system of the increased levels of partisanship that are characteristic of the new local authorities. Because of this it is appropriate to defer much of the examination of this aspect of chief executives' performance to the next chapter. However, it should be noted here that the policy advisory role is one that chief executives, without exception, take very seriously indeed. None would disagree, except perhaps in emphasis, with the following comments from two chief executives, the first serving a major metropolitan district council and the second a predominantly rural district council in a shire county:

I am paid to do a job. I am the principal policy adviser to the Council.

The role of the management team is to help the chief executive take decisions.

There is evidence, also, and this is implied in the second of the remarks just quoted, that the inclusion of the role of principal policy adviser in the chief executive's job description has been employed in some circumstances to justify the imposition of the chief executive's view on the management team. Where this is so, it reinforces the leadership role of the chief executive as performed through such other procedures as agenda management and the direction of discussions in the management team.

THE CHIEF EXECUTIVE AS 'AMBASSADOR'

The third and final substantive role laid upon chief executives by the Bains job description is that of maintaining 'good internal and external relations'. It is unnecessary to devote much space here to either of these ambassadorial roles. The central and powerful postion of the chief executive in the field of external relations, in so far as it applies to inter-authority liaison in the local government system, was considered in Chapter 3, and his role in relations with central government will be examined in Chapter 7. His role in fostering good relations between the management structure and the political structure is central to the analysis of partisanship and the contribution of councillors that is the subject of Chapter 5. In the role of internal ambassador, however, there is one matter that deserves attention here – the question of whether a chief executive should have a department. Bains was quite clear about its preference for a non-departmental or 'free-standing' chief executive, which is to say a chief executive who, though he may have a small personal staff, is not the head of a major department. The clear view of Bains was that the leadership role envisaged for the office would be impossible to perform in tandem with the management commitment implied in the headship of a department. The alternative is suggested by the category 'Bains + clerk' in Table 4.1 and gives the chief executive responsibility for the legal, administrative and secretarial departments of the authority. The majority of chief executive posts were created without departments, but as Greenwood *et al.* (1976, p. 94) discovered, 'the rapidly accumulating research evidence suggests that all chief executives have been aware of the difficulties' inherent in the management and leadership roles implied by the new arrangements. Whether he has a department or not, the basic needs of a chief executive are information and communication and he has to have channels through which he can receive information and communicate with the departments of the authority. As Greenwood *et al.* acknowledge, 'leadership of the management team is insufficient by itself' to fulfil these functions.

Evidence from the interviews conducted for this book is suggestive rather than conclusive. It reveals that whereas there is no case of an authority beginning in 1974 with a chief executive with a department changing to a free-standing chief executive, there are several cases where authorities have changed their arrangements in the opposite direction.

In both Plymouth and Reading, for example, the resignation of the secretary of the authority led to the amalgamation of that post with that of the chief executive, though it is interesting that in one case, Reading, the decision was taken by the council against the advice of the management team and in the other, Plymouth, the chief executive recommended the change to the council. In Exeter the resignation of the chief executive led to the abolition of the post (a decision that had consequences for the system of inter-authority liaison, for Exeter was excluded for a time from meetings of Devon chief executives). And in Birmingham, perhaps the most dramatic and notorious case, the decision of the council, after a change of political control, officially to abandon corporate management of the authority (Haynes, 1978;

Corporate Planning, 1977) led to the chief executive being made redundant and the designation of the city treasurer as 'principal chief officer'. After a further change of political control in 1980 he was redesignated 'chief executive'.

Even among those authorities that have persevered with the institution of a non-departmental chief executive, there are holders of the office who have doubts about its effectiveness, as the following comments suggest.

We started off with a chief executive without a department . . . but [it was] always recognised that there had to be a special relationship between himself and the Director of Administration. (Non-metropolitan county chief executive)

I was given the opportunity of being director of administration as well as chief executive. In retrospect, I think that should have taken place. (Non-metropolitan district chief executive)

Although I didn't totally disagree with Bains, given the choice I would not have wanted to be a chief executive without department responsibility. (Non-metropolitan district chief executive)

Once again, the picture that emerges is of authorities adapting the recommendations of Bains in the light of their own experience, although it must be noted that in some cases the decision to move from a non-departmental to a departmental chief executive owed as much to the search for economies in staffing as to any informed judgement about the effectiveness of the existing management structure. By 1976 the financial squeeze on local authorities was tight enough to make very attractive a change that resulted in the shedding of a chief officer post. Also, as will become clear in the next chapter, many leading members were already sceptical about corporate management and welcomed the opportunity to dismantle some of its institutional arrangements.

However, it remains the case that a very clear majority of English and Welsh local authorities still have a 'free-standing' chief executive and there is much evidence that the need to develop the office in response to changing circumstances is recognised. It may be that the importance of good internal relations is seen to be paramount. If so, then the question of whether a chief executive has, or has not, a department is secondary and subject to decision in the light of the needs and personalities of the particular council.

THE OFFICERS' MANAGEMENT TEAM

It was suggested above that in other than hierarchical terms it is difficult to separate parts played in the process of decision-making by the chief executive and the officers' management team once the Bains recommendations, or some variant of them, are put into practice: both are central to the notion of corporate working and their establishment is at least a minimal test of the intentions of a local authority to move from an iterative, incrementalist policy process to one that is more rational and comprehensive. A more rigorous test of the commitment of an authority, and in particular of its chief officers, to the Bains ideal of corporate management is the extent to which departmental chief officers, are prepared to accept the need, quoted earlier from Bains, 'to subordinate their own particular interest to that of the authority as a whole' (Bains, 1972, para. 5.40, p. 49). A closely related point here is the extent to which the specific views of the Bains Report on the size and composition of the management team have been taken into account by the authority.

In assessing the commitment of individual chief officers to the corporate approach to policy determination, it is important to distinguish between what are often called 'central' departments, on the one hand, and 'service' departments, on the other. The former are almost by definition 'corporate', in the sense that they provide services and/or expertise to the *authority* rather than to the *community*. The most obvious central departments are those of the chief executive (if he has a department), the secretary or director of administration, and the treasurer. It is worth recalling here that treasurers, secretaries and administrators are the professions which, after the law, have provided the largest number of chief executives (see Table 4.3). Other central services include personnel, management services, research and intelligence, computing and land management, although in particular authorities, all, or any of these, may be provided by other central departments rather than by separate departments headed by a chief officer.

The service departments are those responsible for the commitment of resources in the community and for the provision of public services. These include education, social services, housing, highways and planning (although there is an important sense in which planners often provide a central service as well, especially in the field of research and intelligence). These are departments which, in many authorities, have a long tradition of independence, subject only to the restrictions placed upon them by the central determination of their budgets and, more infrequently, to decisions of the council to change their policies. In the old system, also, as Bristow (n.d., p. 7) points out, that independence was enhanced in some cases by the fact that authorities were obliged by legislation to appoint certain officers. It was mandatory, for example, for councils which were education authorities to have a chief education officer and, as late as 1970, the Local Authorities Social Services Act obliged counties and county boroughs to appoint a director of social services. This example of central control of local authorities, which in its effects must be inimical not only to the independence of local government but also to its capacity to work corporately, was carried forward to the new system by the requirement in section 112 of the Local Government Act 1972 that certain officers, including a chief education officer and a director of social services, must be appointed by authorities with statutory responsibilities in these fields. Whether it is created by the requirements of legislation or arises from the leadership of a spending department staffed by committed professionals, departmental loyalty and the standards developed by professionalism may militate against the corporate approach (Stewart, 1976*a–i, passim.*).

It was demonstrated above (Table 4.2) that almost all of the new authorities set up a management team: to that extent there was a general move away from strict departmentalism. But the tensions inherent in the distinctions between corporate working and departmental loyalty, between central departments and service departments, and between major departments and minor departments were manifest in the variations in the size and membership of the bodies that shared the name 'management team'. Bains was less than dogmatic about the ideal size of the management team, although it was quite firm about the existence of a maximum number of individuals that can usefully act in a corporate way in the making of decisions. It seemed to favour a view expressed to the study group 'that a team of nine is probably too large' and it tentatively proposed that 'the team will probably number about six' (Bains, 1972, para. 5.43).

In assessing how any decision-making institution performs, the question of ideal size is less important than that of the relationship between size and efficiency. In other words, and this follows directly from the evidence presented earlier about the need to distinguish between the adoption of Bains forms and the substance of management structures as they actually operate, a descriptive approach to the working of management teams in the process of local authority decision-making is likely to be more rewarding than the prescriptive approach characteristic of the more zealous advocates of corporate management.

Bains was aware that the question of membership of the management team might raise complicated issues of personal and professional relationships. Its preference for a small management team, which was reflected in its sample management structures (Bains, 1972, pp. 104–21), raised the possibility that 'if the management team's activities are not made known to those chief officers who are not members, distrust and suspicion are bound to be created' (ibid., p. 51). The evidence suggests that in many authorities good communication has not been regarded as an adequate substitute for membership of the management team.

There was more scepticism among local authorities about the Bains recommendations on the composition of the management team than about any other of the major recommendations. It is not surprising, therefore, that it is here that they have departed most from the report's prescriptions. Certainly, in those districts based upon former county boroughs, the break with tradition implied in the Bains recommendation for a small management team was often regarded as too traumatic to be contemplated. Bains envisaged two methods of achieving a management team of an acceptable size, neither of which was easily compatible with the traditions of departmentalism and professionalism so characteristic of the county borough system. The first was to group together, under a kind of super chief officer or director, cognate departments which in the old system would each have been headed by a chief officer. Thus, for example, such services as planning, architecture, engineering, environmental health, and estates and valuation might be placed within a department of technical services headed by a director. The second method was to maintain the historic pattern of departments but to include in the management team only those chief officers who headed the central departments together with those in charge of major spending departments, such as education, social services, housing and planning in the metropolitan districts; education, social services and planning in the shire counties; and housing and planning in the larger non-metropolitan districts. In what Bains called an 'average' non-metropolitan district, which is to say those formed from smaller county boroughs and all but the largest urban and rural districts, it was envisaged that all chief officers would be members of the management team.

As Greenwood *et al*. (1976) discovered, there has been a wide variation in the application of the notion of the management team in the new local government system, a variation which is, to an extent, concealed by the fact that only a very few authorities have quite deliberately decided against having any institution with the name 'management team'. Where this has happened, the reasons have been a combination of the influence of the experience in former authorities and the particular nature of the relationship between officers and members, a point to which consideration will be given in the next chapter. Elsewhere, it has been common for the principle of the small management team to be difficult to operate in practice and uncommon for the Bains prescription of a small group to which additional members are invited only when necessary to be strictly adhered to. In discussions with chief executives there were many references to the fact that the Bains idea of a small policy-directing team could not cope with the consequential creation of 'first- and second-class officers' or, as more than one chief executive put it, 'inners and outers'. And even where the management style of the chief executive is dictated by his self-image as a leader, he may find that the smooth running of his authority demands a very liberal interpretation of the process of communication demanded by Bains between management team and departments. Consider, for example, the following remarks (all from the same chief executive in a large shire district) for they illustrate the point being developed here about the difference between the theory and the practice of the management team. It should be added that the chief executive concerned would be classified as 'strong' on both of the criteria identified above.

I was determined not to have a big management team . . .

I had protestations from my colleagues whom I had worked with for ten years that they should be chief officers.

We do have chief officers meetings to decide policy.

Except in some of the metropolitan county councils, with their very restricted range of services, it has been common for a quite formalised two-tier management system to develop, in one of two ways. The first process is where authorities have begun with a strict application of the Bains notion of a small management team of 'central' chief officers together with one or two others, and have found it necessary, as in the example just quoted, to supplement management team meetings by more widely representative chief officers meetings. (A common variation is the small management team to which all chief officers have a standing invitation.) The second process is where the primary management institution is a version of the traditional chief officers' meeting which, in turn, delegates much of its corporate discussion to a small group of 'central' officers.

It is possible that the attachment to departmentalism and the questions of status that affect attempts at corporate working in many authorities may be eliminated as a new generation of local government officers, schooled in new ways of decision-making, emerges. There is, however, much evidence to suggest that the early post-reorganisation enthusiasm has greatly diminished. And despite the arguments of supporters of corporate management and corporate planning that economic stringency makes these processes more desirable and probably more valuable (Stewart, 1976*a–i*; Musgrave, 1978; Howick, 1978), there is little doubt that many chief officers still regard strict departmentalism as the great bulwark in defence of their services. It was clearly the aim of corporate management to break down such departmentalism. The establishment of the management team of principal chief officers was to be both the symbol and the motive force for this process. It is important, therefore, to consider reasons why the aim has not been achieved, to examine once again why there is a distinction to be drawn in many of the new local authorities between the form and the substance of corporate management. The research for this book suggests three reasons.

The first reason has already been implied: the strength of departmentalism and of professionalism in British local government (Hill, 1974, ch. 4; Poole, 1978) is such that it will take more than the paper commitment to the Bains prescriptions to undermine it. Consider, in this connection, the following quotations: the first is from the management proposals accepted by the council of one of the 'big nine' former county boroughs after the first elections to the new authority; and the second is a comment from the chief executive of the same authority after five years operating under the management structure created by these proposals.

These recommendations [from Bains, 1972, paras 5.38, 5.40, 5.42, on the officers' management team] should be given unqualified support since they go to the root of any corporate management system. No chief officer should be appointed unless he is prepared to recognise that he has duties outside his department in the furtherance of the corporate interests of the authority and that he is prepared at all times to play a dual role – of professional officer and corporate team member.

Some officers cannot be made corporate.

Nor is this an isolated example of the representational, status and professional problems raised by the difficulties of the 'dual role' envisaged by Bains. In many authorities these problems were made more acute by the clear implication of the report that, under the new arrangements, the corporate role should take precedence over the professional or departmental one.

The second reason is a natural extension of the first: chief officers, already resentful at the requirement to subordinate their long-term professionalisms to a concept of the corporate interest of the authority to the development of which they have made only a minor contribution, often show further resentment at what they regard as the interference in their professional field by other professionals, or by generalist chief officers from central departments whom they regard as ill-qualified to offer advice. As one chief executive put it: 'I think all of us are a bit inclined to offer advice to other professions and not to take equally kindly to the advice of professionals coming from other professions.'

A closely related point here is that whether an authority has a small management team or a large one, that is to say, whether the management team is composed mainly of central chief officers or of all chief officers, there is often no conviction among team members that they have an equality of influence. Inequality of influence is perhaps inevitable within authorities providing a heterogeneous range of services. In the shire counties and metropolitan districts, for example, the high proportion of the authority's budget claimed by education, and the wide range of statutory obligations of education departments, provide chief education officers with powerful arguments about resource distribution that are not available to directors of social services or surveyors. Perhaps it is for this reasons that the Association of Directors of Social Services has issued advice to its members on how to increase their impact on the management team and in the process of corporate management (Association of Directors of Social Services, 1977). Additionally, central officers such as treasurers, secretaries and personnel officers, by virtue of their positions in both the administrative hierarchy and the decision-making process, have, and are perceived to have, a wider sphere of influence, especially in the crucial area of resource distribution, than have most service department chief officers. This is particularly relevant in periods of economic stringency of the sort that has affected the British public sector since the widespread application of corporate management principles to local government.

It is clear, also, that many chief officers, even when the terms of their appointment oblige them to participate in corporate planning through membership of the management team, feel they have little to offer to the process of management team consideration of corporate objectives and deeply resent the time that such participation obliges them to spend away from their departments. This is particularly the case where the management team operates on the basis of open invitations to all chief officers. In these circumstances, the imperatives of inter-departmental competition for resources compel chief officers to attend lest they lose ground. A combination of such feelings of limited usefulness, resentment at time spent at what are regarded as fruitless management team discussions, and attendance for self-protection has led directly, in many authorities, to the formalisation of the two-tier management structure discussed above. The following remarks, both from chief executives in metropolitan districts, illustrate a not uncommon experience.

I realised that the three chief officers that weren't members of the management team had a bit of a chip on their shoulder . . . and I decided . . . to forget the management team idea in the interests of having a united team of officers . . . But [chief officers] have suggested that we ought to reduce the numbers, probably to about four.

I felt we were getting too much of the inner and outer and so I abandoned it for a while and just had an ordinary management team. It was then the [management team] members themselves who said, 'why don't you revert to the old system'.

The third and final reason for the widespread departure from the Bains prescriptions, as they apply to the institution of the management team, is one that will be introduced here and examined more closely in the next chapter. The whole principle of corporate management, and of the specific institutions it produces, is inimical to one of the central traditions of British local government – the close relationship between a service committee chairman and the head of 'his' department. This, of course, is no unintended consequence of the corporate ideal; it is a fundamental and necessary justification for it. But committee chairmen continue to cherish their independence; and chief officers often, and rightly, see it as being in their departmental interest to encourage it. There is always, in the words of a chief executive deeply committed to corporate working, 'a tendency for a departmental link to creep in'. Or, as another chief executive said, perceptively if a little wistfully: 'Bains . . . makes comments which are not entirely uncritical about the chief officer–department–committee link. Members, however, like it . . .'

And the chief executive of a major city characterised the effect of this factor on the workings of local government by referring to 'the close working relationships between chairmen and chief officers [as] one of the most valuable things we have in local government'.

These points raise the whole question of the link between processes of administrative and political decision-making and the structures created to serve them. They help to explain the wide variation in management structures in the new local authorities. And they signal the possible incompatibility between wholly rational planning and the political will of elected members.

THE POLICY COMMITTEE AND ITS SUBCOMMITTEES

In the analysis of the performance of the new local government system, the third major innovation recommended by Bains, the policy committee, forms a bridge between the management structure and the committee structure. As such, it has to be considered as part of the present examination of the application of corporate management principles to local government. It is also, however, a potentially important vehicle for the participation of elected members in the formation of policy and, in that context, it will be considered in the next chapter.

The development of the policy committee, at least in the major authorities, predates reorganisation (Greenwood *et al.*, 1972*a*) and in a few places it predates even the report of the Maud Committee of 1967. But, as with the office of chief executive and the institution of the management team, its almost universal adoption owes much to the influence of the Bains Report on the structure of the new local authorities. Bains provided model terms of reference for the policy committee (Bains, 1972, app. H, p. 164) and recommended sub-committees that would report to it, and its establishment was seen by Bains and other advocates of the rational/comprehensive approach to policy-making as an indispensable part of a modernised management and decision-making system. According to Bains, the move away from departmentalism demanded that the council, as 'the ultimate decision-making body of the authority', should have available to it 'comprehensive and co-ordinated advice on the implications for the community' of its policy decisions (Bains, 1972, para. 4.14, p. 23) and that advice and co-ordination should go further than the general and detailed oversight of financial matters provided in most pre-reorganisation authorities by the finance, or finance and general purposes, committee. In short, the policy committee would provide the democratic accountability necessary to legitimise the choices generated by a policy-planning process in which the chief executive and the management team were the primary sources of information, detailed technical advice and assessments of alternative policies. It is that crucial relationship, between the permanent official structure and the elective political leadership, that is discussed in the next chapter.

At this stage in the analysis, four aspects of the performance of the policy committee as part of the local government decision-making process should be examined briefly: the experience of authorities with the subcommittee structure suggested by Bains, the size of the main committee, its composition, and the attitude of members to the idea of such a co-ordinating and policy advisory committee.

On subcommittees, Bains argued that the corporate approach demanded centralised control and direction of the three major resources of any local authority – finance, manpower and land – and it recommended that authorities should appoint subcommittees of the policy committee to provide such control and direction. Greenwood *et al.* (1976) discovered that whereas the adoption rate for policy committees in the new authorities was very high (see Table 4.2, above) there was 'rather less agreement' on how to deal with the Bains recommendations for resource subcommittees. Although a very clear majority of the authorities surveyed had a separate body responsible for each of the finance and personnel functions, in a significant number of authorities the body chosen was a full committee rather than a subcommittee. Fewer than half the authorities had appointed a subcommittee (or committee) to deal with land. This is an important finding, for it is further evidence of the reluctance of many authorities completely to abandon the tradition of departmentalism developed before reorganisation. Land and property were regarded by service committees (and their corresponding departments) as being in their ownership rather than that of the authority and, on occasion, committees would go to absurd lengths to protect their interests. An example, albeit an exaggerated one, though not altogether untypical, was the so-called 'ransom strip' system in pre-reorganisation Birmingham, whereby the sale of land between committees often involved the retention by the vendor committee of the ownership of a tiny strip of territory to ensure that it would be consulted on the future use by the purchaser committee (Corporate Planning, 1977, p. 13). That so many authorities preferred not to centralise the land function is further evidence of the lack of total commitment to the new principles of corporate management.

Since reorganisation the pattern has been for the finance and personnel subcommittees (or, in a few authorities, full committees) to become established and powerful and, *prima facie*, this must be evidence of the successful adoption of corporate techniques. Two other influences have to be noted, however. First, control of the finance and manpower resources of an authority are of special significance when the council is seeking economies. Since reorganisation local government in Britain has gone from a financial regime of very limited growth, to standstill budgeting, to contraction, and it is the view of many of the chief executives and members interviewed that it has been the reality of local government's fiscal crisis rather than conversion to the abstract principles of corporate management that has made these subcommittees powerful and successful points in the decision-making processes of most authorities. Stewart argues (1976*a–i*) persuasively that financial stringency proves the value of the prescriptions of corporate management, but in many authorities the line of causality is neither so rational nor so direct. It has been the need to save resources that has made councils corporate rather than the corporate planning process allowing authorities to save resources.

Secondly, the finance and personnel functions differed from the land function in that in many old authorities there existed committees to deal with these resources. It is not suggested that the staffing committees in, for example, the old county boroughs performed the sophisticated manpower planning function expected of personnel subcommittees by Bains, nor that the detailed consideration to individual items of expenditure that typified the agenda of pre-reorganisation finance committees was intended to be the concern of the new finance subcommittees. Nevertheless, their very existence made the process of the adoption of these Bains subcommittees more acceptable, especially where the tradition of departmentalism was very strong.

Bains recommended a fourth subcommittee, performance review, and it clearly regarded the idea of such a subcommittee as an important innovation and one that was central to the move towards rational/comprehensive policy planning. On the analogy of the House of Commons Public Accounts Committee, the performance review subcommittee would have a roving commission as 'a watchdog body . . . with the standing and formal authority to make detailed investigation into any project, department, or area of activity' (Bains, 1972, para. 4.20, p. 25) and to report to the policy committee. The Bains recommendation on performance review received the wholehearted approval of two official inquiries into standards of conduct in public authorities. Both the Redcliffe-Maud report on conduct in local government (Redcliffe-Maud, Cmnd 5636, 1974, para. 130) and the Salmon report on standards of conduct in public life (Salmon, Cmnd 6524, 1976, para. 243) referred specifically to the Bains concept of performance review committees. Despite the unanimity of these external investigating bodies, however, this has been the least successful of the Bains recommendations. Hinings *et al*. (1975*a*, p. 17) reported that only a minority of authorities had set up a performance review subcommittee and the research for this book discovered no authority where a process of performance review external to service and resource committees was regarded as successful. Many authorities have abolished their performance review subcommittees, having found that they were not only ineffective but also deeply resented within the authority. The problem, once again, is rooted in the resilience of departmentalism, for committees typically do not see the value of the examination of their performance, and that of their corresponding departments, by councillors who have neither special expertise nor a commitment to the particular service under scrutiny. Also, there is a general view that, because service committees are now so closely circumscribed in the commitment of resources by the decisions of policy committees and the subcommittees on finance and manpower, further monitoring is both redundant and wasteful. Finally, it may be speculated that the process of performance review was intended for a more expansionary period than the new local authorities have yet experienced.

There remain to be considered the questions of the size and composition of the policy committee and, as a preliminary to the analysis in the next chapter, the attitudes of members to it. As with the management team, the question of size is less important than the relationship between size and the capacity of the institution to do the job for which it was designed. In the case of the policy committee, also, it has proved very difficult in many authorities to separate the question of representativeness from the question of functional effectiveness, other than by the employment of devices such as the creation of an 'inner cabinet' under some such title as 'policy advisory group', or the appointment of a policy committee composed solely of members of the controlling political group. These devices are part of the connecting mechanism between the management and the political structures of local authorities and, as such, they will be examined in the next chapter.

The issues of size, composition and attitude are very closely related. Especially where the idea of a policy committee is entirely new, and this was the case in most of the non-metropolitan districts and some of the other authorities, it was often regarded with suspicion by members who saw it usurping not only the powers of individual service committees, but also the constitutional obligation of the full council to determine policy. It was generally found that acceptance of the new institution depended on a less restricted membership than the Bains discussion implied. It was necessary, in other words, to make the policy committee into a representative institution.

Policy committees have typically become representative in four ways: first, they had to be functionally representative in that membership included councillors who also served as the main spending committees; secondly, they had to be geographically representative, especially where the new authority was formed from more than one former authority; thirdly, they had to be representative of the internal hierarchies of the authority by including both backbench members and committee chairmen and vice-chairmen; and fourthly, in the great majority of authorities, they had to be politically representative of the balance of power on the council as a whole. Elcock (1975) provides an account of the importance of representativeness in Humberside County Council and there is no doubt that experience there, though perhaps exaggerated by the particular difficulties discussed in the last chapter, was not untypical. Satisfaction of all these criteria often made policy committees very large and there can be little doubt that this has reduced their effectiveness in the field of policy initiation and co-ordination. Because of their highly representative character, policy committees have tended to become either duplicates of, or substitutes for, the work of the full council and the function of policy co-ordination has shifted to the political party groups, or to the chief executive and management team, or, increasingly, to both. But that is the subject of the next chapter.

Chapter 5

PARTISANSHIP AND PROFESSIONALISM

The decision, in 1971, that the reorganised system of local government would be a county-based, two-tier one entailing, outside the six metropolitan counties, the absorption of the county boroughs into their surrounding counties raised a general expectation that there would be a rise in the levels of partisanship. There were two reasons for this. First, politics in the county boroughs was almost completely a partisan business. Even where the performance of the parties was uneven, with one or other of the major parties dominating the council over a period of time, electoral competition was typically intense, with only a very few wards in county boroughs going uncontested. Between 1945 and 1970 the highest percentage of uncontested seats in the English county boroughs was just over 18, in 1955, whereas in the county councils the comparable figure was just under 57 per cent, in 1961 (Bristow, 1978, p. 17). It was generally expected that the county borough tradition of high levels of partisanship would be carried forward into the new counties and that it would affect not only the former county borough areas but also those areas of the new counties that had been part of the old, and much less competitive and partisan, two-tier system of county and county districts. This expectation was very plausible, particularly given the need for political parties to reorganise themselves into units to correspond with the new local government structure. For a newly constituted county Labour Party, for example, an undertaking to contest every seat on the new county council might perform two important functions: it would demonstrate publicly its will to be a serious political force throughout the new area; and it would indicate to party supporters in its less favourable wards that their political interests would be considered by the party, an indication that could assist in the creation of a well-integrated and effective party to serve the new structure.

The second reason for the general expectation of a rise in partisanship stems from the structural effects of the 1972 reorganisation. The great reduction in the number of local authorities was accompanied by a great increase in the size of the new authorities. For most authorities there was a very substantial rise in the population and rateable value of the areas they covered when compared with their predecessor councils. As Sharpe has pointed out (1978c, pp. 93–5), one result of the change in the structure of local government has been to provide Britain with local authorities whose average size is very much greater than in most other countries. And the need to provide some form of democratic accountability in these enlarged authorities was thought likely to lead to a greater degree of political organisation within councils. Quite simply, it was unlikely that many councils would find it possible to ensure member control of a large and heterogeneous budget without some kind of member organisation: the days of the independent councillor, and more importantly the independent council, were thought to be numbered.

These expectations have proved to be very well founded. As Bristow shows (1978, p. 18), in the first two rounds of elections to the new authorities there was a very substantial decline in the percentage of unopposed returns with, for example, the figure for the new counties dropping in 1977 to 11·9 per cent as compared with the 1970 figure for the old counties of 49·9 per cent. It is, of course, impossible to ascribe this rise in electoral competitiveness simply to the incorporation of the county boroughs into the counties, although there is evidence (Schofield, 1980) to suggest that the increase was greater in those counties which did include a former county borough than in those that did not.

Also, in the new system many more councils are internally organised on party political lines than in the old system. According to Bristow, in 1974 there were Labour or Conservative controlling groups (or largest single party) in 70 per cent of all authorities in England and Wales; by 1977 the figure had risen to 79 per cent.

It is not the purpose of the present book to analyse the reasons for, nor the course of, the rise in partisanship and party competitiveness in British local government. Rather it is concerned with the effects of increased partisanship on the workings of the new system and, in particular, with the relationship between political organisation and the attempts at corporate working and rational planning systems that were considered in the previous chapter. For, as the discussion there suggested, it is unrealistic in the course of an examination of the workings of the new systems of local government to see the increased partisanship that resulted from the structural changes imposed by legislation as distinct from, and wholly unrelated to, the widespread adoption of the forms and prescriptions of corporate management. Local government had to cope with the two processes at the same time; and the interactions between them are likely to be important to an understanding of how the new local authorities work.

There has been no shortage in recent years of expressions of concern about the nature of the relationship between elected members and appointed officials in local government. Such official inquiries as Maud (1967), Redcliffe-Maud (1969), Wheatley (1969) and Bains (1972) considered the relative roles of officers and members and, in varying amounts of detail, suggested ways in which the relationship might be improved. Some academic commentators have attempted to reveal what Rhodes called 'the lost world' (Rhodes, 1975a) of the officer–member relationship and to examine the nature and extent of the contribution of councillors and professionals to what Dearlove (1973) called 'the politics of policy' in local government. Most of the published material, however, either amounts to a general discussion of the relationship between policy and administration and between politicians and administrators (Poole 1978; Gyford 1976) or deals in great and often revealing detail with the decision-making processes in specific authorities or in specific service areas (Newton, 1976; Lewis, 1975; Dearlove, 1973; Kogan and van der Eyken, 1973). There has been little attempt to examine the general effects on the local government world of these parallel, and very widespread, processes of increased partisanship and reformed and rationalised corporate management structures.

THE SPECIFICATION OF PARALLEL STRUCTURES

The internal organisation of local authorities has always entailed the maintenance of parallel structures, loosely identified as the member side and the officer side. In most pre-reorganisation authorities this general parallel was mirrored at the specific level of the relationship between a committee and the department for which it was responsible and in the more overtly party political authorities there was sometimes a close relationship between the political leadership and the clerk to the authority, this last being particularly common in the county boroughs and the larger urban districts. An important general effect of the twin processes referred to above has been to increase the level of specification in these parallel structures and to reduce the degree of structural variations among authorities (Hinings *et al.*, 1975a; 1975b). Furthermore, the increased levels of specification in their turn generate a need for new processes of communication and interaction between the two sides. The remainder of this chapter attempts to describe and analyse the generality of these new structures and processes in the new local authorities of England and Wales. It is not suggested that all the institutions and interactions are to be found in all authorities, only that, to borrow the word that Bristow (1978) uses in another context, the 'homogenisation' of local government has proceeded far enough to justify generalisation and the aggregation of evidence.

First of all, the most important parallel structures should be identified. Just as almost all the new authorities followed the Bains advice and appointed a chief executive to head the paid staff of the council, so it has become exceptional for local authorities not to have a member who is designated 'leader of the council'. Where the party system within a council is not fully developed, there may not be such a position specifically designated but even here the leader of the majority, or dominant, group will act as a *de facto* leader of the council. Surprisingly, however, there are authorities, mostly shire districts constructed from former rural and urban districts, where there has been considerable, and successful, officer and member opposition to the creation of the post of leader. The implications of the deliberate exclusion of such an office for the interactive processes essential to the operation of an authority are considered later, but the attitude underlying the exclusion is exemplified in the following quotation: 'I resist him being called "Leader of the Council": there is no constitutional basis for that title' (Non-metropolitan district chief executive). Significantly, however, on the council to which this remark refers, the leader of the Conservative group is also chairman of the policy committee and, in operational terms, is the opposite number on the member side to the chief executive on the officer side.

The second pair of parallel institutions consists of the management team on the officer side and the policy committee on the member side. These bodies both have a co-ordinating role, the one in respect of professional advice, the other in respect of political decision, and the attitudes of members to them shed some light on the penetration of the corporate ideal in the reformed local government structure.

It was noted in the previous chapter that 94 per cent of English and Welsh non-metropolitan district councils and all of the county councils and metropolitan districts had established a policy committee (Hinings *et al.*, 1975*a*, p. 17) almost immediately they were elected and it was suggested that this figure might exaggerate the adoption rate among the shire districts. This qualification arises from two findings from the fieldwork for the present book. First, there were a number of authorities where there had been very considerable member resistance to the alleged usurpation of the authority of the full council, and so the exclusion from policy formation of back-bench members, implied in the creation of any institution with the title 'policy committee' or 'policy and resources committee'. Secondly, there were some councils which the survey by Hinings *et al.* (1975*a*, 1975*b*) would have categorised as having the equivalent of a policy committee where, in reality, the committee so classified was set up precisely because members expressed antagonism to the central consideration of policy matters by other than the full council, but where officers led by the chief executive wished to have a public forum where the co-ordinated advice of the management team would be debated between officers and members.

Of the thirty-three English and Welsh non-metropolitan district councils visited during the fieldwork for the present book, seven, or

21·2 per cent, began life in 1973–4 without a policy or policy and resources committee. In Vale Royal District Council in Cheshire, for example, there was a co-ordinating committee of the whole council, and in Neath District Council in West Glamorgan, according to the chief executive:

> The members would not have anything called a policy and resources committee; they have finance and resources. The use of the words 'policy and resources' was anathema to them . . . They said that the council will make the policy, 'We are not having a few members getting into a huddle and doing it'.

In South Oxfordshire, the council established a 'co-ordinating' committee and when back-bench members expressed antagonism to its activities it was renamed the 'co-ordination' committee and subsequently the 'policy advisory committee', changes which arose because 'it appeared to members that it was a mini-council'. And in Kerrier District Council in Cornwall there was still in 1979 no committee that could be identified as the equivalent of a policy committee.

In three of the fifteen English and Welsh non-metropolitan counties investigated there was, at reorganisation, a similar resistance to the idea of a central committee with the function of providing general policy direction for the authority. In one, 'members were very apprehensive about setting up a strong central committee'; in the second, 'the members in 1974 did not like the word "policy" because they were anti-Bains' and so they created a general purposes committee; and in the third 'back-benchers were suspicious of any small group that might arrogate policy-making functions to itself' and so the council established a resource planning committee. By 1977, however, in all three cases these committees were serving the function of the Bains-type policy committee and, indeed, two have now formally established a policy committee.

In some authorities, also, there was strong member antipathy to the establishment of management teams, though no case was found where the council had formally prevented the creation of this corporate management institution, an unsurprising finding given the report by Hinings (1975*a*, see Table 4.2) that, in 1975, management teams existed in 99 per cent of English and Welsh non-metropolitan district authorities and in all of the counties and metropolitan districts. But the attitude of members to the management team should be considered, for it is significant in the analysis of interactive processes later in this chapter. In eleven of the sixty-one authorities investigated, which is to say 18 per cent, there had been a degree of member suspicion and antagonism towards the establishment and functions of the management team, most commonly because it was thought that it

policy committee = Cab ? no.

would constitute a competing centre of power and decision-making to the members themselves. Given the imprecation of Bains (1972, p. xiv) that 'there must be clear understanding by members and officers of their respective roles so they can forge an effective partnership' the attitudes revealed in the following quotations must have a bearing on the success of the interactive processes which are essential to the creation of a partnership in the formulation of policy:

There is among the members a deep-seated fear or suspicion of the administrative side. (Non-metropolitan district/FCB chief executive)

Councillors were extremely suspicious of the structure they had adopted . . . It gradually dawned on them that . . . they had passed all power and control to officers . . . (Non-metropolitan district chief executive)

A number of service committee chairmen . . . would not have wanted the Management Team dabbling in their affairs. (Metropolitan district chief executive)

A mixture of dislike and suspicions of management team . . . These arose from a feeling that officers were making decisions despite the demands of local democracy. (Non-metropolitan county chief executive)

Members never like officer groups and are always slightly suspicious of them. (Metropolitan county chief executive)

The increased significance of partisanship in the new local authorities highlights a third pair of structures that may be seen as parallel: party groups and professional disciplines. The increased domination in local authorities of national parties has a profound effect on the policy process in local government. In many, perhaps most, of the new councils the party group has become the *locus* of political decision. This is a development that has considerable implications for the functioning of the local democratic system, and one that creates a need for interaction between politicians and professionals in order to create a working partnership out of a structure that has traditionally emphasised the fact that professional officers are independent of, and impartial between, political parties. Consider these remarks:

I do not favour officer–member working relationships. The officers' role is not one of politics. It is what is right for the town and the area against what is right for the Conservative Party or what is right for the Socialists. (Non-metropolitan district chief executive)

Often one finds that the political groups make decisions in their group meetings, they do not have officers there, they do not have advice and sometimes they make decisions which would have been better made had they had better advice. (Non-metropolitan district/FCB chief executive)

Members tend, for political reasons ... to go their own way and simply to say to the appropriate officer they are intending to raise certain things ... rather than come along and exercise a true partnership arrangement. Conversely, they become very annoyed if we drop them in it by putting a report to committee without consultation. It's a bit one-way. (Non-metropolitan district chief executive)

The major change in the new system, of course, is the spread of partisanship and the involvement of officers with organised party groups, in many cases for the first time in their professional careers. This is especially striking in those authorities that were formed by the amalgamation of rural districts, smaller urban districts and municipal boroughs. Given the variety of the sizes, composition and institutional history of the new authorities, it would be surprising if the new situation had been coped with identically across the system. However, the spread of party organisation of councils has been wide enough, and the need for a professional response common enough, for this pairing to be regarded as another example of the specification of parallel structures. This view is strengthened by the knowledge that the need for an officer response to increased political organisation arose just as the new principles of corporate management were raising an expectation among officers that their role in the process of policy formation and decision-making would be enhanced rather than diminished.

The contribution of party groups to the process of policy-making, however, is more often than not reactive rather than initiative. Except when the controlling group comes to power with a programme worked out in detail, the relationship between professional expertise and political organisation will ensure that much of the business of the authority will be generated by officers. Even in the minority of cases where the group has a detailed manifesto, the committee system and the non-executive nature of most members' contribution to the work of authorities combine to ensure that policy decisions are usually taken in response to the professionals' need for them. As Green (1980, p. 40) says in his study of Newcastle:

The Labour group was the sovereign body ... But this did not mean that the group itself was an important forum for actually taking decisions. The group acted principally as a receiving shop, serving to legitimise decisions which, in reality, had been taken elsewhere.

In Newcastle, other party organisations and individuals were regarded as being more powerful than officers or officers' groups. In the great majority of councils, however, the work of controlling groups falls into Gyford's (1976, pp. 136–7) categories of 'policy scrutiny' and 'policy acceptance' rather than 'policy initiation'. Very few groups, and those mainly in upper-tier authorities and metropolitan districts, take a strongly initiative stance.

The final pairing is, perhaps, less well defined than the others and might plausibly be argued to be a more localised and specialised version of the relationship between controlling parties and professional officers. But the relationship between a committee chairman and the appropriate chief officer should be considered separately. There are four important reasons for doing this. First, one of the processes whose results are being analysed here, the penetration in the new local government system of the ideals of corporate management, had as one of its objectives the destruction of departmentalism as a determining principle of local government decision-making processes. And the essential operational relationship in an administrative system which is both democratic and departmental is between the political head and the administrative/professional head of the department. Secondly, there is evidence, some of which was presented in the previous chapter, that the reduction in the powers of committees and departments that is inherent in the corporate approach is both unwelcome to many members and viewed equivocally by some professional officers. Thirdly, the strengthening of the influence of party in local government raises the possibility, in a greater proportion of authorities than before reorganisation, of a clash between a chairman who will plead the strength of party and the democratic mandate, and a chief officer who will argue the primacy of his professional expertise. And finally, in those authorities where the Bains recommendations for the creation of super-departments or directorates have been implemented, with the establishment of corresponding programme committees, tensions may arise from the fact that neither chairman nor individual chief officer feels he has adequate control or influence over the committee. Alternatively, as Newton reports from his study of pre-reorganisation Birmingham (1976, p. 150), a committee chairman may recognise how the presence on his committee of several professional experts may give him 'the power . . . to set one expert against another'. For all these reasons, the relationship in the new authorities between chairmen and chief officers is important enough to be identified separately and for the interactive processes it generates to be specifically examined.

PROCESSES OF INTERACTION: THE DIFFERENCES BETWEEN OFFICERS AND MEMBERS

There is no possibility of understanding how local authorities work unless it is accepted that officers and members differ in a number of highly significant ways. Models of the relationship, such as those suggested by Collins, Hinings and Walsh (1978), as ideal types upon which to base research acknowledge the differences, but usually only implicitly. Newton (1976, pp. 148–52) examines some of the differences explicitly but concludes that their significance in Birmingham is less than is sometimes assumed, a finding that may have been either peculiar to that city or restricted, as Newton later implies, to authorities with a very well-defined and long-established party system. It is important for the analysis that follows to identify the main differences between the two groups of actors in the local government policy process, for they constitute the background against which the specific processes of interaction take place. They also identify some of the gaps that must be bridged before the kind of partnership in policy-making urged by Bains is likely to emerge.

The first and most obvious distinction to be made is that local government officers are professionals and local councillors are amateurs. This ensures that any legitimacy that each group may claim for its views will arise, in the case of officers, from professional training and technical knowledge and, in the case of members, from the process of democratic election. If the process by which decisions are taken is made more rational or scientific, if it gives great prominence to the making of plans, the preparing of position statements and the monitoring of performance, then the tensions inherent in the professional–amateur dichotomy may be heightened by the fact that, for the member, the equivalent processes are the preparation of manifestos, the public relations of the party group and the process of re-election. And these are processes more likely to be based on ideology, commitment and political self-interest than on anything that a professional manager would recognise as a rational, planned calculation of priorities. Additionally, it is by no means universally accepted, despite the assertions of local government officers to this effect, that the professional views of officers are free of an underlying ideology. All of this, together with the constitutional supremacy of the members acting collectively, amounts to a possibly formidable distance between the two sides in local government.

The second distinction relates to recruitment. Officers are selected and members are elected or, to quote Bains (1972, para. 5.3, p. 39),

'At officer level . . . the authority has the responsibility of selection; it has no control over the election of its own membership'. The processes of selection for local government officers are usually very rigorous, often involving at the chief executive level the advice and services of outside professional management consultants. The process of election of members, on the other hand, is often rather haphazard, affected by the sometimes wild swings of electoral opinion, by the response of the voters in local elections to national cues such as the popularity or otherwise of the national government, and by the application to the intra-party recruitment process of such unspecific criteria as the general ideological stance of the aspirant and the principle of 'Buggins turn'. It is unusual for a member to be recruited to a local authority to do a specific job or to assume a specific responsibility; it is unknown for a senior local government officer to be recruited on any other basis.

Thirdly, members are transient and officers are permanent. This is not to suggest that local government officers spend their entire career in the service of a single local authority for there is evidence (Poole, 1978; Gyford, 1976) to show that top officers generally move between authorities as they ascend the career ladder. Table 5.1 shows the number of previous authorities served by the sixty-one chief executives in England and Wales who were interviewed for this study. The material point is that whereas the continued service of a member in local government depends on re-election, that of an officer depends on survival and his own perception of his career pattern. Thus members must, to an extent that will vary according to the vulnerability of their wards and the volatility of the electorate, make their political choices with the next election in mind. Officers are

Table 5.1   *Career Patterns of Chief Executives: Number of Previous Authorities Served.*

Number of Previous Authorities	No. of CEs	Percentage of CEs
None	5	8·2
One	7	11·5
Two	10	16·4
Three	11	18·0
Four	10	16·4
Five	9	14·8
Six	6	9·8
Seven or more	3	4·9
Totals	61	100·00

expected, as Bains clearly implies when discussing policy planning and the membership of the policy committee, to take a longer view and to seek to minimise the degree of policy change precipitated by such external pressures as elections. Consider the following quotations from Bains:

> Some policy changes will inevitably be in the nature of a reaction to outside events . . . But we believe that, essentially, policy decisions should be based on planning and analysis of objectives and the means of attaining them. (Bains, 1972, para. 3.24, p. 12)

> It [minority group representation on the policy committee] seems likely to lead to less . . . mistrust . . . and may, in so doing, *avoid some of the more violent reversals of policy which can occur following changes of power*. (Bains, 1972, para 4.27, p. 28. Emphasis added)

In short, while members may expect elections to change everything, officers may hope that they will change no more than some of the personalities on the member side.

Finally, officers are full-time and members, in the main, are part-time. The significance of this divide arises from the impossibility, already noted in this book and remarked upon by almost all students of policy-making in local government, of separating policy and administration. There is a continuous possibility that officers, in the administration of established council policy, may pre-empt or fore-close future policy options. This is a potential cause of tension between officers and members and may be, as will be discussed later, a powerful argument in favour of the introduction of full-time councillors.

PROCESSES OF INTERACTION: COUNCIL LEADERS AND CHIEF EXECUTIVES

The need for close interaction between members and officers, and perhaps also a flavour of the lack of success in bridging the gaps just identified, are neatly encapsulated in the following remark from the chief executive of one of England's biggest non-metropolitan county councils: 'One of the shortcomings of local government practice in the past is that there hasn't been a sufficient measure of cohesion between the work of officers and the views of members.'

There can be no doubt that the most important interactive process in the reformed system is the structure of communication between the leader of the council and the chief executive. The relationship here resembles that between a minister and the permanent secretary of his department, or even between the prime minister and the sec-

retary to the Cabinet, with the important distinction that the traditional committee system by which local authorities organise
decision-making and supervise implementation deprives the political
leader of any formal executive responsibility. There is evidence, however, that the arrival in some authorities of the councillor who is
full-time, or effectively full-time, in his commitment to local government is leading to the development of a kind of *de facto* political
executive and a consequent alteration in the position of the chief
executive as the head of the council's paid service.

Evidence of the growing importance in the internal workings of
local authorities of the continuous, or nearly continuous, presence in
council headquarters of the political leader can be found in the results
of the surveys of councillors and local authorities conducted in 1977
for the Committee on the System of Remuneration for Members of
Local Authorities (Robinson, 1977, Vol. II). The surveys revealed
that back-bench members of councils spent, on average, 70 hours per
month on council duties, whereas majority party leaders spent an
average of 112 hours per month (ibid., Vol. II, table 45, p. 28). The
implications of these figures are clear, especially when they are read
in conjunction with those in table 22 (ibid., Vol. II, p. 20) which
reveal the wide variations in the average time spent on council duties
by members in the various types of authority, from an average of 119
hours per month in the Welsh counties (19 of these hours were spent
on travelling), to 109 hours per month in the metropolitan districts,
to only 65 hours per month in the non-metropolitan districts. First
of all, it is not unlikely that the average for majority leaders is
depressed by the effect in the calculations of the large number of
non-metropolitan district councils, for the average is derived from
a 100 per cent sample of leaders and a response rate of 69 per
cent (ibid., Vol. II, table A4, p. 42). Secondly, the gap between
the 70 hours spent on council duties by the average back-bencher
and the 112 hours spent by the average leader is most likely to
be accounted for, in large measure, by the involvement of the
leader with policy-making and implementation, both of which entail
interaction with officers in general and with chief executives in particular.

Indeed, Robinson (ibid., Vol. II, table 45, p. 28) reveals that of the
112 hours spent per month on council business by the average
majority party leader, 19 were spent on 'preparation for meetings', 13
on 'meeting officers', and 8 at 'party meetings'. The corresponding
figures for back-benchers are 12, 4 and 5. It seems plausible to argue
that all of these categories are concerned with the policy process in
local government and that the first two – 'preparation for meetings'
and 'meeting officers' – involve a large amount of interaction between members and officers. (In those authorities, to be considered

later, where officers attend party group meetings this may also apply to the category 'party meetings'.) If this is so, then it is found that of the 112 hours per month average, majority party leaders spend something between 32 and 40 hours per month 'interacting' with officers. For ordinary members, the average is half of this, from 16 to 21 hours. In percentage terms, time spent with officers is between 28·5 per cent and 35·7 per cent for leaders, and between 22·8 per cent and 30 per cent for back-benchers. For both groups, the figures are significant and the nature and quality of the interaction, particularly at leadership level, is revealed in evidence collected for the present book.

Except in the very few authorities where there is neither an established or developing system of political groups nor a clearly identified elected leader, the primary channel of communication between the member side and the officer side lies in the working relationship between the leader of the council and the chief executive. The relationship between leader and town clerk was well established in many of the former county boroughs, where the participation of members in the affairs of the authority amounted to what the chief executive of Birmingham City Council in the new system described as 'continuous political direction', a view that echoes the findings of Newton (1976, pp. 150–1) that for many years prior to reorganisation a small group of members in Birmingham, both Conservative and Labour, were effectively full-time. What is new in the reorganised and more generally politicised system is the extent and prevalence of the leader–chief executive relationship as a vital lubricant for the operation of the whole machine.

But despite the very general incidence of this interactive process, its quality varies widely and is affected by the attitudes of both members and officers. It is significant that the closest relationships occur where the level of partisanship and of party competitiveness are highest, probably because the possibility of a change in political control is, in itself, a pressure towards close co-operation. For the effectiveness of political direction in a highly partisan authority in a politically volatile area may rely as much upon implementation as on ideology. In an area where the political pendulum does not swing regularly – or does not swing at all – political leaders may feel that they do not need to ensure swift implementation because their re-election is not in doubt. Jones (1979, p. 6) suggests, in an article on the dominant Labour group on Durham County Council, 'that there is a tendency towards the bureaucratic politics of inertia and towards a conservative frame of mind, since there is, and can be, no serious political challenge to the power of the group'. Politicians may also feel that close relationships with paid officials will contaminate their ideological purity or compromise their democratic mandate.

An example of the sort of close relationship that arises in a council that is both partisan and volatile is illustrated in the following remark from the chief executive of a large non-metropolitan district formed from a former county borough with a history of alternation in power between the Labour and Conservative parties: 'The Labour Party did tend to consult informally but very regularly in here [i.e. the chief executive's office] on the basis that we destroyed the minutes after their tenure of office ... great confidentiality with their top five people ...'

In this sort of council it is unusual for contact between the chief executive and the leader of the council to be less regular than daily, and even where the political leader is neither officially nor effectively full-time on council duties, the general pattern is for him to be 'on call' continuously and able to come to the council's headquarters for consultation at any time. And the closeness and frequency of contact is regarded by chief executives as a very positive contribution to the internal management of the authority, as the following remarks indicate:

[The leader] keeps me in touch with group thinking and what the administration wants to see ... (Non-metropolitan district chief executive)

The easy way for a chief executive to maintain his independence is to have nothing to do with the politicians at all, but it seems to me that that is not a satisfactory way to run a business. (Non-metropolitan district/FCB chief executive)

We have a system ... whereby I, in conjunction with the political leader, rewrite the manifesto of the controlling political group in terms of what we want to introduce through the council machine to implement their policies. (Non-metropolitan district chief executive)

I like strong leadership ... I don't have to wait for a committee decision. (Non-metropolitan district chief executive)

If you don't have that relationship [with the leader of the council] your job is a lot more difficult. (Non-metropolitan district/FCB chief executive)

I have always believed in working out with the leader of a council beforehand, not the decisions, but how to get them decided. (Metropolitan county chief executive)

But this sort of *modus operandi* is not universal in the new system.

The most significant exceptions are to be found in some authorities where the political control of the Labour Party is very deeply entrenched, and in some non-metropolitan districts where political control is nominally Conservative but where there is no history of political group organisation. These exceptions are important enough to merit a brief examination of them.

There is some published evidence that antagonism between members and officers is more likely where Labour is in control of the council (Hampton, 1972; Sharpe, 1973; Gyford, 1976) and the data from the fieldwork for this book tend to confirm this view. Labour groups have sometimes been antagonistic to new forms of management and, in a few large authorities, this has led them to maintain a considerable distance between the political side and the officer side. Even when this happens, the chief executive usually resorts to informal, unofficial and sometimes hugger-mugger contacts in order to facilitate liaison: 'I know what's in it, because I have channels unofficially to get it, but there's no official promulgation of the manifesto' (Metropolitan district chief executive).

The motivations for the behaviour of the politicians in councils of this sort are somewhat obscure. Perhaps there is a need, as one chief executive faced with a secretive and detached controlling group put it, to show that 'members made the decisions . . . and must, therefore, be seen to be in control', and there is considerable suspicion among members in some places of the motivations and political inclinations of chief executives and chief officers. Attitudes of this sort are not widespread in the new system but their occurrence is important, as the following remarks show:

I think it was a political thing . . . an emotional reaction to the term 'management'; a lot of the members have a trade union background and management can have certain connotations . . . they don't want to feel they are run by officers. (Non-metropolitan county chief executive)

Corporate planning has been rendered difficult because I have difficulty in getting accurate information on Labour group decisions. (Metropolitan district chief executive)

And consider this, from the chief executive of a metropolitan district that was, at the time of the interview, Conservative-controlled but likely to swing to Labour at the next election: 'I'm regarded as a sort of Dracula-type figure who sits in the background devising horrible policies which the leader of the Conservative Party puts into effect.'

It may well be, as Newton (1976, p. 164) concluded from his study of Birmingham, that in general 'the relationship between elected representatives and appointed officials is rather more equal than Weber's "dictatorship of the official" prophecy suggests'. But, in some places, the fear of such a dictatorship is still a determinant of the nature of the relationship.

The second major exception to the rule of close leader–chief executive relationships is found in those largely rural non-metropolitan districts where political organisation is rudimentary and the stance of the controlling group almost completely non-programmatic. In one such council, the chief executive's contact with his leader amounted to 'about half-an-hour a month' and in another the fact that there was no leader of the council led to 'an absence of a close relationship between the administrative/executive leadership and the political leadership'. That this sort of distance between the sides may be the result, in part, of the effects of institutional history is suggested by this remark from the chief executive of a district in a county with a tradition of low levels of partisanship in local politics: 'Coming from councils before reorganisation where there was no corporate forming of opinion among members, you could never know from one day to another what their views and decisions would be.'

Finally, the situation should be noted where there is neither a *de jure* nor a *de facto* leader of the council. Only one such council was found in England and Wales, but it is noteworthy that even here the chief executive had to set up some processes of interaction. He regarded the senior member from each area of the district as his primary contact and 'seniority' in this case was defined in terms of member service both before and after reorganisation.

PROCESSES OF INTERACTION: OFFICER ATTENDANCE AT PARTY GROUP MEETINGS

A reference was made earlier to the fact that in many, perhaps most, of the new authorities the *locus* of decision has moved from committees of the council and the council itself to the party group meeting. For this reason, the question of whether chief officers in general, and chief executives in particular, should attend such meetings to advise the politicians, especially those politicians who make up the controlling group, is crucial to an understanding of how policy is made in the new authorities.

The *Scheme of Conditions of Service for Administrative, Professional and Technical Staff* – the so-called 'Purple Book' which governs most aspects of the employment of local government white-collar workers – is uncompromising in its attitude to officer advice to political groups. Paragraph 70 (c) of the scheme, drawn up long before reorganisation and not revised since, reads: 'The officer should not be called upon to advise any political group of the employing authority either as to the work of the group or as to the work of the authority, neither shall he be required to attend any political group.'

The Bains job description for a chief executive (Bains, 1972, app. J, p. 165) is silent on the question of attendance at group meetings, although the report, when discussing the roles of officers and members, says (para 3.45, pp. 18–19) that 'the advice of officers must be available wherever effective decisions are taken and if it is the party group that makes these decisions then a way must be found of making the officers' advice available'. It stops short, however, of confronting the question of whether officers should attend private party group meetings. Sir John Boynton, who was chief executive of Cheshire County Council both before and after reorganisation, has, however, published draft guidelines for chief executives (Royal Institute of Public Administration/Policy Studies Institute, 1980, pp. 48–50) which include the following advice:

If a chief executive attends a meeting of any party political group, he should inform the leadership of other parties on the council. He should ensure that the part he plays in the proceedings is consistent with his political neutrality. He should not attend party political group meetings at which there are persons present who are neither elected members nor officials of the authority.

The conditions for attendance specified by Boynton are exactly those suggested by several of the interviewees in the present study: equality of treatment for all parties and the absence from group meetings of non-councillors. The issue is an important one, and the practice of chief executives in the sixty-one English and Welsh authorities investigated for the present book gives a general indication of how this interactive process works in the reorganised system.

Table 5.2 is an analysis of the attitudes of the chief executives of sixty of the authorities studied (the sixty-first had no system of party groups) and it shows that only one-sixth of chief executives interviewed would refuse, as a matter of principle, to attend any group meeting. The table also suggests that reluctance to attend such meetings may be associated with the urbanisation of the area served by the authority – no chief executive in a metropolitan district said he would never attend – and this suggestion is strengthened when the largest group of authorities, the non-metropolitan districts, is analysed further. Table 5.3 disaggregates this group into those new districts that contain a former county borough (FCB) and those that do not. The rationale for this procedure is that the high levels of partisanship typical of the county boroughs would lead to the expectation that the

Table 5.2 *Chief Executives' Attitudes to Attendance at Party Group Meetings: By Type of Authority (England and Wales). Percentages (n's in parentheses)*

	Will Not Attend (n = 10)	Attends Conditionally[a] (n = 15)	Attends Unconditionally (n = 21)	Attends Constitutionally[b] (n = 14)
Metro county (3)	33·3 (1)	—	33·3 (1)	33·3 (1)
Metro district (9)	—	33·3 (3)	55·5 (5)	11·0 (1)
Non-metro county (16)	13·3 (2)	26·6 (4)	33·3 (5)	33·3 (5)
Non-metro district (32)	21·9 (7)	25·0 (8)	31·2 (10)	21·9 (7)
All councils (60)	16·6 (10)	25·0 (15)	35·0 (21)	23·3 (14)

[a]Denotes insistence on right to attend group meeting of all parties and on the absence of non-councillors from meetings.
[b]Denotes insistence that attendance at group meetings by chief executive is formally approved by the council.

Table 5.3 *Chief Executives Attitudes to Attendance at Party Group Meetings: Non-Metropolitan Districts (England and Wales) by Institutional History. Percentage (n's in parentheses)*

	Will Not Attend (n = 7)	Attends Conditionally[b] (n = 8)	Attends Unconditionally (n = 10)	Attends Constitutionally[c] (n = 7)
Districts with FCB[a] (11)	18·2 (2)	9·1 (1)	45·5 (5)	27·3 (3)
Districts without FCB (21)	23·8 (5)	33·3 (7)	23·8 (5)	19·0 (4)
All non-metro districts (32)	21·9 (7)	25·0 (8)	31·2 (10)	21·9 (7)

[a]FCB = former county borough.
[b]See Table 5.2.
[c]See Table 5.2.

new districts of which they became part (or, in six of the cases investigated for this book, which they comprised) would also be partisan to a higher degree than other districts.

This connection between institutional history and levels of partisanship is raised by Bristow (1978, p. 29) though he is concerned with the territorial integrity of new authorities (which is to say the number of former authorities comprising a new authority) and does not, therefore, directly address the question of the influence in the new authorities of the presence of former county boroughs. It is suggested that the longer the history of group organisation, the less likely it is that chief executives will refuse to attend group meetings. The figures in Table 5.3 confirm this expectation, with only 27·3 per cent of FCB chief executives falling into the 'will not attend' or 'attends conditionally' categories, compared with 57·1 per cent of the chief executives of districts not containing a former county borough. Finally, if the authorities are grouped on a rough index of urbanisation, it is found that in the most heavily urbanised authorities, the metropolitan counties, the metropolitan districts and FCB districts, 47·8 per cent of chief executives attend group meetings unconditionally, whereas in the non-metropolitan counties and non-FCB districts the comparable figure is 27 per cent.

Thus the evidence is that in a large majority of authorities provision exists for officers to attend the group meetings of political parties and it also appears that the practice is spreading, possibly because the local government grapevine leads authorities to emulate one another and therefore to continue the process of homogenisation. There are still authorities, however, where the members exclude officers from their group meetings and, in these cases, other devices have to be developed to ease the process of interaction. The most common of these are variations on the theme of the one-party policy committee and these will be examined later under the heading of 'special institutions and processes'. At this point, the consideration of interaction by officer attendance at group meetings is concluded by two quotations from chief executives, the first in a non-metropolitan district based upon a former county borough with unchanged boundaries, the second in a non-metropolitan county which absorbed one of the 'big nine' former county boroughs.

> I don't see any difficulty at all in going to political groups because I believe that I am a fairly independent person and I have no intention of giving my independence away.

> If you had asked me in 1973 I would have been appalled at the fact that I should go into a party caucus meeting . . . We quickly realised, however, . . . that we have to shift our advice giving . . . into the party machine.

PROCESSES OF INTERACTION: MEMBERS AND THE MANAGEMENT TEAM

One of the sets of parallel structures identified earlier consisted of the policy committee on the member side and the management team on the officer side. Because both of these institutions are concerned with the refinement of policy and the setting of priorities the processes of interaction between them are of great significance in the internal workings of local authorities. It was also noted earlier that there was much evidence of member antagonism towards, and suspicion of, the activities of the management team. These two features – concern with policy and priorities and member hostility – go far towards delineating the nature of the interactive process between the two institutions.

In formal terms, the interaction between the management team and the elected membership should take place through the policy committee where, according to Bains, the chief executive should present a management team recommendation on policy arrived at either by consensus or by direction and where only rarely should 'a strongly held minority view' (Bains, 1972, para. 5.42, p. 50) be articulated by a chief officer. In many authorities, however, there is considerable suspicion that the discussion of policy options by the management team leads to a situation where, to quote one chief executive, there is a 'feeling of resentment from members that things have been cut and dried' before reports come to the policy committee. There is a feeling, in other words, that the consideration of policy and priorities by the management team leads to the elimination of possible options before members have a chance to deliberate upon them.

Members' attempts to gain the access to the management team that might allay these fears have fallen into four categories, all of which have met with a degree of resistance from the officer side: the suggestion of councillor membership of the management team, agenda access, leadership liaison and councillor observers.

No council was found where the interaction between members and the management team took the form of permanent, full membership of the management team being extended to councillors. Chief executives and chief officers are typically very jealous of the privacy and confidentiality of management team discussions, and it is difficult not to conclude that those councillors who have pressed for personal access to the management team have demonstrated a degree of naïveté about the behaviour of bureaucratic institutions. For it is likely that the performance of the officer side would adjust to accommodate the presence of members at their hitherto private discussions as this comment, from a chief executive in an authority where there had been considerable member pressure to attend, suggests: 'What would happen is that there would be an agreed front to the elected members, and the management team's real business would be done behind the scenes anyway.' The generally settled and strongly held officer view that the notion of the management team is incompatible with councillor membership of it is further highlighted by the following remarks:

If a member came to the management team, it certainly would destroy it. (Non-metropolitan district chief executive)

There has been, from time to time, a hint that members would like to sit in the management team, but we have been resisting that very aggressively. (Non-metropolitan district chief executive)

We do not have members sitting in at our chief officers' meetings – . . . because there must be a professional discussion without any holds barred and sometimes there would be comments made which perhaps it would be wise not to make in front of members. (Metropolitan county chief executive)

In at least one authority, however, the antagonism of members to the management team has led to its formal abolition. In Cumbria County Council in 1977, the chief officers' management team was abolished and replaced by a new institution called the joint management team, consisting of senior chief officers and senior councillors. This body was described by the chief executive as 'the core of decision-making in Cumbria'. As its workings are described by Ford (1979), it appears to be a successful attempt at officer–member corporate working outside the confines of the conventional committee system. What is not clear, however, is whether chief officers continue to meet informally, without the presence of members. The chief executive described the new institution as being characterised by 'active member leadership' but, significantly, '80 to 90 per cent of its business is generated by officers'. In other authorities, too, new institutions have been created to provide an opportunity for officer–member consideration of policy, but these have involved neither the abolition of the management team nor the presence of members on the management team. They are considered later under the heading of 'special institutions and processes'.

The second interactive process has been to provide members, usually leading members, of the authority with copies of the agenda for management team meetings. This is seldom regarded as satisfactory by members who have sometimes followed up their access to the agenda with a demand for a sight of management team minutes. For some chief executives this has been the sticking point, the place to stand and fight for the privacy, professionalism and exclusiveness of the management team, as this remark indicates: 'The political leader gets a copy of the management team agenda; it is not something I was very happy about but I was forced into either that or something I liked even less – he doesn't get a copy of the management team minutes' (Non-metropolitan district chief executive).

By far the most common interactive process is the creation of formal institutions of liaison between the management team and the members. These bodies are neither decision-making institutions, in the same sense as the policy committee, nor are they priority-setting or inter-departmental negotiating institutions like the management team itself. Rather they are talking-shops, opportunities for communication, and they have two effects: they allay some of the member suspicion of the management team and they enhance the role of the leader of the council and other prominent members in the day-to-day running of the authority. The usual forum for such liaison is a meeting of the management team with all committee chairmen which takes place on an agreed timetable, often quarterly. It is doubtful whether meetings of this sort make any identifiable contribution to the content of policy, but it is certain that they ease the process of decision-making as issues travel between management team and the formal stages of council decision-making.

Finally, a few authorities are attempting to solve the problem of member communication with the management team by having the leader of the council attend meetings (or some meetings) of the team. It is hard to see how the members' position as an observer on the management team can be anything but invidious; he has no formal authority, no vote, and his presence at management team may be both inhibitive of discussion and destructive of the close relationship between the leader of the council and the chief executive, referred to earlier as the primary channel of communication between the officer side and the member side. It is not surprising that this is the least common form of interaction.

To conclude, the relationship here is characterised, in many authorities, by suspicion on the member side and defensiveness on the officer side, although it is now unusual for the exclusiveness of the management team to be carried to the point implied by one county chief executive (now retired) who responded to a question by saying: 'You surprise me by saying "somehow there has to be a member input" in the sense of the goings-on of the management team.'

PROCESSES OF INTERACTION: CHAIRMEN AND CHIEF OFFICERS

The continued importance of the operational relationship between committee chairmen and the appropriate chief officers has already been touched upon in a number of contexts, and little more need be said about it here. Despite the anti-departmentalist thrust of the Bains Report and the partially successful attempt, through the use of management teams and policy committees, to ensure the subordination of these individual actors in the local government process, the system is still characterised by the political and professional specialisation upon which the chairman–chief officer link is based. There are three very important reasons for the resilience of the relationship, quite apart from the fact, noted earlier, that members continue to find it congenial.

First, the continued obligation on major authorities to appoint certain statutorily specified chief officers – chief education officers and directors of social services – makes it impossible completely to downgrade the departmental character of the services these officers administer: they cannot, in other words, be submerged in a super-directorate. Secondly, in the shire districts, where the only major community service is housing, it is very often the case that the director of housing or chief housing officer is a highly visible and influential chief officer administering a service attractive to local politicians and so a close relationship often emerges between the chief officer and the chairman, whatever the Bains prescriptions might envisage. And finally, the effects of financial stringency have led chief officers and chairmen in vulnerable services to co-ordinate their efforts – in management team, in policy committee, in controlling group – to defend their departments and to seek to minimise the effect of economies on the services they provide. Paradoxically, therefore, the corporateness of approach that arises from the need for economy is counterbalanced by the gift of a new lease of life to a relationship that corporate management was intended to replace.

SPECIAL INSTITUTIONS AND PROCESSES

The new local authorities, then, in their attempts to cope with the combined effects of structural reorganisation and the introduction of corporate management have developed and refined a number of interactive processes. They have also been innovative in the sense of creating new institutions and processes, most of which are, to some extent, variations on the theme of the policy committee. The need for new institutions arises directly from the unsatisfactory performance of the processes of interaction just considered. There are three major reasons for dissatisfaction. First of all, members are not convinced that the existing institutions and the interactions between them give them control of the process of policy-making; they believe, in other words, that the officer and member sides run separately, with the officers in the lead. Secondly, officers are concerned that the conventional institutions and their interrelationships do not provide a clear-enough opportunity to offer professional advice at the point of decision. Thirdly, there is a desire on both sides, but especially among officers, to legitimise the provision of advice to political groups, to ensure that the close relationship between officers and members, which is considered to be essential to the efficient operation of the council and to the effective provision of services, is adequately covered by standing orders. Only thus can the conduct of the relationship satisfy the Bains ideal of advice at the point of decision without undermining the protection provided by the 'Purple Book'.

The one-party policy committee pre-dates reorganisation, but its introduction was an integral part of the contribution of several former county boroughs to the drive in the late 1960s and early 1970s to streamline and modernise decision-making processes (Greenwood *et al.*, 1972*a*). A policy committee composed solely of members of the controlling group has several obvious advantages. First, it establishes clearly which political group in a council is responsible for policy. Secondly, it provides a formal institution through which officer advice can be presented to political decision-makers. Thirdly, since the 1972 Act, the requirement that all committee meetings be open to press and public ensures that decisions of the policy committee are open and subject to public scrutiny. And fourthly, by constituting what is, in effect, the collective leadership of the controlling group as a committee of the council, it makes it clear that meetings of this group are 'approved duties' and therefore attract attendance allowances.

But there are also some disadvantages. There can be little doubt that decision-making in a one-party policy committee is, in public accountability terms, preferable to decision-making in a closed party group. In most of the authorities that have experimented with a one-party policy committee, however, members still meet in private, sometimes without officer advice, to co-ordinate their views in advance of the public session. Conversely, of course, it would be idle to pretend that officers do not attempt, often successfully, to reach an agreed view before the policy committee meets; indeed this is an important part of the rationale for having a management team. As the chief executive of a non-metropolitan county put it, commenting on experience with single-party policy committees: 'Very often where there are warring factions within the party . . . they say "We can't discuss that with officers here", so they throw them out and you are back where you were anyway.'

Also, the opposition members, especially in a council where the swing of the political pendulum is uneven or non-existent, may find their exclusion from the authority's most powerful committee hard to accept. They may, therefore, resort to tactics that are at best duplicative and at worst disruptive in order to ensure that they have a chance to comment on policy decisions and options. Not surprisingly, perhaps, opposition groups have been more ready to acquiesce in the creation of a single-party policy committee where they stand a good chance of taking control of the council after a subsequent election.

The effect on the internal workings of an authority of the formal adoption of a single-party, decision-making process can be illustrated by example. In the Metropolitan County of Tyne and Wear, the opposition Conservatives eventually agreed to the establishment of a single-party policy committee to replace the duplication of discussion that was inherent in the practice that the chief executive described as follows: 'A ... two-party management committee with a policy advisory committee being the Labour Party full executive; in the morning we took all the decisions and in the afternoon the Conservatives had an opportunity of asking questions.'

It is worth noting, however, that the creation of the single-party policy committee ensured that opposition scrutiny of policy shifted out of the committee stage and into the more formal, even ritualistic, forum of the full council. In terms of accountability such a shift is significant. Given that a single-party policy committee will only work where there is clear control, it must be very unlikely that discussion in full council will alter the decisions of the policy committee. Thus, effectively, the only meaningful counter-arguments to the views of the majority-group leadership will be presented, albeit publicly, at policy committee by the officers of the council. And officers are accountable only to the authority, not to the electorate. In full council, professional officers, with the exception of the chief executive whose advice may be sought on matters of law and procedure, do not speak. So although the institution of a single-party policy committee may legitimise the provision of officer advice to party groups, it excludes from the possibility of influence at the point of decision the representatives of those electors who did not support the candidates of the controlling group. Thus the procedure emasculates opposition even more effectively in local government than does the winner-take-all system by which parliamentary elections are decided. This is because of the degree to which the agenda for full council meetings are pre-determined by the deliberations of committees. Even where a council's standing orders are liberal enough to allow the introduction of new business at full council, the domination of the committee structure ensures that in most cases such business (if it is not immediately killed by the majority group on council) will be referred back to the appropriate committee.

An interesting variation on the theme of excluding the opposition from the crucial stages of the decision-making process was the decision of the Conservative group on Berkshire County Council to by-pass the policy committee altogether. Berkshire, at the time of reorganisation, constituted a policy committee that was large and representative, suffering many of the defects identified in the previous chapter. This was inevitable, perhaps, in a council where the Conservatives were the largest single group but without a clear majority, and in a county containing both a former county borough and a former municipal borough that had aspired to county borough status. After the 1977 elections, however, the Conservatives were in a heavily dominant position, having a majority of almost fifty over all other groups. They did not, however, establish a one-party policy committee. Rather they removed the vital stages of decision-making on the budget from the committee system altogether. The annual estimates and the rate precept were determined in the Conservative group, with chief officers present, and then presented, for ratification and legitimation, by council in the name of the leader of the council.

The procedural results of this change were predictable. The small body of opposition members used the statutory rate-fixing meeting of the full county council as the only opportunity for line-by-line consideration of the council's estimates as recommended by the Conservative group. In the first year of the new procedure, the council's budget meeting lasted from 10.30 a.m. until 2.50 a.m. the following day, a meeting that is thought to have been the longest local council meeting in modern English history. In the next two years the meeting lasted until 9.00 p.m. on one occasion and until just after midnight on the other.

If the reactions of the opposition councillors were predictable, those of the chief officers were less so. For in 1978, in an action which was probably without precedent, the county's chief officers issued a statement that effectively dissociated them from the guidelines to committees published, at the start of the budgetary process, by the controlling group. This document, 'Chief officers' views on the budget guidelines for 1979–80' (Berkshire County Council, 1978*b*) was published as an appendix to another paper, '1979 budget guidelines: report of the leader of the council' (Berkshire County Council, 1978*a*). The background is an excellent example of how the combination of a developing officer–member relationship and a majority group determined to seize control of the policy process can highlight the problems inherent in coping with the complex issue of measuring professional commitment against political will. Briefly, the course of events was as follows. The leader of the council drew up his budget guidelines and invited the chief officers' group (Berkshire's equivalent of the management team) to comment upon them. These comments revealed a serious difference of view. The chief officers believed, as their document said, that the guidelines would involve 'further reductions in standards which could cause a backlash of public opinion against the Council'. In the absence of agreement between the leader and the chief officers, it was agreed that the guidelines would be submitted to committee in the name of the leader of the council but with the officers' views appended in what was, in effect, a dissenting memorandum. Had this action not been taken there would have been no public opportunity, under the procedures described above, for an officer–member discussion of the overall budget. The next time the budget would be publicly discussed as a whole (as distinct from committee consideration of individual service estimates) would be at the rate-fixing meeting of the council nine months later.

Two further variations on the policy committee theme should be noted, for they are additional examples of the institutional and procedural innovation stimulated by the need to respond to the shift in the *locus* of decision from the committee system to the party group. Many authorities have formally established groups of senior members whose formal duty is to advise the leader of the council, and through him the policy committee, on the establishment of priorities and the making of political choices. These 'leaders' advisory committees', as they are often called, are the formalisation (for reasons of standing orders and the desire to bring its meetings within the definition of 'approved duties' for the purpose of attracting attendance allowances) of the collective leadership of the controlling group. Sometimes the membership is identical to the executive committee or the office-holders of the group, sometimes it is composed of the leader and the chairmen of major committees, but it always excludes minority representation and, despite its function of 'advising' the leader and the policy committee, it is invariably the point in the policy process where the hard decisions are made. It is advised by the management team and it, rather than the policy committee, functions as the member analogue of the management team. Where such a body exists, the procedural consequence is that the deliberations of the policy committee become almost as ritualistic as those of full council. The operations of leader's advisory committees, however, satisfy the need to feed in professional advice at the point of decision and, by preserving the policy committee stage of decision-making (unlike the Berkshire practice already described), an opportunity is provided for opposition scrutiny to take place with officer advice available.

Finally, some councils have experimented with the introduction of a wide range of officer–member working groups to consider policy innovations. Where corporate working has proceeded to the point of producing a policy plan, identifying all the authority's services and objectives and attempting to assign each of these to a priority category, these groups have been generally effective and are regarded by both officers and members as a useful bridge between the two sides. In particular, by involving members at an early stage in the formulation of policy, the danger, identified earlier, of decisions being pre-empted before members have an opportunity for influence is avoided. However, frustrations, for both officers and members, arise when the recommendations on priority categories developed by these necessarily specialist groups are altered or vetoed by bodies further up the line, such as policy committee or controlling group, whose view of the council's business is, perforce, much more generalised.

THE FULL-TIME COUNCILLOR

This section is concluded by a brief consideration of the innovation of the full-time councillor. The Local Government Act 1972 introduced the system of attendance allowances whereby in place of the old financial loss allowance, councillors could be paid an allowance for the performance of any function designated by their council as an 'approved duty'. In practice, for most members of most councils approved duties are confined to meetings of committees, subcommittees, working groups and panels established by the authority, but the discretion left to individual councils in the definition of an 'approved duty' made it possible for some councils to use the maximum level of allowance (as determined by the Secretary of State for the Environment) as a *per diem* payment amounting, at the time of reorganisation, to a maximum annual salary (for a five-day week) of £2,600 plus reimbursement of expenses. Robinson (1977, Vol. II, p. 65) provides examples of approved duties 'which extend beyond those specified by the majority of authorities'.

When the new councils took over in 1974, with a maximum permissible daily allowance of £10, some members were able to choose to become full-time councillors in order to give to council work the sort of continuous political direction that some of the old county boroughs, such as Birmingham, had experienced for years. In Nottinghamshire, for example, the leader of the council and most of the major committee chairmen were full-time during the period of Labour control from 1973 to 1977, and in many other authorities, particularly at the upper tier and in the metropolitan districts, leading members have, as was discussed above, been able to devote most of their working time to council duties. It should be noted, also, that it is not merely the payment of allowances that has facilitated the rise of the full-time councillor. Some leading members are retired, some have private means and some have professional or trade union commitments that allow them to give unlimited time to the council without financial penalty. The material point is not the occasion for the move to full-time status – although there is little doubt that attendance allowances have made the choice of such a move possible for councillors from a broader social range – but the effect of such a move on the workings of authorities. Nor are the numbers large: 95 per cent of councillors in 1976–7 either claimed no allowances at all or claimed less than half the maximum estimated above (Robinson, Cmnd 7010, 1977, Vol. I, para. 83 and table 1, p. 18).

The motivation for becoming full-time is clear enough: it is to assume control of the authority's policy-making and policy implementation. The practicalities are less easy to deal with for, as was mentioned in another context earlier, the committee system of decision-making which predominates in British local government makes no provision for a political executive, either individual or collective. Thus to accommodate the introduction of full-time elected members to the political/administrative structure of a council it is necessary for procedures and relationships, hallowed by time and tradition, to be adapted and modified to fit the new arrangements.

Until the arrival of the full-time councillor, and to some extent thereafter, local government, with its attachment to the committee system and its attendant fusion of legislative and executive responsibilities, was, to quote Regan (1980a, p. 10) 'a headless state'. Regan also says (pp. 9–10), 'Democratic accountability in local government can never be effectively clarified under this amalgamated system. Such clarification requires a more concentrated and visible executive responsibility'. In some authorities, since 1974, such clarification has begun to take place with the public acceptance of responsibility for the effects of policy (which is to say the implementation, as well as the principles) being accepted by leading members who, because of their continuous involvement in the affairs of the authority, are highly visible.

These changes are not unrelated to the mystification and complexity which are often associated with the introduction of more rational policy-planning techniques and a corporate, as distinct from a departmental, approach to policy and administration. Simply stated, under previous dispensations, members could pretend to be in overall control, in a cumulative way, by attending committees which ran departments which were, as was suggested in Chapter 4, often operationally independent of the council as a corporate entity. Any movement away from departmentalism was bound to endanger that kind of control by incrementalism. And where the new arrangements entailed the central establishment of priorities and objectives and the inter-service horse trading that this implied, members who wanted to be in control, and to be seen to be in control, were obliged to work at the centre, in institutions other than committees charged with the provision of particular services. For the establishment of priorities and the definition of objectives are exercises that entail the application to service provision of value judgements and in many major authorities members have been unwilling to allow value judgements to be made under cover of rational planning. This has led to the development of the new institutions and processes under discussion here and also to the commitment, by many leading members, of an increasing percentage of their working day to council business, to the point where they become, either by prior decision or by force of circumstance, as full-time as the officers who nominally serve them.

It was implied earlier that the innovation of the full-time councillor would precipitate other changes in the political/administrative mechanisms of local government. The most obvious of these accommodations is the effect on the position of the chief executive of the superimposition on the existing structure of an embryonic – or in some places quite mature – political executive. The first point to be noted is that, in political terms, the title 'chief executive' is a considerable misnomer. The reason for this is clear: the office was created in local government as the result of analogy not with other political institutions but with corporate business, and its application to democratically and popularly elected bodies ignores the crucial distinction between public and private institutions – the necessity in the former, but not in the latter, of external public accountability. The difficulty of the chief executive's position in relation to accountability is that he is not elected and he cannot, therefore, be directly responsible for the actions of the council: his responsibility is to the elected members though he may, on their behalf, be the initial target for public scrutiny. He acts very much in the same way as does a chief executive in the business world in relation to his board. But, just as in business, where the role of the chief executive must change if the chairman becomes active rather than passive in the affairs of the company, so must the role of a local authority chief executive alter where the leader of the council takes a continuing, positive and, in political terms, executive part in the running of the council. This extension to the business analogy was not foreseen by Bains and the other proponents of the corporate ideal in local government. The change for the chief executive is his reversion to the position of clerk and adviser, his leadership role being largely assumed by the political leader of the council.

There is no doubt that in councils with highly developed political systems, which is to say authorities where control by one or other of the major national parties is deeply entrenched, the combined effect of the arrival of full-time councillors and the close relationship between leaders and chief executives is profoundly altering the position of the latter. In these councils, which are mainly among the Conservative shire counties and the Labour metropolitan districts, though similar developments are occurring elsewhere, too, the relationship between the political and administrative heads of the authority is becoming closely akin to that between a minister and the permanent secretary of his department. At the same time, changes are taking place in the definition of what is regarded as acceptable activity for the politicians, especially in the field of direct, day-to-day intervention in the affairs of departments. In one major metropolitan district, for example, during the period of the joint manpower watch instituted by the Department of the Environment in an attempt to control local authority staffing levels, no vacancy could be advertised, internally or externally, without the approval of the leader of the council. In one shire county, a financial reserve for funding policy innovations was effectively at the disposal of the leader of the council and the chairman of the finance committee. These activities by leading members are increasingly ministerial and executive in nature, and their development is both facilitated and accelerated by the members becoming full-time.

Two final consequences of these developments are a further reduction in the autonomy of committees and additional confirmation of the increasingly formal and ceremonial role of the full council. If political direction from the authority's centre increases (and the Berkshire case cited earlier is a good example of this) and the coordination of professional advice through the management team becomes entrenched, then the capacity of committees to affect the content and nature of policy must decrease: they will, in other words, become more the instruments than the sources of policy. And so the factor identified by Regan (1980a, pp. 9–10) as most inhibitive of the development in British local government of a political executive, the predominance of the committee system, may itself be undermined by changes set in train by the twin processes of corporate working and continuous political leadership.

Chapter 6

SCOTLAND

THE PROCESS OF INQUIRY AND REFORM

The movement towards change in the Scottish local government system ran, in most respects, parallel to the process of reform in England: in both countries the key decision was the appointment by the Labour government in 1966 of a Royal Commission, and in both countries it was a Conservative government that carried through the legislative stages of reorganisation. But the Scottish process differed from the English in two important respects.

First of all, the Royal Commission on Local Government in Scotland, under the chairmanship of Lord Wheatley, began its inquiry only three years after the publication by the Scottish Office of a White Paper (Cmnd 2067, 1963) on the future of local government in Scotland. The White Paper, entitled *The Modernisation of Local Government in Scotland*, was published towards the end of the term of office of the Conservative government but in its radicalism on both the structure and the functions of local government it anticipated the mood of the Labour government that came to office the following year. There was an institutional reason why Scottish Office thinking was so far in advance of that of the Ministry of Housing and Local Government in Whitehall and it is important to recognise it because of the implications it has for the performance of the local government system in general and of the process of central–local relations in particular. Since the end of the nineteenth century British central administration has, in Scotland's case, been decentralised to Edinburgh where a powerful and specifically Scottish bureaucracy can, through a single if sectionalised department, take a comprehensive view of Scotland's needs in local government as in other areas of administration. The 1963 White Paper proposed boundary changes, the abolition of some authorities, the amalgamation of others and a redistribution of powers that was intended to get rid of the high incidence of *ad hoc*-ery, confusion of function and cross-representation that characterised the existing system. In the event, the ideas expressed in the White Paper were overtaken by the change of government in 1964 and they contributed to reform only in so far as they were considered by Wheatley during the Royal Commission's investigations. But, emerging as they did from the Scottish Office, they were an indication that the possibility of major structural change had reached the official agenda in Scotland rather earlier than in England.

The second difference between the Scottish and English reform processes is that in Scotland the proposals of the Royal Commission had a more direct and substantial effect on the eventual outcome than was the case in England. Wheatley produced a report which was unanimous apart from one note of dissent and four notes of reservation, all on matters of application rather than of principle. It recommended a two-tier structure of which the upper tier was to be styled 'region' and the lower tier 'district'. Although the Labour government welcomed the commission's 'fundamental approach . . . and the broad objectives' (*Hansard*, 14 October 1969) it described, no formal or detailed view in the shape of a White Paper was published before the government lost office in 1970. The incoming Conservative government published a White Paper on Scotland (Cmnd 4583, 1971*a*) which appeared on the same day as the White Paper on England and Wales. The proposals for a new system for Scotland departed only slightly from the Wheatley recommendations. Where Wheatley had recommended seven regions, the government proposed eight (subsequently increased to nine in the legislation); the government also proposed to raise the number of districts from thirty-seven to forty-nine (and then to fifty-three in the Act); the government accepted the views of two of the notes of dissent to the report by detaching the Orkney and Shetland Islands from the proposed Highland Region and setting them up as two separate 'most purpose' island authorities, a solution that was also applied to the Western Isles in the subsequent legislation; and, finally, the only major change in the recommended distribution of functions was to make housing (rather than simply housing improvement) a district responsibility rather than a regional one. The reasons for, and implications of, these and other decisions will inform the discussion which follows of the structure and performance of the new system.

THE STRUCTURE AND PERFORMANCE OF THE NEW SYSTEM

The new system of local government in Scotland is, with the minor exceptions of the northern and western isles, a two-tier one, the upper tier being composed of nine regions, the lower of fifty-three districts. This basic configuration is not dissimilar to the county–district pattern in England and Wales, but it is essential to note at the outset how the detailed structure, and by extension its operation, reflects the peculiar demography of a country where about 80 per cent of the population inhabits about 20 per cent of the area. Because of the distribution of the Scottish population, the new system of local government has areas covering a very wide range of populations and territorial sizes. At the district level, the largest authority, Glasgow, at the time of reorganisation had a population eighty-nine times larger than that of the smallest, Nairn; and at regional level Strathclyde had a population twenty-four times larger than that of Borders. In England and Wales, outside London, the comparable figures, by population, are as follows: among metropolitan counties the largest, West Midlands, is 2·3 times larger than the smallest, Tyne and Wear; among metropolitan districts the largest, Birmingham, is 6·3 times bigger than the smallest, South Tyneside; among non-metropolitan counties the biggest, Kent, is thirteen times larger than the smallest English county, Isle of Wight, and 14·4 times larger than the smallest Welsh county, Powys; and among non-metropolitan districts Bristol is 17·5 times bigger than Teesdale, Co. Durham and 22·6 times bigger than Radnor in Powys. The extremely wide range in Scotland is further emphasised by noting that Glasgow, a district authority, has a larger population than any region except Strathclyde of which it constitutes 34·4 per cent, and is almost twice the size of the second largest district in Scotland, Edinburgh in Lothian Region. Finally, when examining size by population, it should be noted that one region, Strathclyde, contains more than 48 per cent of the Scottish population.

When examined by area, a criterion that may be significant in the measurement of performance (Page and Midwinter, 1979, pp. 12–27), the variations, though not so wide, are still important, for they reveal the very great disparities of population density that arise from the demography of Scotland. Highland Region, with an area of some 10,000 square miles has a population density of 18·6 people per square mile, whereas Strathclyde, with an area of some 5,300 square miles, has a population density of 469·5 people per square mile. Lothian, which is very much an Edinburgh city-region created against Wheatley's advice in order to keep the strongly Labour areas of South Fife separate from the more Conservative territory around the capital, has a population density of 1,079 people per square mile. (It has also been controlled by the Labour Party since it was established, despite the motives behind its creation by the Conservative government.) These very wide variations of size are shown graphically in Figure 6.1, and Figure 6.2 shows the regional boundaries, populations and areas.

In the allocation of functions, the new Scottish system is less uniform than its counterpart in England and, once more, this is an institutional and operational consequence of demography. The distribution of the major functions is shown in Table 6.1. Two points about the distribution should be noted. First, there are several functions that are statutorily concurrent, with both tiers of local govern-

Table 6.1 Scotland: Distribution of Major[a] Local Government Functions.

Regions (9) and Island Authorities (3)	Districts (53) and Island Authorities (3)	Concurrent Functions: Regions (9) and Districts (53)
Education	Housing	Derelict land[e]
Social work	Local planning[b]	Industrial development
Roads	Libraries[b]	Amenities and tourism
Strategic planning	Environmental health	
Water and related services	Refuse collection and disposal	
Consumer protection		
Police[c]		
Fire[d]		

[a]For more detailed allocation of functions, see *Scottish Office Brief on Local Government* (Edinburgh: Scottish Information Office, 1975).

[b]In Highland, Dumfries and Galloway, and Borders, these functions are regional.

[c]There are combined police forces serving the following groups of authorities: Lothians and Borders; Highland, Orkney, Shetland and Western Isles (Northern Constabulary).

[d]There is a joint fire brigade for Highland Region and the three island authorities.

[e]Primary responsibility was vested in the Scottish Development Agency in 1975. The agency appoints local authorities to act as its agent in particular schemes.

Note the range of population and population density: Strathclyde, with nearly half the population of Scotland, has twenty-five times the population density of Highland.

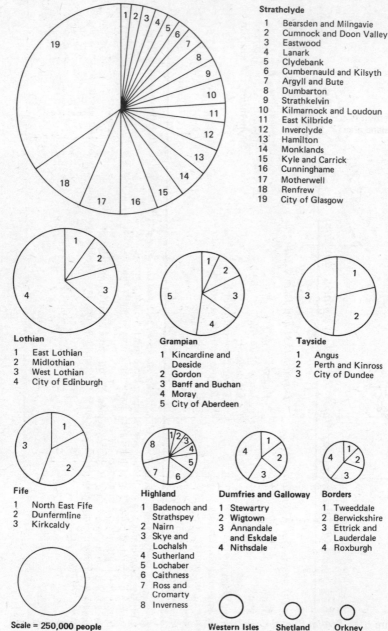

Strathclyde

1 Bearsden and Milngavie
2 Cumnock and Doon Valley
3 Eastwood
4 Lanark
5 Clydebank
6 Cumbernauld and Kilsyth
7 Argyll and Bute
8 Dumbarton
9 Strathkelvin
10 Kilmarnock and Loudoun
11 East Kilbride
12 Inverclyde
13 Hamilton
14 Monklands
15 Kyle and Carrick
16 Cunninghame
17 Motherwell
18 Renfrew
19 City of Glasgow

Lothian

1 East Lothian
2 Midlothian
3 West Lothian
4 City of Edinburgh

Grampian

1 Kincardine and Deeside
2 Gordon
3 Banff and Buchan
4 Moray
5 City of Aberdeen

Tayside

1 Angus
2 Perth and Kinross
3 City of Dundee

Fife

1 North East Fife
2 Dunfermline
3 Kirkcaldy

Highland

1 Badenoch and Strathspey
2 Nairn
3 Skye and Lochalsh
4 Sutherland
5 Lochaber
6 Caithness
7 Ross and Cromarty
8 Inverness

Dumfries and Galloway

1 Stewartry
2 Wigtown
3 Annandale and Eskdale
4 Nithsdale

Borders

1 Tweeddale
2 Berwickshire
3 Ettrick and Lauderdale
4 Roxburgh

Scale = 250,000 people

Western Isles   Shetland   Orkney

Figure 6.1 *Illustration of range of population of the new authorities in Scotland.*
Source: Adapted from Paterson Report (1973), app. 8.

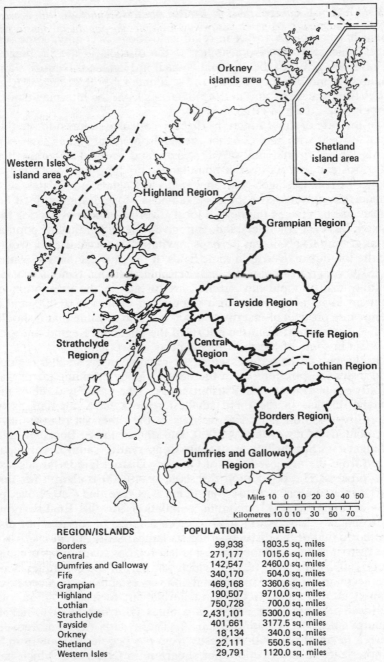

REGION/ISLANDS	POPULATION	AREA
Borders	99,938	1803.5 sq. miles
Central	271,177	1015.6 sq. miles
Dumfries and Galloway	142,547	2460.0 sq. miles
Fife	340,170	504.0 sq. miles
Grampian	469,168	3360.6 sq. miles
Highland	190,507	9710.0 sq. miles
Lothian	750,728	700.0 sq. miles
Strathclyde	2,431,101	5300.0 sq. miles
Tayside	401,661	3177.5 sq. miles
Orkney	18,134	340.0 sq. miles
Shetland	22,111	550.5 sq. miles
Western Isles	29,791	1120.0 sq. miles

Figure 6.2 *Scotland: regions and island areas – boundaries, population and area.*
Sources: Population figures – Stodart Report (Cmnd 8115, 1981). Map and areas – Scottish Information Office Reference Unit, *Scottish Office Brief on Local Government in Scotland* (Edinburgh: Scottish Information Office, n.d.).

ment having powers to act in relation to them. Secondly, some services which are the responsibility of the districts in the six biggest regions are given to the regional council in Highland, Dumfries and Galloway, and Borders. Clearly the rationale for both of these departures from simplicity and uniformity arises from the interplay among population, area and efficiency.

In the case of those functions that are concurrent, it is notable that they all deal with services that are environmental rather than personal. The environmental services concerned demand a combination of consistency across district boundaries and close local knowledge. None the less, like agency arrangements in England and Wales, such concurrent powers have the disadvantages of generating a need for close liaison between the tiers of local government and of making the system less easy to understand. But, given the wide range of populations at both levels, it was perhaps inevitable that concurrence would be the solution arrived at in some fields. If the smallest district, Nairn, is taken as an example, it seems sensible that this famous seaside golfing resort should have some part to play in the promotion of tourism in its area, but with a population of under 10,000 and a penny rate product of just over £4,000 it is also sensible that it should draw some support from the efforts of the Highland Region to foster tourism in some of the most scenic parts of Scotland.

In the case of the services which are regional in the smaller regions and district responsibilities in the others, the determining factor was clearly population and its distribution. For whereas only three of the sixteen districts in the three smallest regions have populations of more than 40,000, only two districts in the other six regions have populations of fewer than 40,000, and one of these, Bearsden and Milngavie in Strathclyde, a strongly Conservative suburb, was separated from the proposed City of Glasgow District late in the legislative process. The population threshold of 40,000 is chosen for this part of the analysis because that figure was regarded (see above, p. 25) as the desirable minimum population for the English non-metropolitan districts which were given a range of services not dissimilar to that of the districts in the six largest Scottish regions. Also, the district councils of the three smallest regions cover areas ranging from 160 square miles (Nairn, which was part of the constituency of the Secretary of State for Scotland and was established as a separate district after a late concession in Parliament to local opinion and political pressure) and 338 square miles (Berwickshire) to 1,930 square miles (Ross and Cromarty). These authorities, moreover, have a range of population density from 6·8 people per square mile (Sutherland) to 86·3 people per square mile (Nithsdale, which has the largest population of all the districts in the three regions). By contrast, Bearsden and Milngavie has an area of ten square miles and a population density of 3,757 people per square mile. The only other district outside the three smallest regions with a population under 40,000 is Kincardine and Deeside in Grampian Region, and because of its historical affinity with the City of Aberdeen it was inevitable that this district would be part of the same region. It is significant, however, that in respect of one of the services not given to the districts in the three smallest regions – libraries – Kincardine and Deeside has joined with two other districts, Gordon, and Banff and Buchan, to create the North East Scotland Library Service to serve a total population of almost 160,000.

In 1979 the Secretary of State for Scotland in the Conservative government appointed a committee of inquiry into local government in Scotland to review the workings of the system in general and, in particular, 'to recommend whether any transfer or rationalisation of functions between authorities is desirable'. The committee, under the chairmanship of a former Conservative MP, Anthony Stodart, reported in January 1981 (Stodart, Cmnd 8115, 1981). Although it conceded that in Scotland there was strong support for all-purpose, unitary authorities to replace the existing two-tier system, it felt unable, because its terms of reference obliged it to ensure the continued viability of existing authorities, to recommend such a change (ibid., paras 15–18). It did, however, recommend an end to all concurrent powers. This would be achieved by vesting existing concurrent powers in either the district or the regional councils. On the other hand, the report did not support the view of the district councils in the three smallest regions that they should become planning and library authorities in their own right (ibid., para. 11 [8]).

Despite these differences in the range of size of authorities and in the detailed allocation of functions between the tiers, the fact that the Scottish system has two tiers, as in England, and Wales, has ensured that liaison between the tiers is essential to the smooth operation of the system. It was inevitable, also, that the process of liaison would be affected by the same contextual factors as were identified in the case of England and Wales: the statutory autonomy of authorities at both levels and the institutional history of the new authorities. To illustrate the similarity between the two new systems (and to indicate that there is no need to repeat in the case of Scotland many of the points about liaison discussed in the consideration of England and Wales) it is useful to look at the relations between Scotland's regions and the district councils that are the successors of the four all-purpose authorities that existed before reorganisation.

Under the County Councils (Scotland) Act 1889 there were established in Scotland four 'counties of a city', the Scottish equivalents of the English county boroughs, as the local government units to serve the largest cities – Glasgow, Edinburgh, Aberdeen and Dundee. Not only had these cities been wholly autonomous local authorities since 1889, they had also been royal burghs since the Middle Ages and therefore had a degree of civic independence. If the recommendations of Wheatley on the allocation of functions had been accepted by the government, the passing of housing powers to the new regional councils would have left the new districts with a very severely restricted range of functions, more akin to those of a parish council than to those of a non-metropolitan district in England and Wales. In the case of the four counties of a city, and in particular of Glasgow, which was by far the biggest of them, this would have added the insult of an unacceptable reduction in function to the injury of their loss of independent status. Thus, partly as a result of pressure from the four major cities, housing became a district responsibility in the new system. This concession, however, was not enough to compensate for their perceived loss of status or to overcome the resentment caused, as in the metropolitan counties, by the degradation of an historic and, it was believed, effective local government unit, and the imposition of a new and powerful upper tier with responsibilities hitherto discharged by the city corporations. As the chief executive of the successor authority to one of the counties of a city put it: 'The region is content to deal identically with all districts but [my council] was resentful of this because of its size, its problems, and its former status as an all-purpose authority.'

As this remark suggests, relations between the tiers in those regions that contain a former county of a city are deeply affected by institutional history and the resentment that arises from loss of status and injured pride. In the course of the fieldwork for this book, interviews were conducted in three of the four regions concerned, and there is no doubt that the entire structure and process of liaison is conditioned by the bad relations between the successor council to the all-purpose authority and the regional council. In Grampian, for example, no regional liaison committee existed until 1977, partly because of an acrimonious and long-drawn-out dispute between the Grampian Region and the City of Aberdeen District over the ownership of property after reorganisation. Also, the initiative for the creation of an Association of Grampian District Councils came from Gordon District Council rather than from the City of Aberdeen, although the latter became an active partner in the association and provided secretarial services for it. In none of the three regions studied (no authority was visited in Lothian Region, which contains the fourth former all-purpose authority, Edinburgh) was the relationship between the region and the former county of a city satisfactory and, in one case, there was an 'almost unbridgeable gulf' between the city and the region.

No assessment of the performance of the new Scottish system can be complete without an examination of the particular problem of Glasgow. For here the additional source of strain identified in the case of the English metropolitan counties – the position of former regional centres – is particularly salient. In its rationale for the creation of its proposed 'West' region, the Wheatley Report laid particular stress on the degree to which that large part of the west of Scotland that became Strathclyde depended upon Glasgow for a wide range of goods and services (Wheatley, Cmnd 4150, 1969, para. 761). Also, as can be clearly seen from Figure 6.1, Glasgow's position in Strathclyde is, on the face of it, a dominant one: it accounts for about one-third of the region's population; it elects more than one-third of the region's councillors; it is almost four times more populous than the next biggest district in Strathclyde and twenty times more populous than the smallest Strathclyde district. And yet under the new allocation of powers it has 'lost' its independent power in such important policy areas as education, social work, strategic planning and industrial development.

In addition to structural and functional changes, and partly as a consequence of them, Glasgow has found itself with a level of influence in the new region that is uncommensurate with its apparently dominant position. There is little doubt that a large number of leading members of the old Glasgow Corporation opted to remain at the district level of local government rather than throw in their lot with an authority they regarded as unnecessary and intrusive. In the period immediately before reorganisation, Glasgow's Lord Provost received a consultant's report which proposed the creation of a Glasgow Region as a unitary authority composed of the old city and its surrounding area. Although the report was never formally considered by the corporation, its commissioning and production are evidence of the hostility of councillors and officials in Glasgow to the creation of Strathclyde. After reorganisation, therefore, the influence of Glasgow councillors in the dominant Labour group on the regional council was less powerful than the apparent status of the district within Strathclyde would imply. The relationship was summed up by a senior official of one of the authorities who said, quite simply, 'the Region distrusts the city and the city distrusts and hates the Region'.

But the acuteness of the difficulties of the relationship between Glasgow and Strathclyde, and indeed between other regions and other former all-purpose authorities, should not be taken to imply that liaison is easy elsewhere in the system. On the contrary, and as was implied earlier, the liaison problems identified in the discussion of England and Wales, and the processes by which they have been overcome, have affected Scotland too. Perhaps the two most significant findings merit mentioning again: formal liaison committees between the tiers and, to a rather lesser extent, among the districts, are generally regarded as being, in the words of one chief executive, 'almost totally useless'; and any liaison that is necessitated by the nature of the system is most successfully undertaken by officers rather than members and as and when necessary rather than on a regular timetable. However, in one region, Tayside, until at least 1979, not only was there no district–region liaison machinery at member level but there were also no meetings of the chief executives of the region and the districts, although there were contacts among the district chief executives. According to one respondent, the town clerk of Dundee had been instructed not to attend any meetings with the region and relations between Dundee and Tayside had been so bad at one stage that the city had threatened to set up its own education and social work committees. It is not surprising that one chief executive in Tayside Region described the process of liaison there as 'very disappointing'. Nowhere in Scotland is there much evidence to support Young's contention (1977, p. 17) that, in the relationship between the tiers, 'the two factors of conflict and delay have their positive side'. The overwhelming impression, as in England and Wales, is of a system that functions because the goodwill and informal networks of members and officers act as lubricants for a structure in which friction is inherent.

The process of liaison between the tiers in Scotland was, however, affected by a particular requirement of the Local Government (Scotland) Act 1973. Under Section 173 of the Act, each of the regions and each island authority was required to submit to the Secretary of State for Scotland a report on its needs and resources. These reports were to be submitted for comment by the Scottish Office rather than for formal approval, and their content, as outlined in 1974 by the chief planning officer of the Scottish Development Department (SDD) (quoted in McDonald, 1977, p. 128) was expected to cover five main subjects. The subjects of the reports were: co-ordination and assessment of resources and demands; identification of major problems and priorities; a judgement of what the authority might accomplish on a realistic view of the availability of money, manpower and management skills; an overview of the development plans of all the authorities in each region; and an indication of what the regional authority might require in the way of guidance and information from central government. It is clear from this contents list that the production of the regional reports would affect the development of interauthority and central–local relations in the early period of reorganisation, for the expectation was that the reports would be submitted to the secretary of state within a year (SDD Circular 4/75, 1975). Also, in its advice to authorities on the preparation of reports, the Scottish Office said, 'Consultations with Districts are mandatory' and, according to McDonald (1977, p. 220), 'districts were approached for information of many kinds and asked to respond to drafts'.

Two points need to be made about the liaison that was stimulated by the need to produce regional reports. First, because of the technical nature of the reports, the need to produce them quite quickly, and the fact that the political responsibility for them (and for their production) lay with the regional councils, any inter-authority liaison necessary in their preparation was at officer level rather than member level. Member involvement was limited to the determination, at regional council level, of the final content of the report before submission to the Scottish Office. Secondly, although it is certainly true that 'the obligation to produce a policy document forced contacts between authorities' (McDonald, 1977, p. 223), these contacts were directed towards a particular purpose whose intention had more to do with improving the quality of central–local relations than with ensuring the smooth and co-operative working of the two-tier local government system. No officer interviewed for the present book mentioned the regional report process as a contributory factor in the development of inter-authority liaison. Nor is this surprising given the fact that the Scottish Office required the preparation of the reports just at the time when the new councils were in the process of setting themselves up and so were often more concerned, at member level, with the internal processes of politics and patronage than with the external consideration of relations with other authorities. The implications of the regional reports for the system of central–local relations in Scotland are considered later in this chapter, together with the further statutory requirement that Strathclyde Region should submit its plans for education and social work for the approval of the secretary of state.

Finally, under the heading of structure and performance, it is necessary to look briefly at the Scottish islands authorities, the only remaining single-tier local authorities in Britain. The three islands authorities – Orkney, Shetland and the Western Isles – provide all local services within their areas, with the exceptions of police and fire cover for which purposes they are joined with Highland Region. It would clearly be less than convincing to build a defence of one-tier local government on the rather shaky foundation of the performance of three differing, but untypical, areas having a combined population of just over 65,000. But equally clearly, the fact that the islands authorities do not independently provide police and fire cover, both of which are services subject to a particularly high level of central direction and a correspondingly low level of local autonomy, does little violence to the view that the Scottish islands authorities are the only remaining all-purpose local government units in Britain. The Stodart Committee (Cmnd 8115, 1981, para 17), moreover, commented that 'it is . . . significant that we received no requests from the three islands councils for any change in their status'. And it went on to say that the success of the islands councils was frequently cited as 'evidence of the merits of a single-tier structure'.

The most obvious consequence of their position as single-tier authorities is that the provision of services by the islands councils neither necessitates nor depends upon liaison with any other local authority. Thus any liaison arrangements they enter into arise from policy considerations rather than from an inherent structural need for them. The Shetland Islands Council, for example, has a sophisticated range of contacts with the companies involved in North Sea oil exploration and production, with the British National Oil Corporation and with the Department of Energy. In particular, the Sullom Voe Association has been established, representing the council and the oil interests, with a brief to control the construction and management of the oil terminal at Sullom Voe. Matters of policy are determined by the council representatives and operational matters by the representatives of the oil industry. The intention of the association, so far successfully achieved, has been to ensure that oil tankers have only restricted access to the islands and to modify charter terms to enable the council to establish 'no-go' areas where tankers may not sail. It is generally believed in the Shetlands that the ability of the authority to regulate the potentially overwhelming environmental impact of the oil boom has been greatly assisted by the council's single-tier status. Comparison of the smoothness of the operation of planning powers and environmental protection policies with the inter-authority wrangling noted elsewhere in Britain lends support to this view. Certainly the old Zetland County Council, with an obligation to deal with one small burgh and fifteen district councils, would have been faced with a more complex task. As the council's chief executive put it: 'There was considerable relief in the islands when the decision was taken not to make the islands part of the Highland Region but to establish them as a separate all-purpose authority.'

Other policy considerations have led the islands authorities to establish liaison arrangements with other public bodies, most notably with the Highlands and Islands Development Board and the Scottish Development Agency. But of particular interest from the point of view of the functioning of the local government system is that they have set up, as part of the Convention of Scottish Local Authorities (COSLA), a 'Policy Committee for the Islands' on which are represented the Orkneys, the Shetlands and the Western Isles. This body meets every two months, weather permitting, and its venue rotates among Stornoway (Western Isles), Lerwick (Shetland) and Kirkwall (Orkney). Each council has six representatives. The committee considers matters of common interest to the islands and its conclusions are transmitted, where appropriate, to the Scottish Office, either directly or through COSLA.

MANAGEMENT AND INTERNAL ORGANISATION

As in England and Wales, the process of change in the structure of Scottish local government was accompanied by a very widespread reorganisation of management structures. These internal changes were stimulated by the attention given to the processes of decision-making in a number of official reports from the mid-1960s onwards. Although the Scottish system of local government is statutorily and constitutionally distinct from that of England, its internal processes are very similar and there has always been a limited amount of interchange of manpower and ideas between the two systems. Only on the legal side is such interchange inhibited by the existence of two quite separate systems of law. Because the two systems share similar concerns, ideas expressed in reports that apply only to England and Wales get considerable attention in Scotland, as can be seen in the frequent cross-references in, for example, the Wheatley Report to the Maud (1967) and Mallaby (1967) reports in England and Wales.

But, as well as being influenced by the conclusions of studies of the English system, Scottish local government had the benefit of the advice of three inquiries exclusively concerned with Scotland. First of all, in 1968, there was the Hughes Report (Hughes, 1968) on the staffing of Scottish local government. This report was produced by a working party, set up jointly by the Scottish Development Department and three of the then existing local authority associations, and its terms of reference included an injunction to have 'regard to the recommendations of the Committee on the Staffing of Local Government in England and Wales' (the Mallaby Report). Hughes was in the mainstream of the movement, noted in Chapter 4, towards rational decision-making and the importation of the practices of corporate business into local government, an emphasis that is clear from the report's leading recommendation that 'the chief administrative officer of a local authority should be designated "General Manager" '. In its outline of the position and functions of a general manager, Hughes accurately anticipated (1968, p. v, para. 2) the job description for a chief executive contained in the Bains Report and in its Scottish counterpart, the Paterson Report (1973). Hughes was, however, published while the Royal Commission was at work, and its recommendations had only a limited effect on the functioning of the old system of local government. As in England, some authorities implemented changes to their structure in the late 1960s – East Kilbride, for example, created the post of general manager, as did Greenock and Coatbridge – but in most places internal changes were deferred pending reorganisation.

Secondly, the Wheatley Report (Cmnd 4150, ch. 30) also considered the question of management and internal organisation and its views contributed further to the creation in Scotland of a consensus in favour of the introduction of a co-ordinating officer – a chief executive – on the professional side and a co-ordinating committee – a policy committee – on the member side. Finally, once the political and legislative stages of reorganisation were underway, the Scottish local authority associations, supported by the secretary of state, appointed a working party, chaired by the Clerk of Lanarkshire County Council, to examine 'the considerations to be borne in mind by local authorities in determining their structures of management' and to 'advise on the formulation of patterns of organisation most likely to be suitable for the various types of authority' proposed in the new legislation. The report of the working party was entitled *The New Scottish Local Authorities: Organisation and Management Structures* and it became known, as had its English counterpart, by the name of the chairman. It is referred to here as the Paterson Report or, where appropriate, as 'Paterson' (Paterson, 1973).

Paterson's recommendations (1973, chs 8 and 9), once allowances are made for the differences of size and functions discussed earlier in this chapter, are very like those made for England by Bains. Like Bains, it envisaged the appointment of a non-departmental chief executive, the establishment of a policy (and resources) committee, and the creation of an officers' management team to co-ordinate the management and advice-giving duties of an authority's paid staff. And, like Bains in England, its conclusions and its prospective influence on the shape of the new Scottish system of local government were endorsed and enhanced by the minister with responsibility for local government. In his foreword to the report, the Secretary of State for Scotland wrote:

> I commend the report to all present councillors, particularly those who will be members of the statutory advisory committees, and to prospective candidates at the 1974 elections. The report will, I hope, be the first paper to be put before those who are elected to the regional, islands and district councils. (Paterson, 1973, p. vii)

Paterson differed from Bains, however, in recognising that the wide disparities in size among the new authorities would affect their requirements for internal administrative structures. Thus, while endorsing unequivocally the notion of the management team, it suggested that in the largest authorities, which is to say the regional councils and the 'larger districts' (although the latter were not precisely defined) a two-level management structure be adopted. This was to consist of a management team of all department heads and an 'executive office', made up of the most senior 'central' chief officers, namely the director of finance, director of administration and, in the four largest regions, the director of policy planning, together with the chief executive. Thus Paterson recommended, in principle, a structure not unlike that which emerged in practice in many of the major English authorities (see Chapter 4). In Scotland, however, the response of the appropriate authorities to the recommendation was more negative than positive with only two regions and three districts opting for the executive office concept (Midwinter, 1978, p. 27, table 6).

In general, however, Paterson's actual influence on the Scottish system has been as strong as Bains's on the English. A survey of all the new authorities, undertaken in 1977, led to the conclusion that 'the bulk of Scottish local authorities have accepted Paterson as a basis for organisation and management' (Midwinter, 1978, p. 36). This conclusion is supported by the detailed evidence. Of all Scottish councils, 90 per cent have adopted a corporate management system 'in principle'; 95 per cent have a chief executive, although in 34 per cent of cases that office is combined with that of director of administration or town clerk; 90 per cent have a management team, with a strong preference (77 per cent) for the model that has all department heads as members; and only 15 per cent do not have a policy and resources committee (Midwinter, 1978, *passim*). Most strikingly, all but three authorities adopted a Paterson-type committee structure, and the three authorities are all former all-purpose authorities, the cities of Glasgow, Aberdeen and Dundee. Midwinter suggests (1978, p. 30), and this is a conclusion supported by the interviews conducted for the present book, that the reasons for this departure from the Paterson recommendations were largely political, having to do with the need to have available, for patronage purposes, a greater number of convenorships (chairmanships) than the Paterson model would allow. As one of the chief executives concerned said: 'It was politically useful to have a large number of "establishment" posts, whose holders would be loyal to the leadership. Thus, in its first three years, the new council had three committees in the housing field and five dealing with civic amenities.' The adherence to a form of internal organisation developed before reorganisation also owed something to the reluctance of politicians and, to a lesser extent, officers to concede that a reform of the local government structure, to which they were fiercely opposed, necessitated any change in their own arrangements. But, as in England, the exceptions to the rule of adoption of the working party's recommendations are numerically insignificant. The broad picture is of a high degree of administrative homogenisation.

There is one aspect in which some of the smaller Scottish authorities differ fundamentally from almost all English and Welsh councils, although in a way that was, to some extent, anticipated by Paterson. The general view of Paterson (1973, para. 8.5) was that no committee should have a membership comprising more than one-third of the total membership of the authority, but it conceded that 'in many of the smaller districts it may be impracticable' so to restrict the size and composition of committees. In fact, in two of the authorities visited, this problem had been resolved by making all members of the council members of all committees. Under arrangements of this sort, of course, the role of the full council, despite Wheatley's assertion (Cmnd 4150, 1969, para. 945) that the full council is 'the hub of the whole machine', becomes almost wholly ritualistic and formal. This is because all councillors are, by definition, involved directly in the consideration of policy throughout the committee cycle. Only one authority was found in England and Wales where all members served on all committees. Also, it can be argued that such an arrangement effectively excludes the possibility that full council, in the exercise of its authority as the legal forum for decision, may act as a check on the activities of committees.

Finally, in this examination of management and organisation a brief word should be said about officers and members. It was argued above that although the structure of the Scottish local government system and the problems of internal organisation faced by its con-stituent councils were the subject of specifically Scottish inquiries, many of Scotland's concerns were similar to those of England and Wales. The relationships between professionals and elected members differ little between the two systems. Both have to fashion a range of interactions between them. Given the degree of correspondence be-tween the recommendations of Bains and of Paterson, and the extent to which these reports influenced management practices in the two countries, it is hardly surprising that much of what was said in Chap-ter 5 about parallel structures applies *mutatis mutandis* to Scotland. There is, however, some evidence that in two aspects of the relation-ship Scotland exhibits a different pattern from that noted in England and Wales. First, members in Scotland are more reluctant to delegate power to officers and it is probable that this arises from the experi-ence of members in small authorities with limited powers in the old system. Secondly, Scottish chief executives are more reluctant to give direct advice to party groups, although the effect of this on the figures given in Table 5.2 would be qualified by the higher number of authorities in Scotland (twenty-five in 1976) that do not have a well-developed system of group organisation.

CENTRAL–LOCAL RELATIONS

It was emphasised earlier that the structure of the new Scottish local government system, and the allocation of functions within it, were conditioned by Scotland's demography. Similarly, the nature of the central–local relationship is conditioned, perhaps even determined, in several senses by scale. First, Scotland's population at the time of reorganisation was just over 5·2 million, approximately one-tenth of the population of England and Wales. It would have been possible, given the norms on size prevailing in the 1960s and the example of the GLC, to set up an upper-tier authority covering the whole of Scotland, a solution considered and rejected by Wheatley (Cmnd 4150, 1969, paras 683–6) on the grounds that it was 'inconsistent with our own concept of local government'. The rejection, however, also owed something to the similarity of such a structure to a form of legislative devolution, an option then under study by the Commission on the Constitution. Secondly, the new structure in Scotland comprised only sixty-five authorities, of which only twelve could be characterised as the 'dominant' authorities in the two-tier system, the nine regions and the three islands authorities. By contrast, in England and Wales outside London there are forty-five upper-tier authorities or, to follow the argument presented in Chapter 3, eighty-three 'dominant' authorities – the English shire counties, the Welsh counties and the metropolitan districts. Thirdly, there was a strong possibility at the time of reorganisation that the whole process of central–local relations would be affected by the sheer size of the Strathclyde Region, a factor that greatly influenced the successful attempt to establish a single local authority association for Scotland (Working Party of Representatives of Regional, Islands and District Council, 1974*a*, 1974*b*). And finally, on the central government side of the relationship, there is only one department, the Scottish Office, which, on the face of it, should find it easier to act corporately than do the five spending departments and the Treasury which are concerned with local government in England. At least one commentator (Page, 1978, p. 12) has, however, cast some doubt on the easy assumption that, to quote the Central Policy Review Staff (1977, p. 41), 'because all Scottish Departments report to a single (and thus highly corporate) Secretary of State' central government in Scotland is necessarily more unified and purposeful in its approach to local government than is the case in England. Certainly the five departments of the Scottish Office do not always ensure that they are acting in concert rather than in ways that are seen by local government as mutually contradictory. There is some evidence, however, that for a number of reasons the relationship between the two levels of government is generally more harmonious in Scotland than elsewhere in Britain.

Layfield (Cmnd 6453, 1976, p. 87) concluded that 'the drift towards centralisation has been even more marked' in Scotland than in England. In support of this view, the report cites a number of ways in which the central–local relationship in Scotland differs from that of England and Wales: the proportion of current expenditure paid for out of national rather than local taxation is higher in Scotland; the process of negotiation of the rate support grant gives 'greater opportunities for ministers to influence local authorities than the formula-based system in England and Wales'; a large proportion of local authority spending is capital expenditure and 'subject to stringent control'; since 1975–6 the Scottish Office has been able to suggest 'appropriate current spending levels for each authority'. This amounts to a formidable array of powers and opportunities for influence available to central government. This account of the potential power and influence of the Scottish Office would lead to the expectation that the operational relationship between local government and the Scottish Office would be a fraught one, characterised by *dirigisme* on the part of the centre and defensiveness on the part of the local authorities. However, the fieldwork for the present book strongly suggests that central–local relations in Scotland are regarded by those involved in them as rather happier than their counterpart in England and Wales. And it is worth emphasising that this comparative conclusion relates to a period before the quality of the relationship in England and Wales was profoundly affected by the introduction and passage of the Local Government, Planning and Land Act 1980.

To what do the participants in the process attribute the generally harmonious nature of the relationship? In the course of the fieldwork for the present book, the chief executives of ten authorities (three regions, six districts and one islands authority) were interviewed, a selection which included both the chairman and the secretary of the Scottish branch of SOLACE. An extended interview took place also with the secretary and treasurer of the Convention of Scottish Local Authorities (COSLA). From these interviews there emerged five features of the central–local relationship to which the respondents attached considerable importance.

First, it was generally thought that the success of the new Scottish local authorities in establishing a single association to represent them had been the single most important factor in determining the nature of the central–local relations. COSLA was set up in 1974 after representatives of all the new authorities had accepted a report and draft constitution prepared by a working party representing all three new classes of authority. The process by which COSLA emerged was clearly affected by the failure of the new authorities in England and Wales to create a single association or even a federation of associations. That failure is considered in the next chapter.

Both Redcliffe-Maud (Cmnd 4040, 1969, Vol. I, para. 107) and

Wheatley (Cmnd 4150, 1969, ch. 31) had strongly urged the formation of a single local authority association. The success of Scottish
local government in following this advice seems to have owed much
to the differing attitudes of Scotland's two largest authorities. Clearly,
the size of Strathclyde could have militated in two related ways
against the creation of a single association. The regions might have
thought that their natural strength as the dominant authorities would
be enhanced by a separation from the districts that ensured that
Strathclyde's strength would be harnessed to their joint interest. And
the districts might have feared that to reflect in local government's
only representative body the dominance of Strathclyde in the structure of local government would not serve their interests as well as
would a separate association of district councils. Certainly, when the
draft constitution was presented by the working party, eighteen
authorities opposed its adoption, favouring instead the creation of
two associations. Strathclyde, however, was in favour of a single
association, a commitment that its dominant Labour Party had
included in its manifesto for the first regional elections. It is evident
from the working party's reports that this commitment was followed
through in the attitude of Strathclyde's representatives in the early
formative stages. At the first representative meeting in July 1974 'it
was made quite clear by certain of the regional representatives . . .
and in particular the Rev. Geoffrey Shaw of the Strathclyde Region,
that it was not the intention of the larger authorities to dominate any
association that was established'. If Strathclyde had insisted on a level
of influence or had claimed a block of representation commensurate
with its population, the prospects for a single association would have
been bleak. It did neither.

The attitude of Glasgow was also influential, though in a more
negative way. The resentment of the city at its loss of status was
reflected at the first representative meeting in July 1974 when one of
its delegates, in the words of another participant 'flayed the regions'
and argued strongly for the creation of separate associations. The
contribution was so intemperate that, to quote one of the respondents
in the present book, 'its vehemence pushed many waverers towards
the opposite view'. Despite this early antagonism, however, Glasgow,
through some of its senior officials, played a positive part in the
introduction of the single association. It is not unlikely that there was
a significant gulf between members' views in Glasgow and those of
the officers.

The internal structure of COSLA inevitably had to reflect the
structure of the local government system it was formed to represent
and this was achieved, primarily, by its having four policy committees: a convention policy committee, a regional policy committee, a
district policy committee, and an islands policy committee. This was
intended to preserve the possibility of different classes of authority

taking different stances, particularly in discussions with the Scottish Office. In fact this has rarely happened and, as the Convention's constitution review subcommittee found in 1979 (COSLA, 1979, p. 10), 'the District Policy Committee seldom meets and is on that account relatively ineffective' and, similarly, 'meetings of the Regional Policy Committee are seldom held'. Despite these findings, the Review Subcommittee recommended, and COSLA accepted, the retention of these committees as a 'reserve to be used in emergency situations'. The islands policy committee is most useful, as was implied earlier, as a forum for liaison among the three islands authorities. It should be noted, however, that when the Stodart Committee, in 1980, sought evidence on the workings of Scottish local government, it was informed by COSLA that it would be impossible 'for the Convention to submit a single Memorandum of Evidence which would be of any value . . . and would, at the same time, be acceptable to a reasonably substantial percentage of the Convention's membership' (Stodart, Cmnd 8115, 1981, para. 8).

Despite its difficulties in responding to Stodart, it is clear that the successful establishment of COSLA, as a single organisation to represent local government, has worked as a continuing pressure towards the creation of a united front, especially in relations with the Scottish Office. It has not been found necessary in Scotland's case to set up a special institution to co-ordinate the process of discussion leading to the rate support grant settlement, as has been the case with the Consultative Council on Local Government Finance in England. The local authority side in such discussions in Scotland comprises the finance subcommittee of the COSLA policy committee.

Thus the creation of COSLA, and the development through it of a wide range of contacts and bilateral negotiations with the Scottish Office, is generally regarded as having created a relationship that is not only good in absolute terms, but very much better than that which existed before reorganisation. As one chief executive put it: 'It used to be said that when the Scottish Office sent out three letters it got six replies: one from each of the association secretaries and one from whichever advisor he consulted.' That said, however, there is some resentment, especially among the smaller district authorities, that the effectiveness of COSLA, together with the dominance of the regions, has made it rather more difficult for them to establish direct links with the Scottish Office. The practice of the Scottish Office in writing to regional councils requesting them, in turn, to seek information from the district councils in their areas was changed when the district councils objected to it. One chief executive had refused to reply to any Scottish Office communication that was not sent directly to his authority.

A second generally accepted factor in producing harmonious central–local relationships in Scotland is, not surprisingly, the small scale of the local government system and the personal familiarities that are possible within it. There are, after all, only sixty-five authorities and, as was suggested above, only twelve of those – the regional and islands councils – can be regarded as dominant. In 1976–7, 'regional services' accounted for more than 81 per cent of net local government expenditure in Scotland (CIPFA, 1976, pp. 8–21). The frequency of contact between the chief executives of these twelve authorities and the senior civil servants at the Scottish Office is surely facilitated by the fact that the former group numbers only twelve. Similarly, contacts among Scottish local authority leaders and Scottish Office ministers are more frequent than is the case in England, although given the spread of partisan support nationally in Britain – Scotland has a permanent majority of Labour MPs – these relations tend to be better when a Labour government is in office. At least once a year (sometimes twice) there is a meeting between the Scottish Office management team and those local authority chief executives who act as advisers to the COSLA policy committee, with the Permanent Under-Secretary of State at the Scottish Office in the chair. Agenda items for this meeting can be submitted by the secretary of COSLA, the secretary of the Scottish branch of SOLACE, and by the Scottish Office itself. In addition, the chief executives have an annual dinner with Scottish Office civil servants and this, in the words of one participant, 'offers a more relaxed opportunity for contact'. Finally, under the general heading of scale, it is worth noting that many of those involved in the continuous process of central–local negotiations share a common social, educational and professional background, and one that is peculiarly Scottish and small-scale.

Thirdly, the creation of a co-operative attitude between central and local government was greatly facilitated by the regional report process mentioned earlier. The time-scale imposed by the Scottish Office on the production of the regional reports was very short indeed: it was announced in January 1975 that the reports were to be submitted by May 1976. Because of this, the production process was very much a collaborative one, with the regions and islands staff working closely with the planning staff of the SDD. During the preparation stage, the SDD suggested that each report should include a summary statement of priorities in a standard format. The result, not surprisingly, was a certain degree of homogenisation in the presentation of these basic planning documents and the creation of 'a distinctive medium of communication between central and local government' (Page, 1978, p. 14). Stewart (1977) makes the even bolder claim that the regional report process 'could be the basis for discussion between the policy and resources committee of an authority and the political leadership of the centre'. As both Page (1978) and McDonald (1977) suggest, the substantive effects of the regional report process are not yet clear. In procedural terms, however, there is little doubt that it has contributed to the creation of a co-operative and harmonious set of relationships between the Scottish Office and Scottish local authorities.

Closely related to the general requirement to produce regional reports, there was in the Local Government (Scotland) Act 1973 a specific requirement that Strathclyde Region should submit to the secretary of state 'proposals setting forth the arrangements made by them for the discharge of their functions under the Education (Scotland) Acts, 1939–73 and the Social Work (Scotland) Acts, 1968–72'. However, whereas the regional reports were to be submitted for comment, these reports on the two most important personal services to be provided by Strathclyde were to be submitted for 'approval' by the secretary of state. This was an unusual requirement for two reasons: first, it applied to only one authority; and secondly, it could have amounted to a considerable departure from the conventional practice that local authorities, as long as they provide services to the minimum statutory level, should be free to make whatever administrative arrangements they find most convenient. On both counts, the nature of the central–local relationship might be affected.

Strathclyde, however, is the biggest local education and social services authority in Britain, perhaps in the world. It was not surprising, therefore, that the government was anxious to be sure that such a fundamental change as that entailed in combining six education authorities and six social work departments into one of each would not have a deleterious effect, either temporary or permanent, on the quality of the service provided. In the event, the requirement was not considered by the regional council to be a significant interference with its autonomy.

Finally, there is the question of the secretary of state's announcement, since 1975–6, of expenditure guidelines for individual authorities. Once again, the assumption is made (Layfield, Cmnd 6453, 1976; CPRS, 1977) that this constitutes a powerful exercise of central government authority. It is not, however, widely perceived as such in Scotland. Perhaps because of the harmony of the general relationship, authorities have accepted the guidelines as indicative only, and indeed the Scottish Office has sometimes seemed to regard them as part of the negotiating process, the secretary of state having told COSLA, on one occasion, that the guidelines were, at the very least 'something for the councils to disagree with'. By 1980, however, partly in response to the actions of some authorities in ignoring guidelines as a matter of policy, the government had decided to introduce legislation to empower the secretary of state to control rather than influence the expenditure of individual authorities. As in England, this move seemed likely to cause a deterioration in the quality of the central–local relationship.

Chapter 7

THE NEW CENTRAL–LOCAL RELATIONSHIP

In any unitary state, the power, influence and effectiveness of local government will be conditioned by the nature of its relationship with the centre and by the particular form of the local government system. Before examining how the relationship between central and local government has developed since reorganisation, it is important to outline its basic characteristics – constitutional, financial and political.

In constitutional terms, local government is a subordinate form of government. Despite the romantic claims of such nineteenth-century champions of local self-government as Joshua Toulmin Smith (1857) that the parish, as a unit of local government, exists as an immutable part of the constitution and the common law, local authorities in twentieth-century Britain exist because their statutory position is affirmed by Parliament and because, in practical terms, the delivery of a wide range of public services is facilitated by the existence of governmental institutions at the local level. Local authorities are legally circumscribed in Britain by the principle of *ultra vires*: they must be able to point to a specific statutory foundation for anything that they do and they must not act without statutory authority. And although it is difficult to envisage that Parliament would act, or be asked by a government to act, to abolish local government, the latter's subordinate position ensures that its sphere of activity can be altered at any time. The reorganisations with the effects of which this book is concerned, as well as the removal in 1974 of health functions and water supply from the control of local government, were in no sense the outcome of an agreed, or consensus, policy: in the end, they were imposed by central government upon existing local authorities, some of whom were relieved that the changes were no worse, others of whom were forced to accept their own demise. Similarly, the changes in the central–local relationship, and by extension in the autonomy and independence of local authorities, caused by the provisions of the Local Government, Planning and Land Act 1980 took effect despite the unanimous opposition of local government as expressed through its national representative bodies.

In financial terms, also, the position of local government is subordinate. Most commentators have argued that the possession of an independent power to tax is a necessary, though not a sufficient, condition for the existence of local government. Local authorities in

Britain have such a taxing power. They levy a rate on the notional rental value of real property, either directly, in the case of the district councils in England and Wales and all the Scottish authorities, or by precepting, in the case of the county councils in England and Wales. But in sharp contrast with other European countries, the rates are the only tax available to local authorities in Britain, whereas central government has a monopoly of all other forms of direct and indirect taxation. The rating system has the merits of being simple to administer and difficult to evade, but it is not progressive, except when its incidence is qualified by rebate schemes, and it ensures that any decision to increase its yield will be a highly visible and palpable political act. As Sharpe illustrates (1980) central government has taxing powers, particularly in relation to income taxation, that are buoyant in that their yield increases without any need for political decisions. Also, the fact that the rates are based on the value of real property inevitably entails inequality of resources in different areas of the country.

These two factors – visibility and inequality – combine to compound the subordinate status that arises from local government's reliance on a single tax. For together they have led, through requests for expenditure to be grant-aided from central taxation and by the need to equalise resources between areas, to a situation where about 60 per cent of the expenditure of local authorities in England and Wales (net of receipts from fees, charges and rents) is met by central government, mainly through the medium of the rate support grant (RSG). Although academic commentators (Ashford, 1974, 1975a; Boaden, 1971) have been unable to show that the financial relationship has decreased the decision-making autonomy of *individual* authorities, it is generally believed in local government that it has led to increased, and increasing, control over local government *as a whole*. It is generally accepted in local government that the aggregate of local government expenditure is such a significant proportion of public expenditure that it is a legitimate concern of central government. What is not accepted, despite the obvious difficulty of completely separating the actions of individual authorities from the aggregate effects of these actions, is that this concern necessitates a high degree of intervention in the decision-making processes of local government.

The political characteristics of the relationship between central government and local authorities are closely related to the constitutional and financial factors just discussed, and they are both complex and varied. As background to developments since 1974 four factors should be noted.

First, because Britain is a unitary state governed by programmatic parties, national government engages in a continuous exercise of goal-setting, often in policy areas where performance depends upon the co-operation and efficiency of local government. This is true both at the general level of macroeconomic management and at the specific level of individual services such as education, social services, housing and physical planning. Since 1974 the balance of power has moved in favour of the centre because of the unwillingness of local authorities to respond to exhortations to contain expenditure, in general, without having specific indications of the government's order of priority among individual services. This point will be elaborated under the heading of 'cash limits and joint circulars' later in this chapter. Suffice to say here that the effect on the central–local relationship of national goal-setting is greater when the principal objective is the containment rather than the expansion of expenditure. This has been the position continuously since reorganisation.

Secondly, the politics of the relationship is affected by the comparative unity of central government and the comparative disunity of local government. The 'corporateness' of central government may, of course, be exaggerated, existing only as a procedural and notional consequence of Cabinet government and collective responsibility. The frequent protests from local government about the receipt of conflicting advice from different ministries suggest such a conclusion. Nevertheless, there are only five service departments in England and Wales (Departments of Environment, Education and Science, Health and Social Services, Transport and the Home Office) with major local government responsibilities, together with the Treasury with its general oversight functions for public expenditure and taxation. On the other side, there are in England and Wales outside London 422 autonomous local authorities represented nationally by three separate representative associations. If the notion of dominant authorities is again introduced here, the number on the local authority side comes down to eighty-three represented by two associations. This factor of unity and disunity may relate more to the existence of several classes of authority than to the number of individual authorities and to the relationship between administrative convenience and the exercise of central government power. In their evidence to Redcliffe-Maud, the major government departments concerned with local government proposed a reduction in the number of local authorities in England and Wales to under forty and it is clear (Sharpe, 1978c, p. 104) that this would have made the central–local relationship simpler for central departments. Also, many people in local government believe that the reduction in the number of local authorities, though not so drastic as departments wanted, in itself increased the power of the centre, because it is easier to control 400 councils than 1,200. The contrary argument, however, is that the centre will have less power over fewer, larger and better-resourced local authorities. But the strength of local government is lessened when it is unable to present a united front to government. For fundamental reasons of structure, such unity was not available in the new system in England and Wales.

Thirdly, the relationship is affected, in a number of ways, by the incidence of partisanship in the British political system. It was noted in Chapter 5 that the new local government system is much more generally partisan than was its predecessor. What needs to be emphasised in the context of central–local relations is that electoral politics in Britain have no developed local autonomy. The voter in local elections responds overwhelmingly to national cues rather than to local ones, to the extent that council elections often amount to mid-term referendums on the performance of national government. The result is that it is not unusual for a majority of the dominant authorities, and so the associations that represent them, to be controlled by the party which is not in power at Westminster. Here the existence of competing mandates, referred to at the beginning of the discussion of the two-tier local government structure in Chapter 2, is again relevant, but it is complicated in this case by a constitutional system that assumes the primacy of the centre.

Finally, the political relationship is inseparable from the financial one. Ever since local government became heavily dependent upon central financial resources, the most significant aspect of the interactions between national government and local authorities has been the consultations on, and settlement of, the annual level of Exchequer support for local government services. Particularly since the introduction of RSG in 1966, and more so in the period of financial stringency since 1973–4, RSG has assumed an overwhelming importance in the 'business cycle' of local government. And however the relationship is organised, the position of local government, in its search for central support for its services, is that of a supplicant, a subordinate rather than an equal.

Local government, then, is subordinate to central government. It is not being argued, however, that the relationship between them is necessarily a master and servant one, or one in which local government can be no more than the agent of central government. The nature of the relationship has been examined from various new perspectives in recent years, and it is difficult to disagree with the view expressed by Rhodes (1980) that to see the relationship only in terms of centralisation and financial dependence is to miss some of its subtleties and sophistication. It is suggested, however, that where conflict arises between the two levels of government its resolution is more likely to favour central than local government. And the level of conflict, as the result of a disputed reorganisation and a continuing economic crisis, has been higher since 1974 than before.

THE NATIONAL REPRESENTATION OF LOCAL GOVERNMENT

In considering local government in Scotland in Chapter 6, it was noted that both Redcliffe-Maud and Wheatley had strongly emphasised the desirability, after any reorganisation, of local government being represented nationally by a single association. In the old system in England and Wales, the four major classes of authority each had a separate representative body and one of them, the Association of Municipal Corporations (AMC) representing both county boroughs and non-county boroughs, was itself a loose federation representing subclasses of authority which often did not share a common point of view (Isaac-Henry, 1980, p. 41). The effectiveness of local government as a pressure group acting upon national government was generally thought to have been undermined and its influence dissipated by this division.

In the two years between the publication of the Conservative government White Paper (Cmnd 4584, 1971b) and the passage of the Local Government Act 1972, a series of consultations took place among representatives of the then existing local authority associations with a view to establishing a single association to represent the new classes of authority and to include the London Boroughs Association and the GLC. It became clear quite early in these discussions that

> ... this could not be agreed by all, the main objection was that whilst agreement between representatives of all authorities on national matters could be anticipated for many or even most occasions, matters of importance could arise when the representatives of a particular type of local authority would hold differing views from their colleagues and that it would be proper for each of these views to be made known. (CCA, 1973, p. 1)

The alternative then considered was a 'local government federation' which would 'maintain a strong single voice' but which would guarantee the right of the representatives of each type of authority 'even when in a minority ... to have their own particular views presented alongside that of the majority' (CCA, 1973, p. 2). Such an arrangement would, of course, have been broadly similar to that adopted by the Convention of Scottish Local Authorities (COSLA). It was, however, vetoed by the representatives of the AMC, who put up their own proposal for three independent associations and a federation with 'certain limited functions that would act as a central discussion forum' (CCA, 1973, p. 3). This was not acceptable to the other three associations. The result of these abortive negotiations was the establishment in 1973 of three quite separate associations, the Association of County Councils (ACC), the Association of Metropolitan Authorities (AMA), and the Association of District Councils (ADC).

The failure to agree upon the creation of a single association was, and is, widely regretted in local government, but it was made inevitable by the nature of the structure introduced in 1973. For that structure built into the local government system a number of major conflicts of interest that no amount of negotiation and constitutional ingenuity could overcome. First, in the non-metropolitan counties, the counties and the districts did not share a common perception of their interests. Although the County Councils Association (CCA), Urban District Councils Association (UDCA) and Rural District Councils Association (RDCA) were in broad agreement during the discussions referred to above, they did not include the representatives of those authorities whose disgruntlement at the outcome of reorganisation would be carried forward into the new system, the county boroughs. They would be district councils after reorganisation, but as was emphasised in Chapter 2, their resentment was directed primarily towards the new counties by which they saw themselves being swallowed up. They found it difficult enough to live at peace with their fellow members of the ADC during the period when 'organic change' was under discussion; their position in a single association would have been untenable.

Secondly, the creation of the metropolitan counties, with their constituent and powerful metropolitan districts, established a clear conflict between the highly urbanised conurban areas and the more rural shire counties. This was probably the single greatest obstacle in the path of the creation of a united association, for it was political as well as structural. It was emphasised in Chapter 5 that the new system was expected to be much more partisan than its predecessor, and it was inevitable that this would be reflected in the new representative body, or bodies, for local government. Put simply, on any conceivable system of representation, a single association would be dominated by the highly Conservative shire counties and districts. If there were a separate association to represent the metropolitan authorities it was likely that it would be dominated, more often than not, by Labour. Isaac-Henry (1980, p. 54) notes that 'Sir Robert Thomas, leader of the Labour group on the AMC . . . objected to the principle of a single voice speaking for local government and suggested that the objective should be a strong voice for the urban areas'. But concern for the distinctiveness of the urban voice can be interpreted as a proxy for the safeguarding of a distinctive Labour input to the process of central–local relations. There is no doubt that the Labour Party opposed, and through its strength on the AMC frustrated, the creation of a single association.

CENTRAL–LOCAL RELATIONS SINCE 1974

The period since the creation of the new local government systems of England and Wales has been one of unprecedented financial stringency in the course of which successive governments, of both major political parties, have become ever more determined to control that large part of public expenditure (31 per cent in 1976) which is directly incurred by local authorities. The consequence of this determination for the quality of the relationship between Whitehall and the local authorities has been an increase in the amount of central control over local government decisions. During the fieldwork for this book, respondents in upper-tier authorities were asked whether they thought that the nature of local government's relationship with central government had materially changed since reorganisation. Of the nineteen respondents, twelve were quite unequivocal in their view that the period had brought a greater degree of central control and a concomitant decline in local autonomy; four expressed no view; and three thought that there had been little change. No respondent believed that the objective of increasing the independence of local authorities, which was frequently expressed by ministers in the pre-legislative stage of reform, had been met. The following remarks are typical of the responses.

As an authority we have been very concerned . . . at increasing interference . . . in all sorts of insidious ways. (Non-metropolitan county chief executive)

The 'grand design' from the Whitehall point of view must be to exert greater and greater control. (Metropolitan county chief executive)

There is a much greater tendency for central government to 'inter-meddle' in local government than there was. The prevailing economic conditions are an excuse for central government to be *dirigiste*. (Welsh county chief executive)

I think that central government is keen on the erosion of local government's responsibilities. (Metropolitan county chief executive)

I detect a consistent and sustained attempt by central government . . . to get a grip on local government. (Non-metropolitan county chief executive)

Some respondents believed that the structure created in 1974 facilitated the increase in central control, both by the reduction in the number of local authorities and by the creation of two-tier systems in which central government can 'play one tier off against the other'. In general, however, there was a perception that the effect of reorganisation had been to render local government less able than before to resist the extension of central control. Local politicians and officers generally regard as legitimate the intention of central government to control public expenditure. But when local government is divided, it is less able to ensure that the activities of central government in the control of local expenditure stop short of direct encroachment on the autonomy of individual authorities. However, the view that local government would have been better placed to resist the centralist trend if it had been united is called in question by its failure to prevent the Conservative government from passing the Local Government, Planning and Land Act 1980, despite the unanimous opposition of the three local government associations.

Since 1974 several new mechanisms and one new institution have been introduced into the central–local relationship, all of which increase rather than diminish the influence of central government: cash limits on RSG and joint circulars to accompany the settlement; Transport Policies and Programmes and Housing Investment Programmes; the Consultative Council on Local Government Finance; and the new financial and administrative arrangements contained in the Local Government, Planning and Land Act 1980. Only by the removal of certain minor controls over local authorities has central government moved in an anti-centralist direction. The developing nature of the relationship is analysed here by looking at these innovations.

CASH LIMITS AND JOINT CIRCULARS

Until 1974–5 the announcement of the RSG settlement by the Secretary of State for the Environment was followed by the publication of circulars by the various departments concerned with the provision of local services. According to local government spokesmen, the advice contained in these circulars was often contradictory, exhorting councils to provide levels of individual services which, in aggregate, were sometimes incompatible with the assumptions underlying the RSG settlement. In an expansionary phase, such as the period from the inception of RSG in 1966 until the oil-led inflation of 1974, local government would grumble about the problem but it could live with it, in the knowledge that the final determinant of the level of RSG was its own spending rather than the targets specified by the government. With the imposition of cash limits on RSG, however, local government was put in the position of having to provide its own hedges against inflation, a new problem in their budgeting. This led them to invite a greater degree of central intervention in their affairs.

Until 1975 the RSG was paid in three instalments: in November a settlement was announced based upon projections of local authority expenditure for the current year, and in the following year there were two 'increase orders' based upon the actual out-turn of expenditure. It was this that gave local authorities the determining influence in the amount of cash paid out in RSG. Rate Support Grant was composed of a needs element (based on assessments of the need for services in particular localities), a resources element (based upon the rateable value and penny rate product of individual authorities) and a domestic element (in effect, an Exchequer subsidy to non-commercial ratepayers). Also, the needs element from 1975 was calculated by a highly complex multiple regression formula which was argued to be objective. None the less it was historic spending patterns that determined the final level of RSG. The imposition of a cash limit on the increase order changed all that: from 1975 the amount available was finite, influenced crucially by the assumptions about inflation built into the process of decision-making at central government level. This faced individual local authorities with the need to budget much more carefully and, by extension, to take harder decisions about the order of priorities within and among services.

The imposition of cash limits was symbolic of the fact that local government was entering a period of consolidation, retrenchment and, eventually, contraction of expenditure. There was no reason, however, why this should inevitably have led to a greater amount of central intervention in the decision-making processes of local government. Local government could have accepted the onset of a more stringent financial regime and the need to take the decisions implied by the change. Instead, through its representative bodies, it persuaded central government that its capacity to respond to the new situation was limited by its receipt of contradictory advice and that it was essential that the individual circulars on RSG be replaced by a joint circular.

The joint circular increases central intervention in two related ways. First, despite the suggestion by the Central Policy Review Staff (CPRS, 1977, para. 5.4, p. 22) that such circulars are often little more than the old departmental circulars with a common top and tail, they introduce into government advice the dimension of relativity – the order of priority that central government expects to see among services. This makes it more difficult for local authorities to choose their own order of priority, as they could more easily do before joint circulars were introduced. Secondly, joint circulars increase the degree to which parts of the RSG are 'hypothecated', which is to say earmarked for individual services, thus compromising RSG's status as general grant and harking back to the days when Exchequer support for local government came in the form of grants for specific services. Under these arrangements, the individual discretion of local authorities to spend a block grant as they will is circumscribed.

There is a strong sense in which local government has been its own worst enemy in this regard, a view that is reflected in the following comments, all from county chief executives:

Local government has to some extent got itself to blame because we asked central government too many questions that we should ourselves be settling within the family . . .

We are our own worst enemies because we are weak-kneed.

I think there was too much readiness to seek guidance from central government.

As far as the internal decision-making processes of local authorities are concerned, the combined effects of joint circulars and cash limits have accelerated the process of what might be termed procedural homogenisation. It was suggested earlier, that the budget cycle of local authorities has always, inevitably, been linked to the process by which RSG (and its predecessors) has been settled; since local government has direct control over the raising of less than half of what it spends, it could hardly be otherwise. But the combination of a lack of intense inflationary pressure, encouragement from central government to improve services, and an open-ended RSG commitment allowed councils to begin the budget process on generous assumptions of Exchequer support. In practice, this meant that they could publicly commit themselves, sometimes in considerable detail, to local targets whose later revision was unlikely, given the prevailing financial regime. Since 1975 authorities have been increasingly unwilling to give any but the most generalised attention to their individual budgets until the level of RSG, and the government's outline of service priorities accompanying it, are known. This is an effective increase in central control and one that bears upon the autonomous power to spend that local authorities, within the constraints of *ultra vires*, have always possessed.

TRANSPORT POLICIES AND PROGRAMMES (TPPs) AND HOUSING INVESTMENT PROGRAMMES (HIPs)

Since reorganisation, the system by which government assistance is allocated in support of local authority expenditure in the fields of transport and housing has been changed by the introduction of the

Transport Policy and Programme/Transport Supplementary Grant (TPP/TSG) and Housing Investment Programme (HIP) systems. In both cases, the stated objective of central government was to remove central controls on individual capital projects and, in the case of transport, to abolish specific grants. These were to be replaced by block allocations and a general grant. The mechanisms are similar: TPP and HIP were prepared by county councils and district councils respectively and they functioned as bids for TSG and for capital allocations in housing. County councils were not obliged to spend TSG precisely according to their TPP, but in the case of housing virement between heads of expenditure (or 'blocks') in the HIP was limited to 25 per cent of each block. Such processes provide central government with the opportunity to reverse in practice, the objective in principle of reducing central control. This point becomes clear when the provision of Exchequer support in response to a programme bid is compared with its provision as a result of the application of published, if not necessarily agreed, indicators of need, as in the case of RSG. In the 'bid–approval–grant' mechanism there is, for central government, an additional opportunity for approving, or disapproving, the priorities established locally. In RSG once the needs element is established, and the resources element calculated, allocation is an administrative act rather than a political one. There is no opportunity for central government to comment upon, or to act against, the specific and published priority decisions of the local authority.

In both policy fields, the twin pressures of national goal-setting and the need to contain public expenditure have ensured that central intervention in local affairs has increased, sometimes quite spectacularly. In 1977–8, for example, the Secretary of State for Transport substantially reduced the TSG paid to the metropolitan county of South Yorkshire because of the council's refusal to heed the government's instructions to reduce its subsidies to public transport. Also, in the HIP process, the Department of the Environment has been able to reduce very substantially the capital allocations of authorities because they were not in housing stress areas – an effect of national goal-setting – or because their bid reflected priorities between aspects of housing expenditure not supported by central government. No judgement on the merits of policy is intended here. It may well be that the priorities and policies of central government are highly defensible as part of its overall national responsibilities. But the effect is to increase the degree of central intervention in local affairs and so to circumscribe further the independence and autonomy of local councils. Thus in these specific fields, for similar reasons but by different means, the centralising trend noted in the consideration of cash limits and joint circulars is replicated.

THE CONSULTATIVE COUNCIL ON LOCAL GOVERNMENT
FINANCE (CCLGF)

The only new institution (apart, of course, from the local authority associations themselves) to be created since reorganisation in the field of central–local relations is the Consultative Council on Local Government Finance (CCLGF). The creation of this body was announced by the Chancellor of the Exchequer in his budget speech in April 1975. Its announcement in this way was significant, for it suggested that the council was intended more to facilitate central control of the economy than to increase local government's capacity to protect its position and to maximise its influence on the government and on individual departments.

The CCLGF has no precise terms of reference, though its general remit is clear: to act as a single and authoritative forum for discussion between central government and local authorities on the nature and development of the financial relationship between central and local government. It is chaired by the Secretary of State for the Environment and is attended by ministers and civil servants from all departments concerned with local government, including the Treasury. Its local authority members are selected by the associations and its secretariat is provided jointly by the Department of the Environment and the associations. Early in its life, the CCLGF had to confront the question of the effects of its existence and working on the many already existing interactions between local authorities and central departments in respect of individual services – between education committees and the Department of Education and Science, social services and the Department of Health and Social Security, protective services (that is, police, fire) and the Home Office, to take three obvious examples. The conclusion arrived at on this question of competence served to define more exactly the role of the council and to emphasise that its concern was primarily financial, concern with the quality and quantity of particular services remaining with individual departments. Thus a note from the Department of the Environment in September 1975 suggested that items for discussion 'should be considered under two headings: "Strategic" and "Tactical/Departmental" ', the former being 'those with which the Council should be chiefly concerned' and the latter those which 'will not normally be the concern of the Council'. The paper went on to say that 'It is not intended that the Council should replace existing lines of communication between individual departments and Local Authority Associations and with related bodies . . . and appropriate professional organisations' (CCLG [75] 15, 1975, para. 4) and to concede that 'wider issues of principle' arising from consideration at departmental level could come to the council. Nor was this a one-sided business: the preservation of departmental links on operational matters was sought by departments as well as by the associations. As Taylor (1979, p. 20) says 'vertical links between Ministries and local authorities have been jealously guarded'. However, as is argued later, the predominance of the associations in the central–local consultative process has led to the virtual disappearance of discussions on policy between individual local authorities and individual central departments.

The effect of the CCLGF on the pattern of official relationships between central government and local authorities may conveniently be examined under three headings: the unity of local government, the relative roles of officers and members in the work of the council, and the views of members and officers on the effectiveness of the council.

The existence of the CCLGF has necessitated closer contacts than before among the local authority associations. The associations, through their secretaries, frequently co-operated before reorganisation as their joint initiatives in the establishment of the Maud, Mallaby and Bains committees show. But since the creation of the CCLGF, the mechanics of the work of the council have propelled the associations into a more continuous co-operative relationship which overcomes at least some of the divisions inherent in the existence of separate representative bodies.

Soon after the CCLGF was set up, the secretaries of the associations and the director-general of the GLC presented a joint proposal for the organisation of the local government side of the council's secretariat. Also, the decision in 1976 to relax the confidentiality surrounding the council's work and to circulate to local authorities a 'narrative report' of its proceedings, involved the associations in agreeing a draft prepared by the local government joint secretary. The report was then published by the associations and the GLC.

More importantly, however, the local authority side in the council, both at member level and at officer level, has developed various processes of co-ordination. On the member side, meetings of the council are preceded by pre-meetings of the local authority representatives. Members are supported by their officer advisers who are, in the main, chief executives, treasurers and other chief officers who advise the functional committees of the associations, together with the association secretaries and their staffs. One objective of such meetings is to explore the possibility of presenting a united front to government in the council itself. This possibility is, of course, limited by the fundamental conflict of interest that arises from the fact that although the associations (as representatives of classes of authority) may share a common view about the desirable level of local authority spending and of central government support for it, they are in competition with each other over the details of its allocation. As Taylor points out (1979, p. 21), these 'disparities of interest' are 'highlighted by . . . a perennial argument on the distribution formula for RSG'.

On the officer side, much of the detailed work of the CCLGF is undertaken by bodies composed entirely of professionals, both from central departments and from local authorities. In particular, the Official Steering Group (OSG) gives detailed, preliminary consideration to all substantive items of business coming before the council. The OSG is composed of civil servants from the Department of the Environment, the Treasury, the Home Office, the Department of Education and Science, the Welsh Office, the Department of Health and Social Services and other departments when appropriate, the secretary of each local authority association, specialist professional staff of the associations, and officer advisers (particularly treasurers). The background work of the OSG entails the preparation and circulation of papers by departments and by the associations, and the whole process has increased the amount of contact and co-operation among the associations. Other bodies, such as the Expenditure Steering Group, Grants Working Group and various functional groups provide further pressure towards co-operation. The degree to which these developments are regarded as, in any way, the embryo of a joint or federated association is, however, slight. Although the matter remains on the agenda of the associations, the general view in local government is that the prospects for unification are no better now than they were in 1971–3. There is, however, general satisfaction that, at this important level, the associations have sometimes been able to act in concert.

The delegation of much of the detailed work of the CCLGF to professionals rather than elected members produces a partial analogue in the field of central–local relations of the largely reactive role of members in many local authorities. With the determination (since 1974) of the needs element of RSG by a highly technical process based upon multiple regression analysis, the consultations on the financial support given by the Exchequer to local authorities have become increasingly complicated. The result has been the exclusion of members from some of the most crucial parts of the process. It can, of course, be pointed out that on the local government side the interests of authorities are served by the activities of their officer representatives, the association secretaries, and the advisers from various disciplines. On the other hand, however, the nature of the accountability of members to their associations and to the member authorities is affected by the degree to which they rely on technical expertise rather than on direct and personal involvement. If it is possible that professional ideologies affect the process of policy formulation in individual councils, it is also possible that they affect the consultative process at national level. And at national level, as at local level, it is only relatively few members – the most senior office-holders of the associations – who can give to the consultative process the sort of sustained attention that would put them on an equal footing with their own officials, with civil servants and with ministers. In short, in the process of consultation through CCLGF that leads to the announcement of the RSG settlement, members are less influential than their constitutional position assumes.

It is difficult to separate the perceptions that local government leaders have of the CCLGF from the expectations with which they greeted its creation. Before 1975 continuous contact between local and central government in the RSG process was wholly at official level, with consultations at the political level occurring *ad hoc* and at the annual statutory meeting where the settlement was announced by the secretary of state. It was not surprising, therefore, that the leaders of the local authority associations were enthusiastic about the establishment of a standing forum where they could discuss local government finance directly with ministers and civil servants.

However, some of that enthusiasm came from an expectation that the CCLGF, despite its name, would be a forum for negotiation rather than consultation. With the creation of fewer and larger authorities, and the natural enthusiasm of newly established institutions, local government, through the associations, anticipated a balancing of the central–local relationship and a halt to the process of centralisation that it felt had been underway for a very long time. As one chief executive put it: 'I think members believe they negotiate RSG, whereas they do nothing of the sort.' Certainly, in the author's personal experience, both as a county councillor and as member of the policy committee of the ACC, leading members, as a matter of course, referred to the 'negotiation' with the government of RSG. In some senses, it was inevitable that such high, and unrealistic, expectations would be unfulfilled. But even after it had been in operation for five years, and in a period of increasing financial stringency and decreasing central support for local services, attitudes to the council remained more positive than negative. In 1980 a questionnaire was sent to twenty leading members of local authorities, all but two of whom had served as representatives on local authority associations. The responses of the eighteen who had served as representatives to a series of questions on the CCLGF are shown in Table 7.1.

Of the respondents, seven were Conservative councillors and eleven were Labour members and it was noticeable that the Labour members were a little less enthusiastic about the council than the Conservatives. Two reasons suggest themselves: first, the questionnaire was administered in early 1980 at a time when the proposals of the Conservative government for changes in the grant system, an increase in ministers' powers over local authorities and further major reductions in local government expenditure were matters of high and bitter controversy; and secondly, the role of the CCLGF in the discussion of reductions in expenditure is probably less palatable to

Table 7.1 Leading Members' (n = 18) Views of the Consultative Council on Local Government Finance (CCLGF).

Questions	Responses				
	Very helpful	Helpful	Neither helpful nor unhelpful	Unhelpful	Very unhelpful
How would you assess the contribution of the CCLGF in the field of central–local relations?	5	10	2	0	0
	Strongly agree	Agree	Neither agree nor disagree	Disagree	Strongly disagree
The CCLGF is a real forum of discussion where local government's views can have a major influence on central government's decisions about local government.	2	7	7	1	1
	Strongly agree	Agree	Neither agree nor disagree	Disagree	Strongly disagree
The CCLGF is a talking shop and local government has no more influence on ministerial decisions than before it was set up.	1	4	4	7	2

Labour local politicians than to Conservative ones. The general conclusion, however, remains: despite the fact that it has not greatly increased the power of local government, the CCLGF is supported by members as a guaranteed channel of access and influence. In particular, members (and officers) have welcomed the way in which the work of the council and the participation of the Treasury in it have allowed local government, as well as central departments, to have an input to the Public Expenditure Survey committee process which results in the annual publication of the government's expenditure plans.

Perhaps because, as professionals, they do not have constituencies to impress or national public reputations to make, officers are more critical, sceptical and cynical about the work of the CCLGF. For although very few of the nineteen upper-tier chief executives interviewed were entirely dismissive of it, almost all of them considered it to be of limited value as the following comments illustrate:

A rather successful charade. It functions as a theatre in which ministers can state what they have already decided and appropriate noises of expostulation can be made. (Non-metropolitan county chief executive)

An interesting mechanism, useful for hammering out RSG, even if it is recognised that the final decision rests with ministers. (Non-metropolitan county chief executive)

A means by which government can say it has taken local government into its confidence. (Metropolitan county chief executive)

It is just window-dressing. (Welsh county chief executive)

A marvellous talking shop. I do not believe it is a consultative council – I think it is a forum for central government to promulgate its views to local government. (Metropolitan county chief executive)

If it is true, as some commentators suggest (Laffin, 1980; Regan, 1980*b*), that the role of professionals in the central–local relationship is in some respects quite autonomous and independent of elected members – and the dominance of professionals in the detailed work of the CCLGF lends support to this view – then the less enthusiastic appraisals given by officers may be due, in part, to the fact that the high visibility of the council has broken their virtual monopoly in the representation of local government in central–local consultations.

One further effect of the work of the CCLGF should be noted.

Since the council began its work, it has virtually displaced the direct contacts on policy between departments and individual authorities that were fairly common before reorganisation. Almost all such contact between local authorities and the government is now channelled through the associations, whether it is on general matters that are the direct concern of the CCLGF or on specific matters where discussions with an individual department are appropriate. Some chief executives and leading members see dangers to individual authorities in channelling all approaches to government through the associations, largely because they believe that the need for an association to form a view may obscure the special needs of specific areas. This danger, of course, would be increased, in the present local government system, if there were a single association. Closely related to this point is the position of certain authorities which, before 1974, were big enough and dominant enough in their regions to command almost instant access to civil servants and ministers. With the abolition of the county boroughs, there are no subnational, all-purpose authorities. Moreover, former county boroughs, such as Birmingham and Manchester, are members of the same association as the metropolitan counties that deprive them of their all-purpose status and position of regional leadership. They are, therefore, inhibited from establishing direct contacts with government because such contacts might threaten the fragile unity of the association.

THE LOCAL GOVERNMENT, PLANNING AND LAND ACT 1980

When the Redcliffe-Maud Commission was set up in 1966, the question of local government finance was not included in its remit. There was, however, widespread concern in Parliament and elsewhere that the system of local taxation should be modernised and that the decline in the power of local government was related to its reliance upon a single tax and upon an increasing degree of financial support from the centre. This concern was acknowledged by the Prime Minister, Harold Wilson, when he told the House of Commons that the Commission was 'not precluded from considering questions of finance' (*Hansard*, 24 May 1966). When Redcliffe-Maud reported, it conceded a need for new sources of revenue but also said (Redcliffe-Maud, Cmnd 4040, 1969, Vol. I, para. 539) that 'the rate . . . will remain the chief local tax'. The legislation of 1972 contained no new provisions on finance, although the Conservative government had published in 1971 a Green Paper (Cmnd 4741, 1971*c*) on the future shape of local government finance. Consultations took place but no legislation emerged. In 1974, in response to general criticism of the level of rate increases, the Secretary of State for the Environment in the Labour government, Anthony Crosland, appointed a committee of inquiry under the chairmanship of Frank Layfield, QC, with terms of reference 'to review the whole system of local government finance in England, Scotland and Wales, and to make recommendations'.

Layfield (Cmnd 6453, 1976) had much to say about the structure and process of local government financial arrangements, about responsibility and accountability, and about the shortcomings of the existing systems of local taxation and national contributions to the cost of local services. It considered in detail the nature of the central–local relationship and presented a clear choice for the future between continuing the process of centralisation, which it saw as an inevitable consequence of 'a system depending on high and increasing grants, and associated with an inflexible and politically sensitive local tax', and the revival of local accountability by making local authorities 'responsible . . . for both the expenditure they incurred and the revenue they raised' (Layfield, Cmnd 6453, 1976, p. 72). The committee proposed the introduction of local income tax (LIT), but it conceded that such a change was dependent upon the choice being made in favour of increasing local autonomy. It also said (p. 293) that 'a unitary grant [i.e. one that did not identify separate needs and resources elements] based on a prescription of the approved expenditure of each authority . . . would be the most appropriate form of grant' if the choice were made in favour of increasing central responsibility.

In 1977 the government published Green Papers (Cmnd 6811, 1977a and Cmnd 6813, 1977b) announcing their response to Layfield's recommendations. They ruled out LIT, and indeed any new source of local revenue, and said that any changes would be made in the context of retaining the rates as the only local tax. At the same time, however, the CCLGF considered in some detail the report and recommendations of Layfield, and the government's preference, expressed in Cmnd 6813, to move away from RSG as it was then constructed towards a unitary grant of the kind described by Layfield. No basic changes were made before the government lost office in 1979, perhaps because of the combination of the absence of a parliamentary majority, a preoccupation with devolution to Scotland and Wales, and the opposition of the local authority associations. When the Conservative government came to power only the last of these obstacles remained and that was overcome by the parliamentary majority that passed, in 1980, the Local Government, Planning and Land Act. The remainder of this chapter considers the effect of this Act on the nature of the central–local relationship and on the political and constitutional position of local authorities.

The Local Government, Planning and Land Act profoundly affects the nature of central–local relations by giving legislative form to the general movement towards centralisation that has been apparent since reorganisation and before. It would be a mistake, however, to see this as a partisan policy, for the Conservative government's legislation differs only in emphasis and detail from the Labour proposals of 1978. And at the heart of it is the questionable assertion that central government's control of the aggregate of local authority spending cannot be guaranteed without a capacity to intervene selectively to control the expenditure of individual local authorities. The Act contains six provisions that materially affect the central–local relationship and reduce the autonomy, independence and authority of local councils.

First, and most significant, is the introduction under Part VI of the Act, of the block grant to replace the needs and resources element of RSG. To understand the implications for local government and central–local relations of this change it is essential to examine the motivations of central government in introducing it. Ever since it became the major objective of government economic policy to contain public expenditure, central government has been anxious to overcome the open-endedness of RSG. The imposition of cash limits was a move in that direction. However, it did not deal with the fact that the calculation of the resources element ensured that, as long as an authority's expenditure was 'relevant', it would attract grant at the current rate, thus depriving central government of control of the amount of grant payable to a particular council. The resources element was designed to be a rate deficiency grant, compensating an authority for the amount by which its rateable value, and hence its available local revenue, fell below a 'national standard rateable value per head of population' established each year, as part of the RSG settlement, by the Secretary of State for the Environment. It allowed central government to determine the level of RSG, but did not give it any power to act against an authority which, by increasing its rate, attracted more grant.

In all but one of the years between 1967–8 (when RSG was introduced) and 1977–8, the aggregate of local government spending at the time of the final increase order paid when the actual expenditure of authorities is known has been within 1·8 per cent of government targets: the exception was 1974–5 when local government reorganisation took place, with attendant additional expenditure, in a period of extremely high inflation. The reason for this has been that high-spending authorities have been compensated for by low-spending authorities. Or to put the matter in terms of politics rather than finance, the result of a range of individual political decisions by autonomous local authorities has been a close correspondence with the overall public expenditure targets of central government. Central government, however, has been unhappy with the level of unpredictability inherent in RSG.

Under the 1980 Act, needs element and resources element were abolished and the block grant payable to an authority is now based upon an assessment by the Secretary of State for the Environment of its 'grant related expenditure (GRE)'. Grant aid may then be reduced, in such a way as the secretary of state decides, if an authority's actual expenditure is greater than its GRE. The significance of the GRE concept is clarified if it is noted that the original term proposed by the government, and changed at the behest of the local authority associations, was 'standard expenditure figure'. This figure is defined as 'the aggregate of the notional expenditure of the authority for the year, having regard to their functions as determined by the Secretary of State'. In other words, the key determinant of grant will be an assessment by central government of what it thinks a local council ought to be spending. As SOLACE (1980, p. 12) said, commenting on the proposed change, 'By stating a figure for each authority the Secretary of State will become answerable for that figure.' Local responsibility is thus replaced by national accountability.

It is significant in this context that this innovation was unanimously opposed by the local authority associations. For although the period of stringency since 1974 has been characterised by frequent expressions of disapproval by low-spending, or conforming, authorities of high-spending, or non-conforming, ones, no national representative body was prepared to pursue the irritation and dismay of some of its members to the point of collaborating with ministers in what they regarded as an attack on local democracy and a considerable turn of the centralist screw. During the legislative process the associations briefed members of both Houses of Parliament in an attempt to prevent the changes, and their arguments showed a remarkable unanimity of view and approach as the following quotations show.

The new provisions . . . will result in a decisive shift of responsibility and accountability from local government to central government . . . Instead of relying on local democratic control within a national policy framework, the government has opted for central control and influence over the spending decisions of individual authorities. (ADC, 1980, para. 2)

The Block Grant System . . . represents a serious threat to local autonomy and to the future of local democracy . . . would result in a major shift in the balance of central–local relationships and as a result . . . local government accountability would be prejudiced rather than enhanced. (AMA, 1980)

The block grant will markedly increase the power of central departments to influence local spending decisions, to the detriment, therefore, of true local democracy. (ACC, 1980)

And, as the AMA pointed out, there was no certainty that the new system would have the desired effect of controlling local government expenditure, for the government's powers depend upon an authority being in receipt of grant. If the GRE figure is regarded by an authority as quite unreasonable, the authority may act in such a way as to invite the secretary of state to deprive it of all grant. It would then finance all expenditure from the rates. In 1981–2 some authorities acted precisely in this way thus, paradoxically, increasing their independence by their response to a statute that was designed to curtail that independence.

Secondly, the 1980 Act introduces a new method of controlling local authority capital expenditure. Until the passage of the Act, central government exercised a control over the amount of money a local authority could borrow for capital purposes. The new provisions entail a control of the level of an authority's actual capital payments in any one year. This change will affect the relative positions of local and central government in two major ways. First, local authorities are no longer entitled to supplement their borrowing by financing some capital expenditure from revenue (that is, from local rates), a significant reduction in local independence and an encroachment on both the autonomous power to tax, and more importantly, on the autonomous power to spend. Secondly, by making the allocations on an annual basis, the ability of local authorities to plan ahead is restricted, subject only to a 10 per cent 'carry-over' from one year to the next. The Act also contains additions to the power of the secretary of state to restrict the use to which a council may put capital receipts (that is, money received from the sale of assets), a further reduction in local autonomy. These restrictions are, however, partly offset by the abolition of controls on the transfer of capital expenditure from one service heading to another. The annual allocation of capital expenditure is a block figure, giving authorities freedom to employ it as they will.

Thirdly, the secretary of state is given wide powers to intervene in the operation of local authority direct labour organisations (DLOs). Many authorities, particularly those which are successors to county boroughs, employ their own labour force, principally to undertake building and maintenance work for the authority. Much concern has been expressed about the alleged inefficiency of DLOs when compared with the private sector of the building industry and about the extent to which some authorities subsidised their DLOs out of the rates. In the course of consultations, the associations accepted the need for separate accounting and competitive tendering. The legislation, however, as well as making these procedures mandatory, greatly increases the power of the secretary of state. He may prescribe for each DLO a rate of return on capital employed and, after the preparation of a special report demanded by him, he may order the closure of any DLO with whose performance he is not satisfied.

Fourthly, the Act gives to the secretary of state a new power to compile a register of the land held by an individual local authority if he believes that the land is not being properly employed by the authority in the performance of its functions. He may also direct a local authority to sell such land and he may specify the terms and conditions upon which any offer to dispose of the land is to be made. As the AMA said in its brief to members, 'Such changes constitute a major extension in the secretary of state's powers and are wholly out of keeping with a Bill which purports to relax controls.'

Fifthly, the Act gives to the secretary of state the power to set up, subject to parliamentary approval, urban development corporations which, in effect, would suspend local government in their area of operation. This part of the legislation was argued by the government to be necessary to give effect to the decision to set up such corporations in the London and Merseyside docklands in order to deal comprehensively with areas of dereliction that crossed several local government boundaries. For procedural reasons, the government thought it necessary to confer upon the secretary of state a general power, for otherwise the Bill would have become a hybrid Bill rather than a public Bill and would, therefore, have been subject to a different, and time-consuming, parliamentary process. However, as the local authority associations pointed out, the power granted is to designate 'any area of land as an urban development area' and there is no guarantee that the legislation will not be employed in the future to remove urban areas from the jurisdiction of local authorities. To quote SOLACE (1980, p. 26):

This is a decision not to rely on local government dealing with critical urban problems. This is itself a change of principle. Merseyside and even the London Docklands are not so different from other areas that the same principle cannot be argued for in other areas and the powers will be available to be used.

Sixthly, the Act gives legislative effect to the decision, announced by the Chancellor of the Exchequer in his budget speech in 1980, to create 'enterprise zones' where inducements, principally exemption from rates and certain planning requirements, would be offered to prospective developers. This provision was generally welcomed by local government but it constitutes, none the less, an encroachment upon the capacity of local councils to act as comprehensive planning authorities for their areas. Also, it is central government, not local authorities, to which the power is given to designate the areas of the country in which enterprise zones are to be set up.

Taken together, these six provisions significantly alter the balance in the relationship between central and local government. And their effect is scarcely offset by the provisions in Part I of the 1980 Act relaxing about 300 specific controls previously exercised by central government over local authorities. An assessment of the changes resulting from the removal of these controls depends upon two considerations: the comparison between their extent and the promises of relaxation of control made by successive ministers in successive governments; and the nature of the controls removed.

In September 1979 the government published a White Paper (Cmnd 7634, 1979*b*) listing the controls over local authorities that it proposed to remove. This list became the basis of Part I of the 1980 Act. This part of the Act was widely supported in local government, though there was a general feeling that it did not go nearly far enough. It fell far short of Peter Walker's 'thousands of controls' (AMC, 1971, p. 11) and it did not measure up to the expectations of the associations as expressed in a joint publication in 1979 (ACC *et al.*, 1979). More importantly, however, the nature of the controls relaxed is such as to have little impact on the substance of central–local relations. While it is true that they will have the effect of reducing administrative and bureaucratic interference with the exercise by local authorities of their statutory duties, they do not increase the general political independence of local government. Many of the controls removed, especially in the fields of housing, planning and highways, were regarded by councils as petty and vexatious; and because they were so regarded their removal will make life easier and day-to-day administration cheaper for local authorities and central government alike. However, their generally trivial nature, when set against the major changes in the balance between two levels of government implied in other sections of the Act, makes the purpose of the Act, as indicated in its preamble – 'to relax controls over local . . . authorities' – seem rather grandiose.

In general then, the combined effect in England and Wales of the structural reorganisation of 1974, the response of both central and local government to economic crisis, and the provisions of the 1980 legislation has been a substantial shift in the balance of power in favour of central government. Perhaps, given the subordinate status of local government, that shift was inevitable in the economic climate of the 1970s. As Stewart (1980, p. 14) points out, there is a 'dilemma of conflicting objectives' at the centre of government policies, between a belief in principle in the extension of local authority independence and a need to control public expenditure wherever it is incurred. The resolution of the dilemma has been achieved by favouring the power of the centre against the autonomy of local authorities. And this has been so whether the government in power has been Conservative or Labour.

Chapter 8

THE FUTURE OF SUBNATIONAL GOVERNMENT

The reorganisation of British local government in the early 1970s was not a spectacular success. Its failures, however, are rather less apparent in Scotland than they are in England and Wales. The reasons for the relative failure of this major exercise in institutional reform have been suggested in the course of the analysis of the performance of the new systems: the two-tier structures throughout Britain were unstable from the moment of their creation because of the combined effects of the dissatisfaction of many urban areas at the loss of their local government autonomy and a distribution of functions between the tiers, especially in non-metropolitan England and in Scotland, that maximised the chances of inter-authority conflict. Thus the capacity of the new systems to pass the tests of efficiency, comprehensibility, autonomy and conclusiveness, outlined in Chapter 1, was compromised from the start.

This is not to say that the system does not function. Children continue to be educated, dustbins to be emptied, houses to be built, home helps to be organised; or if they do not, the reasons are much more likely to be concerned with financial stringency than with the failure of the local government system to work. And yet the system has few defenders and fewer enthusiasts. The overwhelming impression is of practitioners, both members and officers, whose determination to make the system work owes more to a wish to avoid a further reorganisation than to a commitment to the systems that arose from the legislation of 1972 and 1973.

Any further substantial change in the structure of local government is unlikely in the short term, if only because the Conservative Party is committed only to seeking alternative sources of revenue to replace the rates (or to replace the rates in their present form), rather than to a thoroughgoing reform of the structure. The Labour Party, on the other hand, is profoundly unhappy with the present system, especially as it affects the major urban centres, whose exclusion, except in the metropolitan counties, from an independent role in education and social services deprives the party of influence in two policy fields that have traditionally been its major concern. The abortive attempt to change the system piecemeal by the device known as 'organic change' had few friends in local government. 'Organic change' was the name

171

given by the Labour Secretary of State for the Environment, Peter Shore, to his proposals to return to the larger former county boroughs some of the powers they had 'lost' in the 1972 legislation. Even in urban areas that would have benefited from the changes, leading figures supported the proposals in the Labour government's White Paper (Cmnd 7457, 1979a) with the reservation that tinkering with the allocation of functions in the existing system was not, in principle, the best way of dealing with the unacceptable consequences of the 1972 Act. And, of course the proposals were totally opposed by the county councils and by the ACC, thus creating battle lines not dissimilar to those that had characterised the unreformed system almost from its inception until the appointment of the Redcliffe-Maud Commission in 1966.

Certain specific deficiencies of the 1972 Act have been corrected in subsequent legislation. The Housing (Homeless Persons) Act 1977 placed a statutory duty on the district councils to house the homeless. The Local Government, Planning and Land Act 1980 simplified the distribution of planning powers by making the districts responsible for receiving all applications and by greatly curtailing the power of the county councils to insist upon the conformity of district council planning decisions with the structure plan for the county. It can be argued that the change will make strategic land-use planning and structure planning more difficult, but at least it seems likely to reduce the amount of day-to-day acrimony between the tiers of local government.

Any future changes to the structure of subnational government will, perforce, be introduced by central government. It is convenient, therefore, to examine possible developments in the light of the policies of the two major political parties.

Perhaps because of its greater dissatisfaction with the outcome of reorganisation, coupled with its stronger predilection towards institutional change, the Labour Party is more likely to produce a comprehensive policy for changes in the shape of subnational government. 'Organic change' was always envisaged as a short-term measure to ameliorate the worst effects on the urban areas of the 1972 legislation, and one that was limited enough to find a place in a congested legislative programme. Since the general election of 1979, however, organic change has been abandoned, and the Labour Party is now working towards proposals for a major reorganisation. These may involve not only a restructuring of local government but also the establishment in England of regional councils under whose authority might be placed the services that were removed in 1974 from the jurisdiction of elected local government, namely the health service and the water supply and distribution industry. Both of these services are now administered by appointed authorities, and their immunity from local democratic control is widely and deeply resented in local government.

But the establishment of regional government in England would not be easy. First of all, there is no unanimity on what constitutes a region, although the most likely configuration would be a system based upon the existing economic planning regions (Smith, 1972). Also, local perceptions of regional identity vary considerably: the council of the City of Stoke-on-Trent, for example, opposed regionalism because it was unclear whether the city would be part of a region based on Birmingham or part of a region based on Manchester, and because they identified with neither. There is little evidence that local government would be any more enthusiastic about regional government than it was in 1976 when discussions took place on the government's consultation paper, *Devolution: The English Dimension* (Lord President of the Council, 1976). In any scheme of regional government, one of the existing tiers of local government would, in all probability, be abolished and for that reason there is no more likelihood now than there was before the Redcliffe-Maud Commission was set up that reform could proceed with the agreement of existing local government institutions and their representative associations. For the distribution of functions that suggests itself, entails giving to regional authorities responsibility for strategic planning, environmental and emergency services and for the intermediate allocative decisions between national and local government in such fields as health, public transport and the public utilities. This would necessitate the continuation of a system of local councils to provide the personal and local services such as education, social services, housing, development planning, recreation and amenities (Labour Party, 1977).

For every argument in favour of retaining the counties, however, there would be a counter-argument in favour of abolishing them. Finally, there would be no guarantee that relations between regional and local authorities would be any more harmonious than those between districts and counties in the present system. It might be possible, however, to ensure that with a more defensible distribution of functions, together with synchronised election dates for the two levels, the occasions for liaison and dispute were minimised rather than maximised. And the chances of a co-operative response from local politicians and officials would be improved in the unlikely event of the devolution to regional authorities of a substantial amount of the power now exercised at the centre (McAllister and Hunter, 1980).

Conservative Party policy on local government is not concerned with alterations to the structure. Rather it seeks, as in the Local Government, Planning and Land Act 1980, to reduce statutory controls on local government while retaining and reinforcing the capacity of the centre to ensure that local autonomy poses no threat to central management of the economy. (There is, of course, no fundamental division between the parties on this latter point.) The Conservatives, however, also have an outstanding commitment to the abolition of the rates. Margaret Thatcher made this commitment during the election campaign of October 1974, when she was shadow Secretary of State for the Environment. It is difficult to see how abolition of rates can be compatible with the traditional Conservative attachment to local self-government unless some other form of local tax, or a grant system completely free of central direction, is introduced. And because Conservatives are committed to reductions in the burden of direct taxation they are left with little room for manoeuvre. The solution applied in the Irish Republic in 1978 (Alexander, 1979*b*), which makes the central government a substitute ratepayer for domestic assessments, is attractively simple. In Britain, it would be possible to add to the existing domestic element of RSG the costs of the 40 per cent of local expenditure not covered by grant, but such a change would be difficult to square with a defence of the autonomy and continued viability of local government.

In the continuing economic crisis that has beset Britain since local government reorganisation, the contradictions inherent in British attitudes to the role of government are thrown into sharp relief. On the one hand, there is the fact that politicians continue to place a high value upon the notion of local autonomy and its institutional expression as local government. On the other, the expansion of central government, the welfare state, and the continuous goal-setting of national politicians carry with them the possibility that local government's independence will be sacrificed in favour of the efficient delivery of services planned and financed at the centre. At the time of the 1974 reorganisation, health services throughout Britain and the water industry in England and Wales were removed from local control, just as other utilities had been taken away in the years after the Second World War. Many officers and some members believe that the amount of discretion left to local education authorities is now so small that education could conveniently be 'nationalised' rather than left within the purview of local government. The argument here is that with local powers of decision attenuated by successive Education Acts and the negotiation of teachers' salaries (which account for a very large proportion of current educational spending) undertaken nationally, the maintenance of the education service as a local government function obscures the real responsibility for the nature of the service and distorts and complicates unnecessarily the local authority budget process. This is not a majority view in local government but its adherents, on the basis of the research for this book, are growing in number. Similarly, the fire and police services are so hemmed in by Home Office regulations, very few of which were removed in the

1980 legislation, that the scope for local discretion in the provision of these services is very narrow indeed.

The question that arises as a central element of any speculation about the future of local government in Britain is whether local authorities can be much more than the agents of central government. This is to ask in a more simple form the question set by Layfield: Should local government be strengthened by increasing its independence of national financial support and by making it directly responsible for a greater proportion of what it raises in tax, spends on services and decides on policies; or should the strongly centralising trend of the last decade be accepted as inevitable?

As long as the answer to that question lies with central government, and no matter whether national politicians are pursuing the containment of expenditure or the expansion of the public services, the best that local government can hope for is that its position will not be further weakened. A reversal of the process of centralisation, and of the weakening of local democratic government that that process has caused, will depend upon a fundamental change in the conception of government that motivates Britain's national politicians. Such a change is less likely in the 1980s than it has been before. And local government, as a result of the reorganisations of 1974 and 1975 and the changes in the central–local relationship examined in Chapter 7, is in no position to act as a catalyst to such a constitutional transformation.

Appendix

FIELDWORK

During the fieldwork for this book extended interviews were conducted with officers and/or members in the following local authorities

ENGLAND

Metropolitan counties:	Greater Manchester
	Tyne and Wear
	West Midlands
Non-metropolitan counties:	Avon
	Cambridgeshire
	Cleveland
	Cumbria
	Devon
	Dorset
	East Sussex
	Hertfordshire
	Isle of Wight
	Kent
	Lancashire
	Nottinghamshire
	Surrey
Metropolitan districts:	Birmingham (West Midlands)
	Kirklees (West Yorkshire)
	Knowsley (Merseyside)
	Leeds (West Yorkshire)
	Liverpool (Merseyside)
	Newcastle upon Tyne (Tyne and Wear)
	Rotherham (South Yorkshire)
	Sheffield (South Yorkshire)
	Tameside (Greater Manchester)
	Wakefield (West Yorkshire)
Non-metropolitan districts: (with former county borough(s)):	Darlington (Durham)
	Ipswich (Suffolk)
	Hull (Humberside)
	Middlesbrough (Cleveland)

Northampton (Northamptonshire)
Plymouth (Devon)
Reading (Berkshire)
Southampton (Hampshire)
Stoke-on-Trent (Staffordshire)
Warrington (Cheshire)

Non-metropolitan districts (without former county borough):	Aylesbury Vale (Buckinghamshire)
	Beverley (Humberside)
	Bracknell (Berkshire)
	Broxbourne (Hertfordshire)
	Castle Morpeth (Northumberland)
	Chichester (West Sussex)
	Derwentside (Durham)
	Eastleigh (Hampshire)
	Erewash (Derbyshire)
	Guildford (Surrey)
	Hove (East Sussex)
	Kerrier (Cornwall)
	Lichfield (Staffordshire)
	Medway (Kent)
	Nuneaton (Warwickshire)
	Peterborough (Cambridgeshire)
	South Bedfordshire (Bedfordshire)
	South Oxfordshire (Oxfordshire)
	South Norfolk (Norfolk)
	The Wrekin (Salop)
	Thurrock (Essex)
	Vale Royal (Cheshire)

WALES

Counties:	Mid Glamorgan
	Powys
Districts (with former county borough):	Cardiff (South Glamorgan)
Districts (without former county borough):	Neath (West Glamorgan)

SCOTLAND

Regions:	Fife
	Grampian
	Strathclyde

Districts: Angus (Tayside)
                              Dundee (Tayside)
                              East Kilbride (Strathclyde)
                              Glasgow (Strathclyde)
                              Gordon (Grampian)
                              Nairn (Highland)

Islands: Shetland

BIBLIOGRAPHY

Abney, Glenn (1980), 'Local chief executives: roles in the intergovernmental administrative process', *Administration and Society*, vol. 2, no. 4, pp. 393–410.

Alexander, A. (1979*a*), 'Solving the dilemma of party politics in local government', *Municipal Journal*, vol. 87, pp. 1,043–4.

Alexander, A. (1979*b*), 'Local government in Ireland', *Administration*, vol. 27, pp. 3–29.

Ashford, D. E. (1974), 'The effects of central finance on the British local government system', *British Journal of Political Science*, vol. 4, pp. 305–22.

Ashford, D. E. (1975*a*), 'Resources, spending, and party politics in British local government', *Administration and Society*, vol. 7, no. 3, pp. 286–311.

Ashford, D. E. (1975*b*), 'Parties and participation in British local government and some American parallels', *Urban Affairs Quarterly*, vol. 2, no. 1, pp. 58–81.

Association of County Councils (ACC) (1980), 'Memorandum of views on the Local Government, Planning and Land (No. 2) Bill' (London: ACC), mimeo.

Association of County Councils *et al.* (ACC) (1979), *Review of Central Government Controls over Local Authorities* (London: ACC *et al.*).

Association of Directors of Social Services (1977), 'Directors of Social services in the local authority management structure', mimeo.

Association of District Councils (ADC) (1980), 'Local Government, Planning and Land (No. 2) Bill: Second Reading Debate, House of Lords, 5 August 1980 – Views of ADC' (London: ADC), mimeo.

Association of Metropolitan Authorities (AMA) (1980), letter and annexes to AMA vice-presidents in the House of Lords, 28 July.

Association of Municipal Corporations (AMC) (1971), *Annual Conference 1971: Report* (London: AMC).

Bains, M. A. (chairman), Working Group on Local Authority Management Structures (1972), *The New Local Authorities: Management and Structure* (London: HMSO).

Barlow, Montague (chairman), Royal Commission on the Distribution of the Industrial Population (1940), *Report*, Cmd 6153 (London: HMSO).

Berkshire County Council (1978*a*), '1979 budget guidelines: report of the leader of the council', mimeo.

Berkshire County Council (1978*b*), 'Chief officers' views on the budget guidelines for 1979–80', mimeo.

Boaden, N. (1971), *Urban Policy Making* (Cambridge: Cambridge University Press).

Boyle, Lawrence (1967), 'British and American city government', *Local Government Finance*, vol. 71, pp. 147–53.

Boyle, Lawrence (1969), 'Politics and the Royal Commission on Local Government', *Local Government Finance*, vol. 73, pp. 414–21.

Boyle, Lawrence (1970), 'Budgetary reform', paper to Rating and Valuation Association conference.

179

Brand, J. (1974), *Local Government Reform in England 1888–1979* (London: Croom Helm).

Brazier, S. and Harris, R. J. P. (1975), 'Inter-authority planning', *Town Planning Review*, vol. 46, pp. 255–65.

Bristow, S. L. (n.d.), 'Entrepreneurs, brokers and agents – the changing role of chief officers in English local government', mimeo.

Bristow, S. L. (1978), 'Local politics after reorganisation: the homogenisation of local government in England and Wales', *Public Administration Bulletin*, vol. 28, pp. 17–33.

Bulpitt, J. G. (1967), *Party Politics in English Local Government* (London: Longman).

Buxton, R. (1974), 'Planning in the new local government world', *Journal of Planning and Environment Law*, pp. 66–72.

Central Policy Review Staff (CPRS) (1977), *Relations between Central Government and Local Authorities* (London: HMSO).

Chartered Institute of Public Finance and Accountancy (CIPFA) (1976), *Rating Review* (Glasgow: CIPFA, Scottish Branch).

Cockburn, Cynthia (1977), *The Local State: Management of Cities and People* (London: Pluto Press).

Collins, C. A. (1978), 'Considerations on the social background and motivation of councillors', *Policy and Politics*, vol. 6, pp. 425–47.

Collins, C. A., Hinings, C. R. and Walsh, K. (1976), 'The best politician in town', unpublished paper, INLOGOV, University of Birmingham.

Collins, C. A., Hinings, C. R. and Walsh, K. (1978), 'The officer and the councillor in local government', *Public Administration Bulletin*, vol. 28, pp. 34–50.

Command Papers (1963), *The Modernisation of Local Government in Scotland*, Cmnd 2067 (Edinburgh: HMSO).

Command Papers (1970), *Reform of Local Government in England*, Cmnd 4276 (London: HMSO).

Command Papers (1971*a*), *Reform of Local Government in Scotland*, Cmnd 4583 (Edinburgh: HMSO).

Command Papers (1971*b*), *Local Government in England: Government Proposal for Reorganisation*, Cmnd 4584 (London: HMSO).

Command Papers (1971*c*), *The Future Shape of Local Government Finance*, Cmnd 4741 (London: HMSO).

Command Papers (1977*a*), *Local Government Finance in Scotland*, Cmnd 6811 (Edinburgh: HMSO).

Command Papers (1977*b*), *Local Government Finance*, Cmnd 6813 (London: HMSO).

Command Papers (1979*a*), *Organic Change in Local Government*, Cmnd 7457 (London: HMSO).

Command Papers (1979*b*), *Central Government Controls over Local Authorities*, Cmnd 7634 (London: HMSO).

Confederation of British Industry (CBI) (1979), *Value for Money: Report on Cheshire County Council Carried Out by P. A. Management Consultants* (London: CBI).

Consultative Council on Local Government Finance (CCLGF) (1975), 'The nature of business to be discussed by the Consultative Council: a discussion paper', CCLG(75)15, mimeo.

Convention of Scottish Local Authorities (COSLA) (1979), 'Report by constitution review subcommittee', mimeo.

Corfield, F. V. (1976), *A Guide to the Community Land Act* (London: Butterworths).

Corporate Planning (1977), 'The Birmingham saga: 1 – background, 2 – the actors speak', *Corporate Planning*, vol. 4, pp. 1–22.

County Councils Association (CCA) (1973), 'The future of the local authority associations' (Note of inter-authority discussions), mimeo.

Crossman, R. H. S. (1975), *The Diaries of a Cabinet Minister: Vol. 1, Minister of Housing 1964–1966* (London: Hamish Hamilton and Jonathan Cape).

Datson, G. G. (1976), 'The management of local government: a stocktaking', paper to SOLACE conference.

Davey, K. J. (1971), 'Local autonomy and independent revenues', *Public Administration*, vol. 49, pp. 45–50.

Dearlove, John (1973), *The Politics of Policy in Local Government* (Cambridge: Cambridge University Press).

Dearlove, John (1979), *The Reorganisation of British Local Government* (Cambridge. Cambridge University Press).

Department of the Environment (1971), *Local Government Reorganisation: Areas and Names*, Circular 58/71 (London: HMSO).

Department of the Environment (1972), *Arrangements for the Discharge of Functions*, Circular 131/72 (London: HMSO).

Department of the Environment (1973*a*), *Status of Authorities, Civic Dignities, Etc.*, Circular 51/73 (London: HMSO).

Department of the Environment (1973*b*), *Co-operation between Authorities*, Circular 74/73 (London: HMSO).

Department of the Environment (1974), *Homelessness*, Circular 18/74 (London: HMSO).

Department of the Environment (1975*a*), *Community Land – circular 1: General Introduction and Priorities*, Circular 121/75 (London: HMSO).

Department of the Environment (1975*b*), *Transport Supplementary Grant Submissions for 1977/1978*, Circular 125/75 (London: HMSO).

Department of the Environment (1976), *Capital Programmes*, Circular 66/76 (London: HMSO).

Dixon, E. S. (1978), 'Management in local government in West Yorkshire, April 1974–March 1977', M.Sc. thesis, University of Bradford.

Eddison, Tony (1979), 'Corporate planning in British local government – some developments after the Bains and Paterson Reports', background paper to Labour Party local government conference.

Elcock, H. (1975), 'English local government reformed: the politics of Humberside', *Public Administration*, vol. 53, pp. 159–68.

Else, Roger (1975), 'Corporate planning and community work', *Community Development Journal*, vol. 10, pp. 30–7.

Ford, John (1979), 'A forum in which earlier discomforts have been dispelled', *Public Finance and Accountancy* (October), pp. 19–20.

Freeman, R. (1979), 'Ill-prepared, and looking for a guide to the job', *Municipal Review* (August), pp. 103–4.

Friend, John (1976), 'Planners, policies and organizational boundaries: some recent developments in Britain', *Policy and Politics*, vol. 5, pp. 25–46.

Green, D. G. (1980), 'Inside local government – a study of a ruling Labour group', *Local Government Studies*, vol. 6, pp. 33–50.

Greenwood, R. *et al.* (1969), 'Recent changes in the internal organization of county boroughs', *Public Administration*, vol. 47, pp. 151–68.

Greenwood, R. *et al.* (1971), *New Patterns of Local Government Organisation* (Birmingham: University of Birmingham Institute of Local Government Studies).

Greenwood, R. *et al.* (1972a), 'The policy committee in English local government', *Public Administration*, vol. 50, pp. 157–66.

Greenwood, R. *et al.* (1972b), 'The local government councillor', *Local Government Studies* (first series), vol. 2, pp. 77–80.

Greenwood, R. *et al.* (1976), *In Pursuit of Corporate Rationality: Organisational Developments in the Post-Reorganisation Period* (Birmingham: University of Birmingham Institute of Local Government Studies).

Greenwood, Royston and Hinings, C. R. (1972), 'The comparative study of local government organisation: 1972–1976', *Policy and Politics*, vol. 1, pp. 213–21.

Grugeon, John (1978), 'Council leaders', *County Councils Gazette* (March), pp. 320–1.

Gyford, John (1976), *Local Politics in Britain* (London: Croom Helm).

Hambleton, Robin (1979), *Policy Planning and Local Government* (Montclair, NJ: Allanheld Osmun).

Hampton, William (1972), 'Political attitudes to changes in city council administration', *Local Government Studies* (first series), vol. 2, pp. 23–35.

Harris, R. and Shipp, P. J. (1977), *Communications between Central and Local Government in the Management of Local Authority Expenditure* (Coventry: Institute for Operational Research).

Haynes, R. J. (1978), 'The rejection of corporate management in Birmingham in theoretical perspective', *Local Government Studies*, vol. 4, pp. 25–37.

Heclo, H. Hugh (1969), 'The councillor's job', *Public Administration*, vol. 47, pp. 185–202.

Hender, J. D. (1976), 'The chief executive in action', *Local Government Chronicle* (20 August), pp. 769–72.

Hender, J. D. (1980), 'Whatever happened to corporate management?', paper presented to 107th annual conference of Institution of Municipal Engineers.

Herbert, Sir Edwin (chairman), Royal Commission on Local Government in Greater London (1960), *Report*, Cmnd 1164 (London: HMSO).

Hill, D. M. (1974), *Democratic Theory and Local Government* (London: Allen & Unwin).

Hinings, C. R. *et al.* (1975a), 'Contingency theory and the organization of local authorities: part I – differentiation and integration', *Public Administration*, vol. 53, pp. 1–23.

Hinings, C. R. *et al.* (1975b), 'Contingency theory and the organization of local authorities: part II – contingencies and structure', *Public Administration*, vol. 53, pp. 169–220.

Honey, Michael (1979), 'Corporate planning and the chief executive', *Local Government Studies*, vol. 5, pp. 21–34.

House of Commons (HC) Papers (1948), *Local Government Boundary Commission: Report for 1947*, HC 1947–48 (86) (London: HMSO).

Howick, Cristina (1978), 'Budgeting and corporate planning in Cheshire', *CES Review* (May), pp. 45–62.

Hughes, A. A. (chairman) (1968), *Report of Working Party on the Staffing of Local Government in Scotland* (Edinburgh: Scottish Development Department, Association of County Councils in Scotland, Convention of Royal Burghs, Counties of Cities Association).

Isaac-Henry, K. (1980), 'The English local authority associations', in G. W. Jones (ed.), *New Approaches to the Study of Central–Local Government Relations* (Farnborough, Hants: Gower), pp. 40–58.

Jones, Alan (1979), 'The politics of educational planning in County Durham: dominant party politics in the local state', paper to the Northern Association of Politics and Sociology, mimeo.

Jones, G. W. (1963), 'The Local Government Commission and county borough extensions', *Public Administration*, vol. 41, pp. 173–87.

Kogan, Maurice and van der Eyken, Willem (1973), *County Hall: The Role of the Chief Education Officer* (Harmondsworth: Penguin).

Labour Party (1977), *Regional Authorities and Local Government Reform* (London: Labour Party).

Laffin, M. (1980), 'Professionalism in central–local relations', in G. W. Jones (ed.), *New Approaches to the Study of Central–Local Government Relations* (Farnborough, Hants: Gower), pp. 40–58.

Layfield, Frank (chairman) (1976), *Local Government Finance: Report of the Committee of Enquiry*, Cmnd 6453 (London: HMSO).

Leach, S. N. (1977), 'County–district relationships in shire and metropolitan counties', M. Soc. Sci. thesis, University of Birmingham.

Leach, S. and Moore, N. (1979*a*), 'County–district relations in shire and metropolitan counties in the field of town and country planning: a comparison', *Policy and Politics*, vol. 7, pp. 165–79.

Leach, S. and Moore, N. (1979*b*), 'An interaction approach to county/district relationships', *Policy and Politics*, vol. 7, pp. 271–9.

Lewis, Janet (1975), 'Variation in service provision: politics at the lay–professional interface', in K. Young (ed.), *Essays on the Study of Urban Politics* (London, Macmillan), pp. 52–77.

Local Government Boundary Commission (1972), *First Report*, Cmnd 5148 (London: HMSO).

Lord President of the Council (1976), *Devolution: The English Dimension* (London: HMSO).

McAllister, R. and Hunter, D. (1980), *Local Government: Death or Devolution* (London: Outer Circle Policy Unit).

McDonald, Shiela T. (1977), 'The Regional Report in Scotland: A study of change in the planning process', *Town Planning Review*, vol. 48, pp. 215–32.

Madelin, K. B. (1980), 'Whatever happened to corporate management? – (an operational view)', paper presented to 107th annual conference of Institution of Municipal Engineers.

184   *Local Government in Britain since Reorganisation*

Mallaby, Sir George (chairman), Committee on the Staffing of Local Government, (1967) *Report* (London: HMSO).

Maud, Sir John (chairman), Committee on the Management of Local Government (1967), *Vol. 1: Report* (London: HMSO).

Midwinter, Arthur F. (1978), 'The implementation of the Paterson Report in Scottish local government, 1975–1977', *Local Government Studies*, vol. 4, pp. 23–38.

Musgrave, Terry (1978), 'Management modes and management codes . . . 1', *Local Government Chronicle* (7 July), and 'Management modes and management codes . . . 2', *Local Government Chronicle* (14 July).

Newton, Kenneth (1976), *Second City Politics: Democratic Processes and Decision Making in Birmingham* (Oxford: Clarendon Press).

Page, Edward (1978), *Why Should Central–Local Relations in Scotland Be any Different from that in England* (Glasgow: University of Strathclyde, Centre for the Study of Public Policy, study no. 21).

Page, Edward C. and Midwinter, Arthur F. (1979), *Remote Bureaucracy or Administrative Efficiency: Scotland's New Local Government System* (Glasgow: University of Strathclyde, Centre for the Study of Public Policy, study no. 38).

Paterson, I. V. (chairman), Working Group on Scottish Local Government Management Structures (1973), *The New Scottish Local Authorities: Organisation and Management Structures* (Edinburgh: Scottish Development Department).

Poole, K. P. (1978), *The Local Government Service in England and Wales* (London: Allen & Unwin).

Redcliffe-Maud, Lord (chairman), Royal Commission on Local Government in England (1968), *Research Studies 2: The Lessons of the London Government Reforms, Research Studies 3: Economies of Scale in Local Government, Research Studies 4: Performance and Size of Local Education Authorities* (London: HMSO).

Redcliffe-Maud, Lord (chairman), Royal Commission on Local Government in England (1969), *Vol. I: Report*, Cmnd 4040; *Vol. II: Memorandum of Dissent*, Cmnd 4040–I; *Vol. III: Research Appendices*, Cmnd 4040–II (London: HMSO).

Redcliffe-Maud, Lord (chairman), Prime Minister's Committee on Local Government Rules of Conduct (1974), *Conduct in Local Government: Vol. 1 – Report of the Committee*, Cmnd 5636 (London: HMSO).

Regan, David E. (1980a), *A Headless State: The Unaccountable Executive in British Local Government* (Nottingham: University of Nottingham).

Regan, David E. (1980b), 'The myth of professional consensus: the policy process and professional links between central and local government', paper presented to Urban Politics Group of the Political Science Association (draft).

Regan, D. E. and Morris, A. J. A. (1969), 'Local government corruption and public confidence', *Public Law*, pp. 132–52.

Richards, P. G. (1975), *The Local Government Act 1972: Problems of Implementation* (London: Allen & Unwin).

Rhodes, R. A. W. (1975a), 'The lost world of British local politics', *Local Government Studies*, vol. 1, pp. 39–60.

Rhodes, R. A. W. (1975*b*), 'The changing political-management system of local government', paper to ECPR, London joint sessions: European urbanism; policy and planning workshop.

Rhodes, R. A. W. (1980), 'Analysing intergovernmental relations', *European Journal of Political Research*, vol. 8, pp. 289–322.

Robinson, D. (chairman), Committee of Enquiry into the System of Renumeration of Members of Local Authorities (1977), *Remuneration of Councillors, Volume I: Report*, Cmnd 7010; *Remuneration of Councillors, Volume II: The Surveys of Councillors and Local Authorities* (London: HMSO).

Royal Institute of Public Administration/Policy Studies Institute (1980), *Party Politics in Local Government: Officers and Members* (RIPA/PSI, 1980).

Salmon, Lord (chairman), Royal Commission on Standards of Conduct in Public Life, 1974–1976 (1976), *Report*, Cmnd 6524 (London: HMSO).

Schofield, M. I. (1980), 'The English independent county councillor and local government reorganization: an analysis of aggregate electoral data', M. Phil. thesis, University of Reading.

Scottish Development Department (SDD) (1975), *Town and County Planning – Regional Reports*, Circular 4/75 (Edinburgh: HMSO).

Seebohm, Lord (chairman), Committee on Local Authority and Allied Personal Social Services (1968), *Report*, Cmnd 3703 (London: HMSO).

Self, P. (1971), 'Elected representatives and management in local government: an alternative analysis', *Public Administration*, vol. 49, pp. 269–78.

Senior, Derek (1966), *The Regional City* (London: Longman).

Sharpe, L. J. (1973), 'American democracy reconsidered', *British Journal of Political Science*, vol. 3, pp. 1–28, 129–68.

Sharpe, L. J. (1978*a*), 'Are we obsessed with bigness', *Municipal Review* (May), pp. 32–4.

Sharpe, L. J. (1978*b*), 'Smaller can be beautiful', *Municipal Review* (July), pp. 77–8.

Sharpe, L. J. (1978*c*), ' "Reforming" the grass roots', in D. Butler and A. H. Halsey (eds), *Policy and Politics* (London: Macmillan), pp. 82–110.

Sharpe, L. J. (1980), 'Is there a fiscal crisis in Western European local government', *International Political Science Review*, vol. 1, pp. 203–26.

Smart, Gerald (1972), 'Deployment of staff in the new authorities', *Royal Town Planning Institute Journal*, vol. 58, pp. 353–4.

Smith, B. C. (1972), 'Regional administration and the reform of local government in Britain', *Rivista Trimestrale di Dirrito Publico (Milan)*, vol. 22, pp. 335–50.

Society of Local Authority Chief Executives (SOLACE) (1977), *Recruitment and Training of Chief Executives* (Lewes, Sussex: SOLACE).

Society of Local Authority Chief Executives (SOLACE) (1980), *The Local Government Bill: No. 2 – An Appraisal Prepared in Collaboration with INLOGOV* (Lewes, Sussex: SOLACE).

Stanyer, Jeffrey (1971), 'Elected representatives and management in local government: a case of applied sociology and applied economics', *Public Administration*, vol. 43, pp. 73–97.

Stanyer, Jeffrey (1973), 'The Redcliffe-Maud Royal Commission', in R. A. Chapman (ed), *The Role of Commissions in Policy Making* (London: Allen & Unwin).

Stewart, John (1976a), 'A different world', *Municipal Journal*, vol. 84, pp. 100–1.

Stewart, John (1976b), 'Redefining the CEO role', *Municipal Journal*, vol. 84, p. 148.

Stewart, John (1976c), 'From luxury to necessity', *Municipal Journal*, vol. 84, pp. 206–9.

Stewart, John (1976d), 'Opportunity for growth', *Municipal Journal*, vol. 84, pp. 276–7.

Stewart, John (1976e), 'Challenging the norms', *Municipal Journal*, vol. 84, pp. 331–2.

Stewart, John (1976f), 'Fruitful administration', *Municipal Journal*, vol. 84, pp. 377–8.

Stewart, John (1976g), 'Corporate planning now', *Municipal Journal*, vol. 84, pp. 452–3.

Stewart, John (1976h), 'Corporate planning how?', *Municipal Journal*, vol. 84, pp. 509–10.

Stewart, John (1976i), 'Questions for our times', *Municipal Journal*, vol. 84, pp. 653–4.

Stewart, John (1977), 'Have the Scots a lesson to teach?', *Municipal Journal*, vol. 85, p. 38.

Stewart, J. D., *et al.* (1978), *Organic Change: A Report on Constitutional, Management and Financial Problems* (London: ACC).

Stewart, J. D. (1980), 'The new government's policies for local government', *Local Government Studies*, vol. 6, pp. 7–14.

Stodart, Anthony (chairman), Committee of Inquiry into Local Government in Scotland (1981), *Report*, Cmnd 8115 (Edinburgh: HMSO).

Taylor, John A. (1979), 'The Consultative Council on Local Government Finance – A critical analysis of its origins and development', *Local Government Studies*, vol. 5, pp. 9–35.

Tilley, John (1975), 'Local government councillors and community work', *Community Development Journal*, vol. 10, pp. 89–94.

Toulmin Smith, J. (1857), *The Parish* (London: Sweet).

Turton, R. (1975), 'Two-tier local government: a happy marriage or a field sport', Royal Town Planning Institute, summer school report, pp. 16–21.

Ward, F. W. (1976), 'The chief executive role against a changing background', *Local Government Chronicle* (20 August), pp. 789–90.

Wheatley, Lord (chairman), Royal Commission on Local Government in Scotland (1969), *Report*, Cmnd 4150 (Edinburgh: HMSO).

Wood, Bruce (1976), *The Process of Local Government Reform, 1966–1974* (London: Allen & Unwin).

Woodman, J. B. (1976), *Management in the New Authorities: A Stocktaking*, paper to SOLACE conference.

Working Party of Representatives of Regional, Islands and District Councils (1974a), 'A possible structure for an Association or Convention of Scottish Local Authorities', mimeo.

Working Party of Representatives of Regional, Islands and District Councils (1974*b*), 'A Convention of Scottish Local Authorities: second report', mimeo.

Young, Ronald (1977), *The Search for Democracy: A Guide to Scottish Local Government* (Milngavie, Dunbartonshire: Heatherbank Press).

INDEX